SAINTS
AND
SINNERS

To Jane

This book is also written in memory of
John and Piers,
who inspired the affection and respect
of all who knew them

SAINTS
AND
SINNERS

HOW ONE FAMILY SURVIVED A
THOUSAND YEARS OF HISTORY

NICHOLAS ST AUBYN

PEN & SWORD
HISTORY
AN IMPRINT OF PEN & SWORD BOOKS LTD.
YORKSHIRE - PHILADELPHIA

First published in Great Britain in 2025 by
PEN AND SWORD HISTORY
An imprint of
Pen & Sword Books Ltd
Yorkshire – Philadelphia

ISBN 978 1 03613 149 4

Typeset in Times New Roman 11/14 by
SJmagic DESIGN SERVICES, India.
Printed and bound in the UK by CPI Group (UK) Ltd.

The Publisher's authorised representative in the EU for product safety is Authorised
Rep Compliance Ltd., Ground Floor, 71 Lower Baggot Street,
Dublin D02 P593, Ireland.
www.arccompliance.com

For a complete list of Pen & Sword titles please contact
PEN & SWORD BOOKS LIMITED
George House, Units 12 & 13, Beevor Street, Off Pontefract Road,
Barnsley, South Yorkshire, S71 1HN, England
E-mail: enquiries@pen-and-sword.co.uk
Website: www.pen-and-sword.co.uk

or

PEN AND SWORD BOOKS
1950 Lawrence Rd, Havertown, PA 19083, USA
E-mail: uspen-and-sword@casematepublishers.com
Website: www.penandswordbooks.com

CONTENTS

PART FOUR: PATRICIAN HEIRS
The hazardous path from baronet to baron

PART FIVE: SCIONS OF EMPIRE
Surviving the tumult of the modern age

(Author's note, references, bibliography, glossary and indices)

𝕴𝖓 𝕾𝖊 𝕿𝖊𝖗𝖊𝖘

LIST OF ILLUSTRATIONS

FAMILY TREE

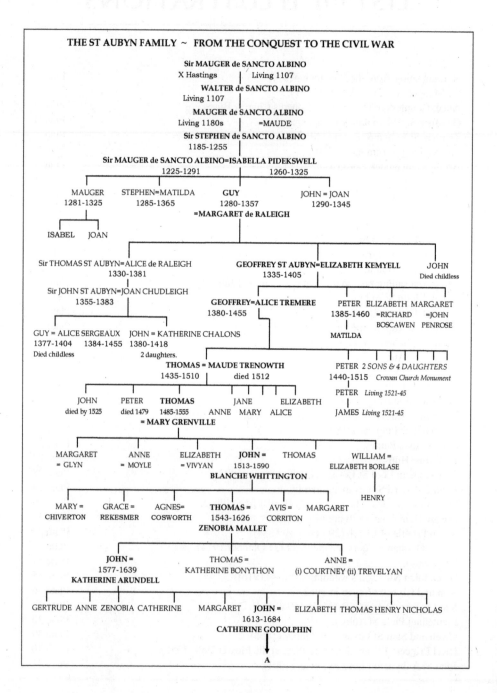

THE ST AUBYN FAMILY ~ FROM THE CONQUEST TO THE CIVIL WAR

Sir MAUGER de SANCTO ALBINO
X Hastings | Living 1107

WALTER de SANCTO ALBINO
Living 1107

MAUGER de SANCTO ALBINO
Living 1180s | =MAUDE

Sir STEPHEN de SANCTO ALBINO
1185-1255

Sir MAUGER de SANCTO ALBINO=ISABELLA PIDEKSWELL
1225-1291 | 1260-1325

MAUGER 1281-1325 | STEPHEN=MATILDA 1285-1365 | **GUY** 1280-1357 =MARGARET de RALEIGH | JOHN = JOAN 1290-1345

ISABEL JOAN

Sir THOMAS ST AUBYN=ALICE de RALEIGH 1330-1381 | **GEOFFREY ST AUBYN=ELIZABETH KEMYELL** 1335-1405 | JOHN Died childless

Sir JOHN ST AUBYN=JOAN CHUDLEIGH 1355-1383 | **GEOFFREY=ALICE TREMERE** 1380-1455 | PETER ELIZABETH MARGARET 1385-1460 =RICHARD =JOHN BOSCAWEN PENROSE

GUY = ALICE SERGEAUX 1377-1404 1384-1455 Died childless | JOHN = KATHERINE CHALONS 1380-1418 2 daughters. | MATILDA

THOMAS = MAUDE TRENOWTH 1435-1510 died 1512 | PETER 2 SONS & 4 DAUGHTERS 1440-1515 Crowan Church Monument

JOHN died by 1525 | PETER died 1479 | **THOMAS** 1485-1555 = **MARY GRENVILLE** | JANE ANNE MARY | ELIZABETH ALICE | PETER Living 1521-45

JAMES Living 1521-45

MARGARET = GLYN | ANNE = MOYLE | ELIZABETH = VIVYAN | **JOHN =** 1513-1590 **BLANCHE WHITTINGTON** | THOMAS | WILLIAM = ELIZABETH BORLASE

HENRY

MARY = CHIVERTON | GRACE = REKESMER | AGNES= COSWORTH | **THOMAS =** 1543-1626 **ZENOBIA MALLET** | AVIS = CORRITON | MARGARET

JOHN = 1577-1639 **KATHERINE ARUNDELL** | THOMAS = KATHERINE BONYTHON | ANNE = (i) COURTNEY (ii) TREVELYAN

GERTRUDE ANNE ZENOBIA CATHERINE | MARGARET | **JOHN =** 1613-1684 **CATHERINE GODOLPHIN** | ELIZABETH THOMAS HENRY NICHOLAS

A

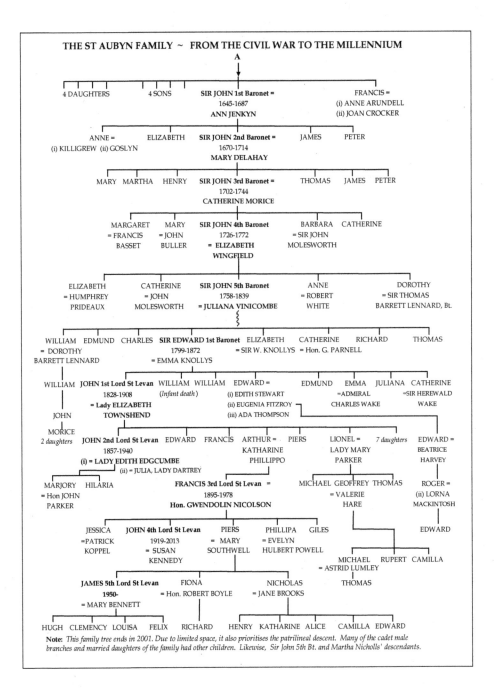

THE ST AUBYN FAMILY ~ FROM THE CIVIL WAR TO THE MILLENNIUM

A

4 DAUGHTERS	4 SONS	**SIR JOHN 1st Baronet** =		FRANCIS =
		1645-1687		(i) ANNE ARUNDELL
		ANN JENKYN		(ii) JOAN CROCKER

ANNE = | ELIZABETH | **SIR JOHN 2nd Baronet** = | JAMES | PETER
(i) KILLIGREW (ii) GOSLYN | | 1670-1714 | |
| | **MARY DELAHAY** | |

MARY   MARTHA   HENRY   **SIR JOHN 3rd Baronet** =   THOMAS   JAMES   PETER
1702-1744
CATHERINE MORICE

MARGARET   MARY   **SIR JOHN 4th Baronet**   BARBARA   CATHERINE
= FRANCIS   = JOHN   1726-1772   = SIR JOHN
BASSET   BULLER   **= ELIZABETH**   MOLESWORTH
WINGFIELD

ELIZABETH   CATHERINE   **SIR JOHN 5th Baronet**   ANNE   DOROTHY
= HUMPHREY   = JOHN   1758-1839   = ROBERT   = SIR THOMAS
PRIDEAUX   MOLESWORTH   **= JULIANA VINICOMBE**   WHITE   BARRETT LENNARD, Bt.

WILLIAM   EDMUND   CHARLES   **SIR EDWARD 1st Baronet**   ELIZABETH   CATHERINE   RICHARD   THOMAS
= DOROTHY   1799-1872   = SIR W. KNOLLYS   = Hon. G. PARNELL
BARRETT LENNARD   = EMMA KNOLLYS

WILLIAM   **JOHN 1st Lord St Levan**   WILLIAM   WILLIAM   EDWARD =   EDMUND   EMMA   JULIANA   CATHERINE
1828-1908   (*Infant death*)   (i) EDITH STEWART   =ADMIRAL   =SIR HEREWALD
JOHN   **= Lady ELIZABETH**   (ii) EUGENIA FITZROY   CHARLES WAKE   WAKE
MORICE   **TOWNSHEND**   (iii) ADA THOMPSON
2 daughters

MARJORY   HILARIA   **JOHN 2nd Lord St Levan**   EDWARD   FRANCIS   ARTHUR =   PIERS   LIONEL =   *7 daughters*   EDWARD =
= Hon JOHN   1857-1940   KATHARINE   LADY MARY   BEATRICE
PARKER   **(i) = LADY EDITH EDGCUMBE**   PHILLIPPO   PARKER   HARVEY
(ii) = JULIA, LADY DARTREY

FRANCIS 3rd Lord St Levan =   MICHAEL   GEOFFREY   THOMAS   ROGER =
1895-1978   = VALERIE   (ii) LORNA
Hon. GWENDOLIN NICOLSON   HARE   MACKINTOSH

JESSICA   **JOHN 4th Lord St Levan**   PIERS   PHILLIPA   GILES   EDWARD
=PATRICK   1919-2013   = MARY   = EVELYN
KOPPEL   = SUSAN   SOUTHWELL   HULBERT POWELL
KENNEDY   MICHAEL   RUPERT   CAMILLA
= ASTRID LUMLEY

JAMES 5th Lord St Levan   FIONA   NICHOLAS   THOMAS
1950-   = Hon. ROBERT BOYLE   = JANE BROOKS
= MARY BENNETT

HUGH   CLEMENCY   LOUISA   FELIX   RICHARD   HENRY   KATHARINE   ALICE   CAMILLA   EDWARD

Note: *This family tree ends in 2001. Due to limited space, it also prioritises the patrilineal descent. Many of the cadet male branches and married daughters of the family had other children. Likewise, Sir John 5th Bt. and Martha Nicholls' descendants.*

MAPS OF CORNWALL, DEVON AND SOMERSET

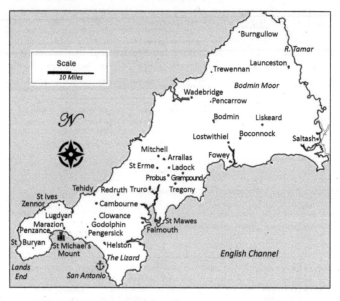

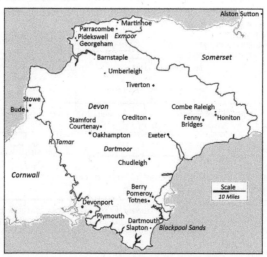

PREFACE

I have imped some feathers of the wings of time
John Aubrey
Brief Lives

*The genius of these people was exercised not in great
services to the state, or to literature, or to
humanity, but in the art of living.*
Muriel St Clare Byrne,
The Lisle Letters

This history of my family is no eulogy, but nor have I sought to impose contemporary values on past members, which would only cloud our appreciation of the context of their times. Humanity's capacity for change, as their story unfolds, speaks for itself.

This is rather the study of one family and their changing world, as seen through twenty-seven generations, whose outlook evolved in step with the times they lived through and the society they and those around them unconsciously helped to form.

Nicholas St Aubyn
November 2024

PART ONE

GIANTS FROM THE SEA

CHAPTER 1

LIEGEMAN

Vous que desyrez assaver
Le nons de Grauntz de la mer,
Que vindrent od le Conquerour,
William Bastard de graunt vigoure

Seint Aubyn, et Seynt Omer,
Seynt Filbert Fyens, et Gomer

You who wish to know
the names of the Giants from the sea,
Who came with the Conqueror,
William Bastard of great valour

St Aubyn[1] and St Omer
St Filbert Fyens, and Gomer
Chronicum Johannis Brompton[2]

In September 1066, a herald attired in the livery of the Duke of Normandy rode up to the Bastille of Judhael of Mayenne in Brittany and demanded entry. Unfurling his banner in the great hall, in the name of William the Bastard, he announced the Pope's support for the duke and his campaign to seize the Saxon throne from 'Harold the oath-breaker'. His sensational banner bore not only the coat of arms of his Seigneur, but also the white and black ensign that proclaimed the Pope's blessing.

At this point, Brittany found itself caught in the throes of a dynastic dispute, through which William had divided its barons for the past three years. Judhael of Mayenne was one of those barons who supported the duke's faction; and into his retinue he had admitted a young page called Mauger. He came from the nearby settlement of Saint-Aubin-du-Cormier,[3] one of many places named after the local sixth-century patron saint of hostages and refugees. 'Mauger' meant 'council spear' in German; in this case indicating the size of the young soldier whose fortunes would be tied to his lord and master Judhael for the next sixty years. The Norman duke's reckless venture – to seize the English crown – came with the lure of riches for all who would risk joining his invasion. But for Mauger, later taking his surname from the place whence he came, this promise of riches was not his first motive, nor had the divisions of the past three years bred any loyalty to William the Bastard.

What stirred in Mauger was the deep-seated desire to restore his family, like so many other Bretons, to those lands in the West Country which their forefathers had been forced to leave by the ruthless Saxon suppression of the Dark Ages. Brittany, first known as the land of the Armoricans, had taken the names of its regions from the origins of its Christian inhabitants. Cornouaille was settled by migrant princes from Cornwall, an independent realm founded by Rivelen Mor Marthou, with its own Bishopric of Cornouaille led by the earliest Cornish saints. The larger adjacent region was occupied by the Domnonians, which had likewise been filled by those fleeing the even earlier Saxon wave into Devon and Somerset. Centuries had now passed, but each generation was still reared on the ancient promise of return, whether instilled through the fabled prophecies of Merlin, the Auguries of the Eagle, or above all the legend of the Voice. It was said to have spoken to Cadwallader, leader of the exiled Britons, before his journey to Rome and blessing by Pope Sergius. So for centuries, from a host of sources, these Bretons had known that one day, the sign to return would come from God.[4]

That September, for thousands of young Bretons like Mauger, it was the Pope's ensign more than the duke's banner, which propelled them to attend their rollcall of fate. So it was that just one month later, Mauger found himself in the heat of the Battle of Hastings, fighting *ex parte militum*[5] beside Judhael, among the serried ranks of Bretons on the left flank of the Norman cavalry. They bore the brunt of the first Saxon onslaught and they played a decisive role in the Conqueror's victory.

Judhael and his retinue, fired by the validation of their cause at Hastings, returned to their south-western roots. They took Exeter and over the next three years, they completely displaced the Saxon elite in ownership of land and control of the Church. William awarded Judhael with the Barony of Totnes, along with lands in the south-east of England, a signal mark of his role in the Conquest.

Among the Breton family names which, as Camden tells us in 1605, now followed into the West Country and who would long prosper in its history were St Aubyn, Morley, Dinham, Conquest, Valtort and Bluet.[6] Their fellowship in arms and the ties, of blood and language, would continue to bind them, by marriage and service, for generations to come.

In these first unsettled years after the Conquest, when the invaders were regarded as aliens living among a defeated and hostile people, Mauger de Sancto Albino (as he was recorded in the formal Latin documents) remained a personal retainer in Judhael's household. As the years passed and the occupation became more settled, some barons gave to their knights portions of their lands, where they could live apart from their lords, holding those lands in exchange for their military services. But while Judhael did likewise for some knights to whom he was liege, their names appearing in *Doomsday*, Mauger remained a key member of his household militia.

Then in 1087, just as he had founded the Abbey of Totnes out of his wealthy spoils of war, disaster struck Judhael. In October, the Conqueror lay dying in Rouen from his war wounds and his barons were forced to choose, as successor to the Crown, which of his two sons to support. The internecine rivalry between the king's victorious followers over the division of the kingdom had already cost many their preferment. By supporting the younger son Henry, Judhael now seemed to seal his fate, when it was the reckless and greedy son, William, who first heard the news of his father's death and sped to Winchester, where he seized control of the Treasury and all the trappings of office. From Devon, the baron from Mayenne and his cohort slipped away to the coast of Brittany, and at the same time so did the fruits of their twenty-year long adventure. William II dispossessed Judhael of all his lands.

In this feudal world, as espoused by the Normans in England and France, William II, as the king of England, was by virtue of the Conquest, lord paramount. To this day, all land tenure still rests upon this principle. Until the development of freehold, ownership was held on certain conditions and if those conditions were breached, the land reverted to the king, who was the real owner; his barons were mere tenants. Siding with William II's rival to the throne was a breach of Judhael's tenancy agreement, just like the Saxon overlords who had opposed his father. All were dispossessed, although leaving their sub-tenants with simply one master in the place of another.

This whole scheme of land tenure and the ranks within it was founded on the supreme importance of military values, softened only by the code of chivalry. Barons were the leaders; knights were the skilled fighters, trained from boyhood; the cloister of the monastery beckoned for any man of this class not up to the mark. If this was the age of chivalry, it was also the age of serfdom, when the lowest in society were treated as goods. This Cornish case, from the Launceston Assizes,[7] illustrates some of the harsh realities of life in 1201:

'William de Ros appeals [that] Alward Bere, Roger the bald, Robert the merchant and Nicholas the tailor ... came to his house and wickedly in the king's peace carried away from him a serf of his whom he had in chains because he wished to flee.' The felony is denied. In front of the Sheriff, Roger of Prideaux, twelve men had sworn and a jury had agreed that the serf was not William's, but the king's; 'wherefore Roger, the serjeant, sought that he should be returned to him.' So 'let the king have his chattels from William.'

Serfs were not often held in chains and the Normans eradicated pure Anglo-Saxon slavery. But treating men as chattels was not fully abolished until after the Peasants' Revolt, nearly 200 years later. This was a time when life was Hobbesian – 'nasty, brutish and short' – at all levels of society. As Polwhele tells us, 'For the mode of holding land, and the services and prestations to which the holders were subject, the observations on aids, scutages, tallages, fines, amerciaments and a variety of other particulars ... Madox's *History and Antiquities of the Exchequer* ... will curiously illustrate the subject'.[8]

'Adam Blund of Bodmin, fined in 6 marks, that there might be a duel between him and Walter de Solde, for 200 pieces of tin, which Walter said that Adam had stolen from him.'

'William Fitz-Richard gave 46 marks and a palfrey, to have his land, and for his relief, and that he might marry whom he please.'

'The wife of Hugh de Nevill fined 200 hens that she might lie with her husband one night.'

'Reginald de Tewaden gave 20 marks, to have his land and inheritance, that he might not abjure the realm, he having undergone the judgement of the hot iron.'

'Richard de Luci was charged with 14s. 2d. being amercements of former years for murders. But he was acquitted thereof, because they fell upon the king's demesne-lands.'

'Robert Francis was charged with 20 shillings, for hanging a robber unjustly.'

The Norman hierarchy appeared rigid, but a person and his family's position within it was always precarious. In an agricultural economy, this created the territorial imperative.[9] Yet there would be no free market in land until the sixteenth century, even if the king might sell his land to his highest bidder when it fell back into his hands. Money was for purchasing goods and chattels, to pay taxes and fines, or in lieu of some service owed. The only coin was a silver penny. To acquire land, in other words, there were only three practical means available: by marriage, by inheritance, or by service to the Crown or to a local lord.

If landing with the Conqueror was the defining step onto the chivalric ladder for St Aubyn, the soldier of fortune and his heirs, then marriage was the prudent means of advancement. However, as in Chaucer's *Knight's Tale* and the letters of the Paston family in Suffolk, even in this harsh existence love and desire sometimes trumped cold dynastic calculation. A medieval inquisition in Southwark, in February 1353, provides a case in point[10]:

> Thomas Staple offered a suitable marriage to John, son and heir of Edmund Amory, a minor, on the second Sunday in Lent ... in the house of the bishop of Winchester at Southwark, viz. Alice daughter of John le Cleet of co. Berks., or Isabel daughter of Adam de Sancto Albano [*sic*] of co. Surrey; he utterly refused both and of his own accord married Eleanor, daughter of Thomas de Baryton, knight. The loss of his marriage amounts to £200.

Mauger must have felt that his dream of reclaiming his forbear's West Country roots had died with his master's political misfortune; he would have returned to duty in Mayenne with a sunken heart, albeit one which had probably already found solace in the arms of a wife.

But thirteen years later, the projection of an arrow flying through the woods of the New Forest would alter that of Mauger's dynasty as well. That arrow, whether by accident or design, pierced the breast of the hunting fanatic William; and this time his brother was well poised to pre-empt all rivals to the throne. The swiftly crowned King Henry I promptly invited Judhael de Totnes to return to England as tenant-in-chief of the Barony of Barnstaple; and this is where Mauger was at last granted his holding, albeit still subordinated to de Totnes in knight service, in the lowest form of 'tenure in chivalry'.

We know this because seven years later, in 1107, Judhael founded the Priory of St Mary Magdalene in Barnstaple. After the clerical dignitaries, among a long list of witnesses to his charter appear '*ex parte militum*' Mauger de Sancto Albino and Walter de Sancto Albino, his son.[11] Later, Brother Pascasius, the prior, granted a tenancy of land which was witnessed by 'Mauger de Sancto Albino, John de Charteray, John de Punchardun, knights' (the last two having held land since *Doomsday*).[12]

Hereon the St Aubyn story plots itself, the path of one family of middling rank through a thousand years of history, which had quickly absorbed the Norman patrilineal custom of surnames followed in the male line; a custom which at times would assume a mystifying importance.[13] Owing to its singular name and the fact that even its earliest members enjoyed sufficient status to be glimpsed in the record books, the footprint of them all can now be traced through twenty-seven generations of social change.

CHAPTER 2

DEVONSHIRE KNIGHTS

A knight there was, and that a worthy man,
Who from the time that he first began
To ride out, he loved chivalry.

Chaucer, *The Knight*
(Prologue, ll.43–45)

After Sir Mauger de Sancto Albino and his son Walter, there came another Mauger, who in 1216 was living on the vivid North Devon coast.[1] He held the manor of Martinhoe, a village set on the edge of Dartmoor, with a thousand acres of open fields and a wooded valley[2] leading down to a hidden cove, facing the Bristol Channel and the Welsh coast beyond.

Those fields were worked by villeins, who made up half the population and held their land off Mauger; in return, they worked for him a set number of days and performed a variety of other services. They could not leave the manor, nor marry outside it, without their lord's permission. Their produce formed his main income and Mauger may well have spent his whole time managing Martinhoe affairs, when not attending his own liege lord under the feudal barony of Barnstaple.

This was one of the eight feudal baronies in Devonshire, and by this time it covered a large area, comprising fifty-six individual manors like Mauger's. After Judhael's death in about 1130, the barony was split between his two daughters and devolved onto their husbands' families. Individual knights owed them 'knights' fees'; a full 'knight's fee' meaning they could be called upon to serve their overlord for forty days a year. But by the middle of the twelfth century, such military service had often been commuted for a payment in lieu called 'scutage'.

By 1228, Martinhoe was in the hands of Mauger's son Stephen,[3] who saw the opportunities offered by changes since the Conquest. One reason to abandon the requirement for strict military duty was the Norman powers of organisation and zeal for legal detail, exemplified by the efficient execution of *Doomsday*, with its myriad of statistics. This required a whole new class of professional officials, an alternative career to the Church and without the tiresome requirements of celibacy, however much honoured in the breach.

Yet ecclesiastical careers had a ladder of their own. In 1210, William de Sancto Albino was Dean of St Buryan, near Land's End, when he witnessed an endowment to St Michael's Mount. In 1218, he moved from this lucrative benefice to serve Henry III in Rome, as Royal Proctor to the Vatican. He stayed in this trusted diplomatic post until 1232.[4]

His brother, Stephen, also appears to have prospered. In 1244, he was serving as attorney to John Lestrange III,[5] one of the Marcher Lords governing Wales under Henry III; and by 1256 he was dubbed a knight.[6] This could be an elaborate ceremony in the case of men of great rank, but an account by Guillaume le Marechal of the dubbing of Henry II's son in 1173 suggests that it could also be quite an impromptu event, even for one who was himself already the ruler of one of his father's kingdoms:

> His friend William Marshal, a landless knight, held out the sword to him, and said: 'From God and from you, gentle sir, I would have this honour…' William girded the sword about his young master's waist and kissed him, and thus the young king became a knight.[7]

By 1244, Sir Stephen also held Henstridge in Berynarbour, a few miles from Martinhoe.[8] He had married and now had four sons, three of whom would earn their spurs. Martinhoe went to Sir Gilbert,[9] where his son Stephen was rector for thirty-one years; 'certain land' out of the family inheritance was given to Sir William, whose descendants migrated to Wales and Ireland; another son John had a daughter who wed in Ireland. But the one who commands our attention was another Mauger.

This son was born in the manor of Hamme in about 1225, the same time as Henry III's heir to the throne, Prince Edward. Like his Breton forbear, Mauger was a man of remarkable physique and great strength, who once threw a huge stone an immense distance, which centuries later was still marked by two monuments in the village of Georgeham.[10]

In his twenties, seizing his chance by supporting Henry III in supressing the wars of the English barons, Mauger took Esse and Bara, manors in the North Devon Hundred of Braunton, displacing two local backers of Simon de Montfort.[11] He then joined Prince Edward on the Ninth Crusade to Jerusalem, part of a contingent of about a thousand men, including over two hundred knights.[12]

Prince Edward sailed to Acre in the spring of 1271, with a fleet of eight sailing vessels and thirty galleys. But his force was not sufficient to take on the Mamluks in a straight battle, and settled for launching a series of raids, capturing Nazareth. Edward, stabbed by a poisoned dagger, was saved, according to legend, by his wife Eleanor of Castille,[13] who 'daily and nightly sucked out the rank poison, which love made sweet to her'. News of the death of his father, Henry III, forced Edward's return to England, to claim the throne, with Eleanor in his heart and Mauger among his band of devoted followers.[14]

Mauger was tenant of the manors of Slapton and Hamme. The additional manors of Pidekswell and Gratton would come through marriage, along with the manors of Parracombe and Hole. All of these were held by the service of the 'knight's fees' owed to an overlord. Among other lands he held as rewards for his service were Nitherham, Twangelegh, Prestlegh, and Sturdeton. Here he stood as 'tenant-in-chief' directly from the king,[15] the role often described as the backbone of the militarised rule of the Norman regime.

By this time, for most knights their military duty to their overlord had largely been replaced by 'scutage', the payment in lieu. But evidently Mauger had made his mark in the Holy Land, for he was twice summoned to perform his knight's service in person, when Edward, as king, was drawn into war by rebellion in Wales. Mauger was a part of the feudal host which gathered before the king at Worcester, on 1 July 1277.[16] Aided by a fleet from the Cinque Ports, this army had reached Conwy by the end of August. Soon the Welsh leader, Llywelyn Gruffyd, was besieged and in November he surrendered and a peace was agreed.

After becoming a tenant in chief, Mauger was formally knighted by the king in March 1279.[17] Three years later, with a second campaign in Wales just beginning, writs were issued which ordered those holding land worth £30 or more to 'meet the scarcity of the great horses suitable for war, by procuring such a horse with appropriate horse-armour' and to keep it in readiness for active service. Sir Mauger was among those summoned to join the king's cavalry,[18] and so was involved in the decisive battle of Edward I's conquest of Wales.

The Welsh troops prepared to meet the English at Orewin Bridge near Builth. But Welsh supporters of the English showed their infantry a ford upriver, which they crossed in order to attack the Welsh on their flank. The cavalry such as Sir Mauger, riding their sturdy and short-backed Destriers, could now cross the bridge unopposed, as the Welsh army retreated up the hill. In a classic manoeuvre, the English advanced their bowmen, who proceeded to shoot the Welsh spearmen caught in tightly packed schiltrons. These battle arrays then faced the charge of the English knights and their mounted cavalry. The Welsh were routed.

Llywelyn was killed, leaving his brother Dafydd as leader of the fugitive remnants of his rebellion. Once he was captured, the following June, Edward summoned a parliament at Shrewsbury to put Dafydd on trial and to raise money for his Exchequer. Sir Mauger was one of the knights called to this third parliament of the reign.[19]

Dafydd was found guilty of treason. As a mere knight, Mauger would not have attended the trial by the barons. But he would have witnessed the sentence – to be dragged at a horse's tail through Shrewsbury, hanged, cut down whilst still conscious, disembowelled, and his body cut into quarters and fed to the dogs. As the chroniclers noted with unease, it had been 'in previous times unknown' for so degrading a punishment to be inflicted on so high ranking a figure as Dafydd.

The meeting of Lords and Commons followed straight after this execution. It marked the first occasion when they met separately, with the knights of the shires taking the historic decision to put themselves among the town burgesses in the Commons. In Devonshire, remote from the seat of power, Sir Mauger had already been tasked as a commissioner in 1274 with collecting the king's taxes.[20] He no doubt welcomed the practical advantages of assembling with his fellow taxpayers, rather than being patronised by his property overlords. He proved to be the first of twelve generations to be a member of the House of Commons, between 1283 and the present day, a record number in one patrilineal descent.

As was the custom of his times, Sir Mauger took the much younger heiress, Isabella Pidekswell, as his wife after his knighthood, although their marriage had been arranged with her father while she was still a child. His heir was only 12 on his death in 1291, and Isabella married again. Sir Mauger's effigy, in Georgeham Church, shows him resting cross-legged, the traditional sign of a crusader. Two lions lie at his feet and his head is supported by angels.

Nicholas Trevet, the distinguished Dominican friar and Anglo-Norman chronicler, was born nearby in Somerset in the 1250s. Through this friar's eulogy to King Edward, we can readily conjure the image that this trusty Devonshire knight also projected in his lifetime:

> He was a handsome figure and so tall of build that he stood head and shoulders above ordinary people. A fine head of hair which in youth turned from almost silver to flaxen, grew black in his young manhood and distinguished him in old age when it had become greyish white. His long arms were in proportion to his lithe body and his muscular strength could not have been more adept at using a sword.

CHAPTER 3

SIR MAUGER'S HEIRS

Nowhere a man so busy of his class,
And yet he seemed much busier than he was.
All cases and all judgments could he cite
That from King William's time were apposite.

Chaucer, *The Man of Law*[1]

Sir Mauger's eldest son, who lived until he was 45, had two daughters. They passed on the greater part of their grandmother Isabella's inheritance to their husbands' families. The *De Donis Conditionalibus* statute in 1285 had loosened the common law of primogeniture, allowing for the wider distribution of family estates in this way. In 1318, Isabella's remaining sons agreed between them[2] who would inherit the manor of Parracombe, where St Aubyn descendants remained until the mid-1400s, when they moved to Alfoxton in Somerset.[3] Guy de Sancto Albino, Sir Mauger and Isabella's second son, waived his stake in Parracombe for 100 marks but inherited his father's Cornish manors. In Mitchell and Arrallas[4] in mid Cornwall, in Lugdvan in the west, they comprised 1000 acres and related dwellings.

In 1315, in order to manage the villeins on this estate at first hand,[5] Guy purchased 'La Medishol', a manor house in mid-Cornwall.[6] Guy was introduced to Eleanor de Knovill, who came from a knightly family near Honiton, and entered a contract to entrust 'all his lands of inheritance or purchase in the realms of England' to their proposed marriage. But on coming of age, Eleanor rejected a move to Cornwall and married a Devonian Mr Dun instead.[7]

By now, every manor court recorded its proceedings, every bishop kept a register, every judge, sheriff or coroner kept clerical staff.[8] Scriveners and lawyers were much in demand. One of these was Walter de Sutton, who came from Alston Sutton in Somerset.[9] After making his mark as a young scribe in the Devon household of the Pole family, he had soon earned renown as the tactful facilitator of delicate legal matters for all the leading families in the county.[10] Walter calls to mind Chaucer's Man of Law, who 'rode but badly in a medley coat, belted in a silken sash, with little bars'.

He was married to Joan de Langford, who had inherited several estates from her acquisitive grandfather, the Devon High Sheriff of his day. Walter and Joan's daughter, Rosea, married John de Raleigh of Beaudeporte,[11] who lived not far from Sir Mauger's manor of Parracombe. She in turn produced a granddaughter, Margaret de Raleigh, who by the 1330s had reached 'dowable age'. The watchful de Sutton eye[12] now fell on Guy de Sancto Albino, jilted by Miss de Knovill, as an eligible match for Margaret.

The wily de Suttons appointed the rector of St Erme, another parish in mid-Cornwall near to Guy's residence 'La Medishol', as trustee of Margaret's inheritance, while the proximity of Beaudeporte to Parracombe no doubt gave Guy the occasion first to meet his intended bride. Walter and Joan, such a part of the bedrock of country living, had set him up.

By 1332, Guy and Margaret were married. On the one side, Joan de Sutton's brother stepped in at this point and released de Langford lands in Boracots and Boradoner to his niece Margaret and her heirs.[13] On the other, in October 1332 at Westminster, with the help of Walter and rector of St Erme, Guy settled his Cornish manors 'to have and to hold to Guy and Margaret & the heirs of their bodies of the chief lords of that fee by the services which to the said tenements belong for ever. Should Guy & Margaret die without heir of their bodies then the tenements shall revert in their entirety to the right heirs of Guy.'[14]

The family home remained in mid-Cornwall. But for John and Thomas St Aubyn, two sons of Guy and Margaret, their mother's Devon estate became the draw. From 1337 to 1340, their maternal grandfather, John de Raleigh, was appointed Keeper of Exeter Castle and would retain an apartment there.[15] Visiting as young boys, they would have found plenty of adventure in exploring the Crown's stronghold in the west, with its history of sieges and rebellions. In 1440, the appointment as Keeper passed to John de Raleigh of Charles. He was another of the five de Raleigh 'chevalers' in Devon at this time, whose daughter Alice was introduced to the St Aubyn boys. When she became engaged to the eldest John, his grandfather, Sir John de Raleigh (as he had become) settled his Beaudeporte, Streete and other estates on his daughter, Margaret St Aubyn, for life, then onto her son, John.[16]

This was 1348 and by now Walter and Joan de Sutton had died, along with their daughter Rosea. Their son-in-law, Sir John, had changed the name of Joan's inheritance to Combe Raleigh and remarried. But as this was her bequest, on his death it would still be entailed to his and Rosea's daughter

Margaret, and then onto her St Aubyn children. Walter had no doubt been delighted by this outcome. As well as a share from his own father Guy, his great-grandson, John St Aubyn, now stood to inherit three estates: Walter's Somerset lands, his wife Joan's Langford estates including Combe Raleigh, and the Beaudeporte inheritance.

———————◆———————

The first of many clouds now arrived over this happy corner of Devonshire, which had been so much Walter and Joan's creation. In 1348, Sir Henry Medecroft, who had succeeded Walter's kinsman as rector of Combe Raleigh in 1334, died. Sir John de Raleigh, as patron of the church, installed Sir William Toustreyn as priest. Within six months, the new rector was also dead. The Black Death, the pestilence which had spread from central China across all of Europe, had finally arrived in East Devon. Just the other side of Honiton, Colyton lost four vicars in seven months. By March 1349, across the county fifty-seven clergy had died of the plague and in April alone Devon lost a further fifty-one. The plague now took Sir John de Raleigh himself, then his son-in-law young John St Aubyn as well, leaving his widow Alice devastated.

Administering to the dying was never so deadly a calling. But the next rector at Combe Raleigh, Sir Nicholas Mileward, realised the need for precautions, as he obtained a licence of absence for a year.[17] A survivor, it was 1361 before his replacement was installed.[18] Thomas St Aubyn was now the patron, the middle son of Guy and Margaret, who not only stepped into his older brother John's inheritance, but also took the hand of his widow. They had a son called John, after the two men they had lost. Thomas had also by now received his family inheritance from his father, Guy. In 1364, he let houses, four acres of land and a corn mill near St Agnes in Cornwall, for 26s 8d a year to one Robert Meddelond.[19]

But the quiet role of a country squire was not suited to Thomas, reared on tales of his ancestors' exploits and castle visits. Moreover, the mid-century military success of the English against the French, at the Battle of Crecy, in the capture of Calais and at Poitiers, where the Anglo-Gascon forces under the Black Prince prevailed against a French army three times their size, had inspired a new generation of warriors. By the humiliating Treaty of Bretigny, in 1360, vast areas of France were ceded to England and the captured French king, John II, was ransomed for three million gold crowns. Knights returning from these campaigns boasted not only of their valour, but also of the bountiful ransoms they had wrung from French captive nobility.

So when the Black Prince planned a new Aquitaine campaign, in January 1369, Thomas rallied to the cause.[20] He now needed trusted attorneys to manage his affairs during his absence. For his Cornish estates, Thomas nominated Ralph Tredenen and Henry Tyrel.[21] For his Devon estates, he first chose Stephen Trevanion, the vicar of Ladock where his father had settled with Margaret thirty-five years before. His other attorney was John de Mohun, a hero of Crecy, a founding member of the Knights of the Garter and a descendant of one of the leading Norman barons at Hastings.

Baron de Mohun was the uncle of the 26-year-old Leonard de Carew, who had recently inherited Monkton, the manor adjacent to the St Aubyn home of Combe Raleigh. Leonard and Thomas' applications for attorneys reached the king's clerk on the same day.[22] It is likely that Baron de Mohun played a much needed hand in recruiting them both. By 1369, both old age and plague had thinned out the ranks of the knighthood who had helped Edward III to his stunning victories in the first decades of the Hundred Years' War, while the next generation had no more escaped the ravages of the plague than the rest of the country.

His effort was also no doubt a welcome diversion for de Mohun, from his domineering wife Joan. She forced the sale of his vast estates in Somerset to provide for her three daughters' exalted marriages and for her tomb at Canterbury, where her effigy still rests in the cathedral chancel; but his does not.

Whatever hopes spurred the enthusiasm of these two fresh volunteers, Thomas and Leonard, they belied the harsh reality which would soon face them. The humiliations inflicted on France in mid-century had forced a radical change of strategy. In the 1340s and 1350s, the main military operations had been conducted by massive armies operating for short periods, mostly in the summer season. At Crecy, the French army of 20,000 men had been corralled for only a month.

But by 1369 the French realised that they could never win massive encounters by opposing hordes, not least because of the fatal impact of English archers. Relative peace may have conditioned many of the knightly class to prefer scutage over service, but the legacy of the Norman militarised state lived in England's cadre of archers. Almost from birth, their physique was developed in tandem with their technique. France could never hope to develop such an asset, in the short interludes which punctuated a century of war.

So the French now rejected the pitched battle as their objective, in favour of effective control of territory, by the use of smaller armies composed of professional fighters, who remained in the field for far longer periods. The financial ability to support such a policy proved an unbeatable strategic advantage. About two thirds of the tax revenues of the French state were available for the prosecution of war. This was three times the amount that England could afford. In the words of Jonathan Sumption's masterly summary, 'The whole history of these years is written into these figures'.[23]

The expeditionary force joined by Thomas St Aubyn and his friend, Leonard de Carew, began to assemble in Southampton under the command of Edmund Langley and John Hastings. Langley, Earl of Cambridge, was an easy-going mediocrity of 28, with almost no military experience. Hastings, Earl of Pembroke, was intelligent, self-confident and ambitious, but at 22 had even less experience. However, by March, Thomas and Leonard were among 800 to 1000 men setting out for the north coast of Brittany, whence they made their way down to England's possession of Aquitaine, through the perfidious dukedom of Simon de Montfort.

The expeditionary force reached the Black Prince in late April, at his capital in Angoulême, and were immediately tasked with a punitive raid into French territory. Destroying property as they advanced on Bourdeilles, a formidable thirteenth-century castle, its siege lasted a month, before falling to an intrepid sortie. Young Pembroke won his spurs in this engagement and quite possibly this is also when Thomas and Leonard were knighted by their commander.

But in the strategic province of Poitou, the French combined the force of several large contingents to arrive without warning. Heavily outnumbered, the English were caught between this attacking force and the enemy troops in the besieged town of Compeyre. As darkness fell, the remnants of the bloody encounter tried to slip away but were pursued. Many more men were lost, along with their baggage train. One to suffer was the mortally wounded Sir Leonard de Carew. He barely made his way home, where he finally died in October just short of his twenty-eighth birthday, leaving a widow and a one-year-old son.[24] Such news would have reached Devon soon enough. Two months later, pride in her newly knighted husband was no doubt mixed with foreboding for Alice St Aubyn, when she learnt that Thomas was to remain on active service in Aquitaine for another year.[25]

In the first half of 1370, a series of skirmishes harassed the English contingent, while depleting the resources of the French. Then John of Gaunt arrived to support the floundering Langley and Hastings. 1600 men landed with him at Bordeaux and by early September, his troops were assembled at Cognac. Here he met these two commanders and his brother, Prince

Edward. No longer at the height of his powers, Edward 'the Black Prince' was now being carried in a litter, surrounded by interfering councillors.

As the enemy melted away, the English commanders' attention fell on the city of Limoges, supinely surrendered by its bishop in the course of the French advance. A retaliatory expedition was launched, to teach other Aquitaine cities a lesson, not to open their gates so easily to the enemy. By mid-September, a 3000 strong Anglo-Gascon army had arrived outside the city walls. Limoges was defended by a garrison of just 140 men. The siege was over in five days.

According to the polemical account of Froissart, Sir Thomas St Aubyn and the other knights under Prince Edward's command then committed one of the worst atrocities. Their actions went well beyond the routine sackings of the times. He described the English seizure of Limoges thus:

> All of them were equipped for evil and ready to spread out across the city, killing men, women and children as they had been ordered to…There is no man who, if he had been at Limoges and remembered the name of God, would not have wept over the tragedy that happened there.[26]

But this report, which for centuries blackened the reputation of one of England's greatest warriors and the men like Sir Thomas whom he led, is recently discredited.[27] The first casualties, it has emerged, were the supporters of the English, who opened the gates and were then killed by the French garrison in revenge. The leaders of the city were taken prisoner not killed, to be ransomed in the normal way, and the citizens ordered to pay a fine of 40,000 gold crowns to the prince. Such penalties were the custom of the age. It would hardly help to persuade other cities to return to the English fold, if its army went beyond the chivalrous bounds of behaviour.

As for Froissart's most egregious allegation, that 3000 inhabitants were slaughtered, this has long been disputed and the true number was around 300, at least half – as it now appears – killed by the French themselves. But the enamel industry took a century to recover from the sacking, a far more obvious cause than massacre, of the rapid decline in population.

Prince Edward was carried back from Limoges in his litter, unaware that Froissart's libel would haunt his reputation for centuries. By the start of October, Thomas had arrived in Cognac, where the Gascon forces were disbanded. The prince's doctors ordered a return to England and the rule of Aquitaine was transferred to his brother, John of Gaunt. Thomas joined those accompanying the Black Prince home, and the long sea journey from Gironde to Plymouth was completed by the end of January 1371. No doubt Alice and his son John, just reaching maturity, were there waiting anxiously on the Devon shore to greet the family hero. He had survived.

Thomas had learnt the hard way that by the 1370s, the glamour and prizes his grandfather had won by knightly endeavour were no longer on offer. Even professional war profiteers were confounded by these straightened times. In the words of Froissart, it was 'one time lost, another time gained'.[28]

By now, three quarters of all English knights and squires had never served in France and most of the others for one campaign at most. As Geoffrey Chaucer, who had fought for Edward III in his heyday, observed: 'there is full many a man that crieth "War! War!" hat woot full little what war amounteth'.[29]

So it may seem surprising that Thomas was prevailed upon to serve again, a decade later when he was nearing his sixtieth birthday. But by the end of 1380, England's financial and military resources were being stretched to the limit, with 8000 men serving across France, 1000 in Ireland and 3000 men defending the Scottish border. With men-at-arms and archers in short supply, the Council advising the new child-king, Richard II, nevertheless committed to sending another 2000 men to Britany and the same again to Portugal, in the following spring.

Sir Thomas Felton, former Seneschal of Gascony, ordered Sir Thomas St Aubyn and his retinue to muster with the rest of his army at Dartmouth, fifty miles down the coast from Combe Raleigh.[30] But before they could sail to the Loire, the Council in London was frozen by indecision, as the position in France had unravelled, with the defection of the slippery Simon de Montfort.

As Felton's men awaited orders, they were joined by 3000 troops heading for Portugal, under Edward Langley, the Duke of York. The Duke of York's men-at-arms included Geoffrey St Aubyn, Thomas' younger brother summoned from Cornwall, who had no military experience at all.[31] As two armies competed for food and lodging around Dartmouth, the St Aubyn brothers attended their retinue, but no doubt sought their own shelter with local friends. There, before the Council finally ordered Felton's army to stand down, Thomas could pass on some harsh lessons of his previous campaign experience under Langley.

In aid of John of Gaunt's claim to the throne of Castille, supported by Portugal, Geoffrey sailed with the rest of Langley's army to Lisbon. But this proved yet another abortive expedition when a decisive naval defeat of the Portuguese fleet forced King Ferdinand into a humiliating peace treaty. The Duke of York's men sailed home discontented.

Felton's army had also been disbanded. Thomas would have returned to his family with uneasy feelings, anxious at leaving his brother en route to Portugal, but also relieved. For by now he must have known that he was not in good health. Many knights returned from war nursing wounds which never fully recovered and eventually claimed their lives. Four thousand rough troops mixing in close quarters for months on end was an ideal breeding ground for the plague – which still lurked in the general population – and for pervasive dysentery. For whatever reason, within four months of his return to Combe Raleigh's restful pastures, Sir Thomas was dead.[32]

CHAPTER 4

THE WIDOWS OF WAR

... the apostle says that I am free
To wed, in God's name, where it pleases me.
He says that to be wedded is no sin;
Better to marry than to burn within.

Chaucer, *The Wife of Bath's*
Prologue (ll. 49–52)

There were some aggressive magnates in Devon at this time. Their acquisitive instincts were frustrated by the dismal military prizes abroad, so they cast around for opportunities at home, without regard for the niceties of the law, its enforcement often resting in their own hands. The death of a knight such as Thomas St Aubyn, with estates in Devon, Cornwall and Somerset, often provided the chance for meddling in a family's affairs, especially when a complex inheritance involved a widow who remarried, a minor's wardship for sale, or a daughter's hand.

One of those who might keep these machinations in check was Sir James Chudleigh.[1] He had begun on foot as a modest esquire but had risen through service at Poitiers and then under Gaunt in Spain, while amassing substantial properties in the county including the overlordship of Shirwell in North Devon, where the St Aubyns had originated. As it happened, some years earlier his daughter Joan Chudleigh had married John St Aubyn, the son and heir to Sir Thomas.[2] By 1382, John had reached 30, had served as a Devon commissioner and had earned his spurs as well.[3] His father-in-law was keen for Sir John, as he now was, to take up arms again. In fact, he may have been obliged to satisfy the conditions tied to his feudal tenures, and which arose when he inherited them from his father, Sir Thomas. Trusted attorneys, which Sir James Chudleigh could help him to find, would take care in his absence to provide for Joan and their children.

The manor of Alston Sutton in Somerset, those of Combe Raleigh, Beaudeporte and Streete in Devon, as well as property in Honiton and elsewhere were all entrusted to John de Blake of Loddeforde, as lead attorney.[4] This was a curious choice. Blake was clerk to Sir Robert Tresilian, the Chief Justice of the King's Bench since 1381, when his predecessor had been killed during the Peasants' Revolt. At Sir Robert's 'Bloody Assizes' which followed, thirty-one rebels were executed. As well as lacking in mercy, Tresilian was also known for his flagrant corruption, abusing his position to advance his own fortune in court cases across Devon and Cornwall.

John de Blake's and his co-attorneys' indenture was witnessed by Joan St Aubyn's father, Sir James Chudleigh, and his brothers-in-law, Sir John and Nicholas de Pomeroy. As well as murky dealings with the Tresilian family, Sir John Pomeroy had also helped the judge's clerk, John de Blake, by giving him the wardship of one of his tenants. One of Pomeroy's close friends was Sir John Dynham, who in 1381 had unscrupulously sought to claim 'the wardship of the land and heir of Thomas St Aubyn'[5] and who was later found by a Cornish inquest to be receiving 'the issues of the manor of Arrallas ... by an unjust title'.[6] This was one of the St Aubyn family's earliest and most valued tenures, held as tenant-in-chief. Sir John St Aubyn had placed his family estates into the hands of a nest of vipers.

But as soon as these arrangements were made, the political dynamic in London compelled Sir John to fulfil his knightly duties abroad.[7] The Peasants' Revolt had been aggravated by the poll taxes to pay for war; while its failures had left both the House of Commons and the mob in the street bereft of confidence in the king's council.

Now Henry le Despencer, Bishop of Norwich, proclaimed a 'holy crusade', financed by the Church and endorsed by Pope Urban, to liberate Flanders, recently seized by the French. His campaign was swiftly approved by parliament and funds poured in from the sale of indulgences; to these, the Commons needed to add only the paltry subsidy they had already raised. In March 1383, messengers were dispatched to every county town in a call to arms. Within two months, Sir John St Aubyn was among 8000 men-at-arms and archers who had sailed to France, where Bishop le Despencer joined them.

Caught up in this mêlée, John must have realised the risks of being led by a bishop with no military expertise. Even though he had secured the counsel of five seasoned lay captains, including Sir Robert Knolles, none of them enjoyed sufficient standing to counter the bishop's whims.

Without waiting for all of his army to arrive, le Despencer led his troops out of Calais and immediately seized Bourbourg, a major fortress on the road to Bruges. The seaport of Gravelines fell at the first assault. The army entered Dunkirk unopposed a few days later. South of the town, they engaged the Flemish army in a rout, with many thousands of the enemy dispatched, none more savagely than by the priests, monks and friars in the English columns. This undeserved success bred a fatal overconfidence.

Just as France raised a more disciplined force to meet them, le Despencer marched his men on Ypres. Their initial assault was obliterated by a barrage of deadly cannon fire and they settled back for a siege of the town. But after a further month of preparations, a major assault on the city gates was even more disastrous, over 500 crusaders dying in a single day. The tide of the campaign had changed, morale was broken and the following month, after a final and failed assault lasting six days, le Despencer's army beat a ragged and ignoble retreat all the way home. At least they had averted a decisive encounter with Charles V's army of 30,000 men, drawn from every part of his realm. The French were left complaining of 'heavy losses and little honour'.[8]

But for Joan St Aubyn and her two young boys under ten, Guy and John, the heaviest loss of all was felt at home. Just two years after their grandfather Sir Thomas, the boys' brave father had fallen in a field of Flanders.[9]

***

For Sir John's heirs, ahead lay all the vicissitudes of wardship and disputed estates. It appeared at least that Sir James Chudleigh, Joan's father, was there to help them. Except that his instinct was to help himself as well.

Sir James was at this moment involved in a bitter dispute with Baron Bryan, whose influence in Devon exceeded even his own.[10] Three years after Joan had lost Sir John, her father proposed to settle his dispute with the baron, by arranging her marriage to the baron's son, Philip Bryan. Such had been the enmity between them that a papal dispensation for this marriage had to be granted, to heal the 'wars and discencions' between the fathers. Yet within two years, Philip had died childless, leaving Joan now as the beneficiary of two 'dowers' (as a widow's claim on her husband's estate was known).

At this point Sir Thomas Pomeroy, a cadet member of the same family which had witnessed Sir John St Aubyn's settlement, found himself in the first of the many dire financial predicaments of his life.[11] He saw in Joan an immediate solution to his problems. Quite apart from her St Aubyn and Bryan dowers, she was also one of the heiresses to the manor of Berry Pomeroy, through her Pomeroy mother. Sir Thomas knew this because he was one of the trustees of this valuable manor and would control how and when it would revert to the sisters and heirs, when the senior Sir John Pomeroy might die.

Sir Thomas' only difficulty was that the twice-widowed Joan Chudleigh had apparently, by common fame, already secretly married one William Amadas. But this most ambitious member of his generation of Pomeroys, lacking any real ability, was not to be deterred. In September 1388, at Chudleigh, the vicar of Berry Pomeroy was summoned before the Bishop of Exeter's court accused of celebrating a clandestine marriage between Pomeroy and Joan. A penance was imposed upon the vicar, but Pomeroy had to obtain the king's pardon, for which, in October 1389, he paid £10 into the hanaper of the chancery. Amadas meanwhile disappeared. A private marriage, contracted by a simple exchange of words, at this time counted as valid; but was hard to prove with no priest to swear it.

His mother's conjugal career must have deeply embarrassed her eldest son, Guy St Aubyn, now 12 years old, not to mention his younger brother John. This was only to be exceeded by anxiety over the portents for Guy's wardship, estates and choice of bride, now that this mercenary and controlling stepfather was on the scene.

In the summer of 1388, Sir Thomas Pomeroy felt confident that however high-handed his conduct, his family's close connections to John de Blake and Sir Robert Tresilian would place the law on his side. But as he wooed Joan the widow, fortune was turning against the king and his favourites. The 'Merciless Parliament', summoned to prevent Richard II's attempt at a secret peace treaty with France, usurped his power. It put the kingdom into the hands of a regency of so-called Lords Appellant, who convicted the king's advisers of treason. Some were exiled but most were executed. Tresilian was among those found guilty of 'living in vice, deluding the said king ... embracing the mammon of iniquity for themselves'.

The purge penetrated the king's administration, with dozens of retainers, clerks, chaplains and secretaries summarily condemned and executed. Tresilian was dragged out of sanctuary in Westminster and dispatched on the spot. His vast lands in Buckinghamshire, Berkshire,

Oxford and Cornwall were forfeited to the Crown, with most sold to John Hawley, an enterprising Dartmouth privateer. John de Blake, the St Aubyn family trustee, was hanged as a traitor and his property also forfeited.

Sir John Pomeroy would not die until 1416 and as for the Bryan inheritance, it was only after the accession of Henry IV, with whom the Pomeroys found favour, that Joan considered risking an inheritance claim. Litigation dragged on for another dozen years.

In the meantime, the mere income from Joan's estates was not sufficient to support Pomeroy's extravagance. Shortly after his marriage, he entered into a recognizance before the mayor of the Staple of Westminster in September 1388 for more than £83; when payment became overdue and a writ was issued threatening his property in Somerset, Oxfordshire, Dorset and Devon, the St Aubyn manor of Alston Sutton was used to pay off the debt.[12]

At regular intervals after this, Pomeroy received royal pardons of outlawry for failure to appear in court to answer his creditors, usually London merchants. Six such pardons alone related to debts amounting to more than £120, owed to city vintners, saddlers, drapers, tailors, armourers, a mercer and a fishmonger, as well as to the receiver of the Duchy of Cornwall. For Guy St Aubyn, his stepfather was proving the darkest of knights.

Healthy members of the upper echelons of country society attained the age of 70 or even 80, if they managed to avoid the medieval hazards of war and disease. Marrying later in life idealised the chivalric code, that a woman should scorn to give her love to any man who had not proved himself three times in battle. More prosaically, old men liked to marry young maids, who could provide them with sons in their fifties or even later, stretching the span of each generation. But by the turn of the fourteenth century, confidence in their lifespan, shaken by the Black Death and heavy military fatalities, meant this 'chivalrous' custom was in abeyance.

In August 1390, an inquest had been held to determine 'whether the marriage of Guy son and heir of the said John Seint Aubyn ought to pertain to the king ... by reason of the tenure of the said messuages and hamlet' in Mid Cornwall.[13] It was determined that, as these properties were held 'in socage' of Sir John Pomeroy and others, 'the marriage of the said Guy ought not to pertain to the king'. The result was that while Guy was out of the king's hands, he was still in the clutches of his stepfather. But in 1398, he would reach maturity and so would the beautiful young girl of 14 who had caught his eye.[14]

Alice Sergeaux was the daughter of Sir Richard Sergeaux of Colquite, in Cornwall,[15] who had accumulated great wealth, both by his own machinations and through his wife, a granddaughter of the Earl of Arundel.[16] In 1393, after both Sir Richard and his son had died in quick succession, his estates were left to be shared between his four daughters, including Alice.

Six years later, Alice and Guy were married and in November 1400, at a hearing in Westminster Hall, the following order was granted:

> … to give Guy de Sancto Albino and Alice his wife seisin
> of her purparty of the lands of Richard Sergeaux knight and
> Philippa his wife … with the proviso that each of the heirs and
> parceners should have a share of the lands held in chief and
> be a tenant of the king and the said Guy has proved the age of
> Alice before the escheator of Cornwall, and the king has taken
> his fealty.[17]

They were now both of age, both at last free of their meddling parents' generation and both free to enjoy the income from their substantial family estates. This couple presented themselves as a young love match and there seemed no reason why they should not have continued to enjoy their happiness.

But the costly burden of supporting his mother and her dissolute husband, obtaining the king's consent to his inheritance and securing Alice's hand, meant that Guy could scarcely afford to defer his 'fealty' to the Crown by paying scutage, even had he so wanted.[18] Before Alice could produce a child, Guy was called away in the king's service, as his father and grandfather had been called before him.[19]

———◆———

In 1388, John Hawley – the enterprising Dartmouth privateer – could afford to buy the estates of Sir Robert Tresilian, the corrupt Chief Justice. By the first years of the new century, his profitable assaults on enemy shipping vessels in the English Channel had provoked the rising anger of the French and in August 1403, William du Chastel led a devasting raid on Plymouth.[20] Hawley responded two months later, seizing seven merchant ships in the Chanel and in November, Sir William Wilford launched a revenge raid on Brittany, taking forty ships. An attack on the Isle of White by Count Waleran of St Pol in December was beaten off, but French raids on Portland and Weymouth followed in the spring. In March, the French declined the offer to renew their truce with England, where a full-scale invasion was now feared imminent.

Henry IV appointed two new admirals, Sir Thomas Beaufort for the east and Sir Thomas Berkeley, a flamboyant soldier with a flair for naval warfare, for the west and south. Berkeley promptly requisitioned 20 knights, 280 esquires, and 600 archers.[21] A third were assigned to Dartmouth and the rest to individual ports along the coast. Guy was one of those commandeered, under the captaincy of his recently knighted brother-in-law, William Marney, married to Alice's elder sister. Letters of protection, safeguarding their estates from lawsuits, were granted to them both in May 1404 while they were 'going on the king's service in the company of Thomas, lord of Berkeley'.[22]

Meanwhile, Chastel had assembled a fleet of 300 ships in St Malo and 2000 knights and men-at-arms. But this crew lacked discipline, some of the fleet breaking away as soon as they set sail to maraud some Spanish wine ships. Chastel sailed on for Dartmouth with reduced forces and arriving at Blackpool Sands, between Dartmouth and Slapton, waited six days for his fleet to reassemble.

This gave John Hawley time to muster his local defences, digging a water-filled moat across Blackpool Sands as they prepared for the French assault. When Chastel leapt ashore, he killed the first three men he encountered and his side quickly established a foothold. A fierce battle commenced as the Bretons charged at those defending their ditch, but it proved an impenetrable front. Seeking to come round its side through the sea, many Bretons attempted to swim but were dragged into the depths by the weight of their armour. Those that emerged, covered in mud, were assailed by arrows and even Dartmouth women pelting them with stones. According to the contemporary *Chronique de St Denis:*

> Those who had made the direct assault, seeing that they could not escape and must fight for their lives, they sustained for long every effort of the English and killed about fifteen hundred men. William de Chastel ... distinguished himself ... his great axe swept right and left ... all that were struck were slain or mortally wounded. In the end ... he fell pierced with wounds.[23]

The enemy ships managed their escape, leaving behind a scene of carnage. It seems among those 'pierced with wounds' was Guy St Aubyn. He may have survived for a few months, as in March 1405 he was still listed as the patron of St Erme, when a new chaplain was installed.[24] But eventually, after two years of mourning Guy's death, while her dower was settled, his attractive widow met Richard de Vere. He owned the neighbouring estate in Essex to her brother-in-law Marney, who had survived his tour of duty.

De Vere's much older cousin had been the widely despised favourite of Richard II, another one of those condemned to death by the Merciless Parliament, albeit *in absentia* as he had escaped abroad. The family estates were confiscated and only partially restored by the time Richard inherited the family title of Earl of Oxford in 1400, at the age of 15. Seven years later, also widowed after a childhood betrothal, he became Alice's second husband.[25] On the eve of Agincourt, nine years on, he would write his will, leaving everything to her and their son.

Guy's death left his younger brother John as the sole survivor of the senior St Aubyn family line, with their substantial estates in Somerset, Devon and Cornwall. His mother Joan's dower gave her the right to the income from the manors of Alston Sutton and Combe Raleigh; this was probably even greater than the dower of his sister-in-law, Alice, which in 1417 was found to be £10 a year, taken from his Cornish manors of Arrallas, Trewennan and Burngullow.[26] Given that a knight was required to show an income of at least £40 a year, these dower obligations may well explain why John remained an esquire.

Yet he was still able to support the family's position in the county and he found a good friend in Sir Robert Chalons, a coming man in Devon and a favourite of Henry IV.[27] Only five years older than John, he offered him the hand of his daughter, Katherine. In December 1409, Chalons was High Sheriff and he used his position to nominate his new son-in-law in the election for Devon, held at Exeter Castle on Christmas Eve, to the parliament in January 1410. But John may merely have been put up as a foil to assist the election of his stepfather, Pomeroy, and the habitual Devon MP Robert Carey, with whom Chalons had had dealings.

Across the county border, the MP elected for the borough of Taunton that year, the administrative centre of the vast manor of Taunton Deane, was Thomas Bacot. Since the eighth century, this manor had belonged to the

See of Winchester, whose bishop was now the powerful Henry Beaufort. The second son of John of Gaunt, he was engaged in a bitter dispute with his half-brother, Henry IV. As the bishop's 'bailiff of the liberty', a vital role in running Taunton and licensing its tradesmen, Bacot carried his master's animosity to the king on his sleeve. Conversely, on the king's side, so did the royal favourite Sir Robert Chalons and his son-in-law, John St Aubyn.

We can only imagine the immediate provocation between these two rival camps. But shortly after Bacot's return home from the parliament, at Ilchester on 21 May 1410 there followed an affray between Bacot and John.[28] Bacot was so badly wounded that his recovery was deemed a miracle and even so, he died within three years. Yet the following February, John St Aubyn was granted a 'pardon of outlawry' after 'not appearing to answer Edward, Duke of York, touching a debt of 1,000 marks.'[29] This debt of £670 was exceptional; the dozens of other debts dealt with by the Westminster court in that session were typically between two and twenty pounds. Evidently, the extraordinary fine imposed on John, for his part in the Bacot affray, had been promptly rescinded.

This sign of royal favour towards John St Aubyn, as one who had taken the side of the Crown, may have assisted when he was again proposed for parliament in 1414. Bishop Beaufort had now been reconciled by Henry V's succession to his father's throne, while John's political rival, Carey, was temporarily indisposed. In the second parliament of that year, John St Aubyn was elected as MP for Devonshire.[30]

By now, his marriage to Katherine had produced their first child, Joan, born about the time he was molesting the Taunton burgess. The Cornish estates were settled on John and his wife and heirs in 1412, his father-in-law, Sir Robert, assisting in the transaction. Katherine gave birth to their second daughter, Margaret, at the abbey of the minoresses of St Clare outside Aldgate, in January 1415. John was probably there with her in London.

Already, the drumbeat of war could be heard on the street, as the recently crowned Henry V mobilised his military resources. It may even have been at Margaret's christening, that John and Sir Robert both decided to enrol – John under the banner of the king's brother, the Duke of Clarence; Chalons under Thomas Beaufort, who was now the Earl of Dorset.[31]

The king had resolved to take Harfleur. He would then provoke the enemy into that definitive pitched battle, which the inconclusive campaigns of the past forty years had avoided, leaving the knightly forces on both sides simmering with frustration.

On 13 August 1415, the English fleet reached the coast just below Harfleur, after two days at sea, catching by surprise the French army positioned further south. The landing of 12,000 men-at-arms and 8000 archers went unopposed. The enormous expense of their invasion was being financed by Henry V largely on credit, not least that of the soldiers themselves, who had agreed to be paid in arrears. There was hardly an item of jewellery or plate in the Crown's possession which had not been hocked to them in some way.

Sir Robert Chalons, providing a contingent of three men-at-arms and nine archers, was delivered of a gold cup and two bowls and a basin of silver gilt as security for payment of £45 6s 10d, the wages of his small force for the second quarter of the year.[32] The Duke of Clarence, John St Aubyn's commander, with the largest company in the army after the king's, had taken the great crown of his father, Henry IV, and broken off its gold fleurons and precious stones, to pledge to his retainers as security for their wages. John's retinue, one other man-at-arms and eight archers, would have been paid £22 15s a quarter.[33]

The town was only defended by its citizens and a small garrison of thirty-four men-at-arms with some crossbowmen. To these the French now quickly added some seasoned captains and 300 men-at-arms hurriedly gathered from Normandy and Picardy. The English took four days to organise themselves and to invest the town on its westward side. Then Clarence's company was ordered to the eastern ridge. John St Aubyn was one of the 240 men-at-arms, with 720 archers, who marched through the night. The chronicler of *Gesta Henrici Quinti* takes up the story:

> And that night the Duke captured on his march certain carts and waggons belonging to the enemy, with a great quantity of guns and powder-barrels and missiles and catapults, which were thought to have come from Rouen for the defence of the town. And on the Monday, at dawn in clear sunlight, he made his appearance over the crest of the hill facing the town on that side, not without causing real fear and dread among the besieged.[34]

The town was now almost completely isolated. But it took a battle of attrition until 22 September, in which Clarence's company made a notable contribution, before the keys of the town were silently delivered up and Harfleur surrendered to the king's mercy.

Victory was bittersweet. Five weeks in waterlogged meadows had proved a breeding ground for disease and for the 'bloody flux', a fatal form of dysentery which soon reached epidemic proportions. About 2000 men died from it, far more than were killed by the enemy, while 5000 more were now too ill to fight. Henry V had lost half the fighting strength which had sailed with him from Southampton.

The sick list included the Duke of Clarence and John St Aubyn.[35] While Chalons and a small company under Thomas Beaufort stayed to protect Harfleur,[36] the remaining army began the dogged march which would lead to their heroic victory at Agincourt a month later, on 25 October. By then, the ships taking the sick home had made a stop in Calais. This confused the enemy, who fearing a rearguard action, tied down troops who might otherwise have tilted the battlefield in France's favour. But the fleet carrying the sick sailed on home, unaware of this incidental part they had played in England's greatest feat of arms.

'What wise man', Bishop Beaufort asked, 'looking back on this campaign, will not stand amazed and attribute it to the power of God?' The House of Lancaster's claim to the throne appeared divinely blessed and would remain unchallenged for fifty years. Henry landed at Dover in November and a week later made a triumphant entry into his capital, which felt an exuberance unknown since Poitiers a half century before.

The effect was a surge of support, to complete the task of conquest the king had set himself. Like so many others, John St Aubyn, recovering for a year with his young family and attending the day-to-day business of his estates,[37] would answer the renewed call to arms when it came.[38] But without a son and heir, on his life stood most of his inheritance, as was the case for so many knightly descents already destroyed in the war with France. If he were killed, his St Aubyn cousins in Cornwall would inherit from him little more than the mantle of the family name.

———————

When Sir John Pomeroy finally died in 1416, his lordship of the manor of Tregony was placed in John St Aubyn's hands, while his mother and her dissolute Pomeroy husband remained at Combe Raleigh, to be nearer the heart of the Pomeroy estates, which now offered her husband rich pickings of its own. Today, the riverbed at Tregony has long been silted up by tin washings drawing water from the river. But at this time, it was still an active seaport, on a tidal creek of the Fal estuary.

So from there, in July 1417, John would have sailed round the coast to join the army assembling at Southampton, one of 4000 men-at-arms and 8000 archers, for the conquest of Normandy.[39] The alarm was raised that some men-at-arms were sporting armorial bearings, who had no right to do so.[40] The king ordered the sheriffs of the surrounding counties to enforce a prohibition on assuming such arms, unless the bearer possessed these 'either by ancestral right or by the grant of someone who had adequate power to make such grant'. On the day of the muster, each man-at-arms had to show by what grant he held such bearings, the one exception being for those who had 'borne arms with us at the battle of Agincourt'.

John St Aubyn could no doubt flourish the proof of his crusading forebear, as well as the service to the Crown of his father and grandfather. But those who could not do so faced 'the stripping off and breaking up of the said arms and tunics called coat armours'. They even risked exclusion from the campaign and the loss of their wages. Henry was determined to monopolise the grant of arms and to impose his Statute of Additions, the law passed four years earlier with its rigid feudal structures.

At the end of July, the Earl of Huntingdon returned in triumph from a decisive sea battle at the mouth of the Seine, bringing four Genoese carracks in tow. These vessels of about 500 tons each were promptly absorbed into the Royal Navy, which had become one of the most powerful fleets in Europe. On 1 August, Henry's task force set sail, at least 233 ships in the line under his 1000-ton flagship the *Jesus*. They landed in Normandy just south of Honfleur, at the small port of Touques. John was not among the twenty-eight new knights dubbed at the water's edge[41]; his dissapointment no doubt designed to spur him on, along with his fellow men-at-arms.

The inhabitants of the local towns fled before the victor at Agincourt, who skirted around Honfleur as smaller settlements fell at his feet. An advanced guard of about a thousand men-at-arms was led by the Duke of Clarence – who had already commanded John at Harfleur, two years before – on an assault on Caen, seizing the towers overlooking the old town before the French could demolish them. Surrender was now inevitable and despite stiff resistance, the keys to the city were given up on 20 September.

But the death or departure of a quarter of its 6000 population, following a brutal reckoning, brought home an emerging problem across Lower Normandy. 'The most pressing need now is for people to inhabit these places', as Clarence reported back to the City of London; otherwise the conquest was not sustainable.

This at last presented John St Aubyn with his opportunity for promotion, along with dozens of other aspiring officers. Lisieux and Bayeux, the two cathedral towns of Lower Normandy, had flung open their gates soon after the sack of Caen, to avoid a similar fate; the surrounding countryside was dotted with surrendered towns, where the invaders urgently needed to impose good governance, if they were to win the battle for hearts and minds. So Henry now granted chosen men-at-arms the custody of more than 140 settlements in the region.

According to the chronicles, among those whom Clarence now appointed captain were: *At Faugernon [sic], John St Albones; At Courtonne, John Aubyn*.[42] These two communities lay either side of Lisieux. Fauguernon was only eighty miles from Mayenne; the bastille where eight generations earlier, Captain John St Aubyn's ancestor, Mauger de Sancto Albino, had first sought adventure as the servant of Judhael de Totnes. Just for now, John savoured the role of being one of the masters himself. But this was hostile territory. His commander, the Duke of Clarence, leaving church on Easter Day, was nearly hit when 'a great stone with great force' was hurled 'from a cannon to kill him'. The duke, 'who was greatly enraged' sought out the perpetrator and 'ordered him to be hanged on a high gallows before all the people'.[43] Three months later, following Henry's decision to besiege Rouen, the duke took an advanced guard which may well have included John, and invested the city on the west side.[44]

Henry's arduous siege of the city would take seven months, again an opportunity for disease and dysentery to flourish. We can only speculate as to what befell John St Aubyn, whether as the captain of his Normandy towns, at the hands of a would-be assassin, or during this siege of Rouen. But we know for certain that by October 1418, he had returned home to Tregony a broken man. On 12 November, the Escheator in the counties of Devon and Cornwall was ordered:

> ...to take into the king's hand and keep safely until further ordered all the lands in his bailiwick whereof John Seynt

Aubyn, who held of the king in chief, was seised in his demesne and of fee on the day of his death; and to make inquisition touching his lands and heir.[45]

It would have been John's dying wish to sire a male heir to inherit 'his lands'. Sadly, a year later, his wife Katherine was buried just a mile and a half from St Clare outside Aldgate,[46] where previously she had given birth but where it seems likely that a miscarriage had left her mortally ill. Her father Sir Robert Chalons' hopes of a grandson now dashed, he ceded the management of John and Katherine's affairs to Sir William Bodrugan,[47] on behalf of the young St Aubyn orphans, Joan and Margaret. As soon as Joan reached maturity, she would marry Bodrugan's son, Otto.[48]

Close ties ran between the St Aubyn and Bodrugan families.[49] But their joint dynastic ambitions could not survive the blow of Otto's death, within a few years of this promising alliance. So the resourceful Sir Robert Chalons now found his St Aubyn granddaughter Joan a second husband, William Dennys, who came from an old Devon family. By now, both her grandmother Joan and the insufferable Pomeroy were gone. Combe Raleigh, nestling in its tidy valley with views stretching far beyond to the south, supported by a thousand acres above Honiton, beckoned as this couple's home and for succeeding generations.[50] The long surviving Sir Robert only died in 1445, having seen his Dennys offspring born there.

In 1498, the Crown granted the children of Joan and William a licence:

> ... to found a perpetual chantry of one chaplain in the new aisle, gild or chapel of St Mary and St Erasmus the Matyr, situate in the northern part of the chancel of the parish church of Combe Cofyn, *alias* Comb Ralegh, co. Devon, newly built by William Denys and Joan his wife, both deceased...[to pray] for the souls of the said William and Joan Denys, Gilbert Denys and Margaret his wife, John Seyntabyn and Catherine his wife, Robert Chalons and Blanche his wife ... and all the faithful dead.[51]

Bodrugan had introduced Joan's sister Margaret to a Cornish husband, Reynold Tretherf, whose family's tenure in the manor of Ladock dated from before the Conquest.[52] The Parracombe branch of the St Aubyns had by now migrated to Somerset. So this chantry marked the last stamp of the family's presence in Devon and the extensive lands which they had once accumulated in the course of four centuries.

The St Aubyn name now faced the dismal prospect of the rest of the knightly class across England, a fate which would befall the Bodrugans soon enough. But in Cornwall, an earlier generation had planted their Breton roots in the indigenous ground of the far west. Here they had found fertile soil.

PART TWO

CLOWANCE

CHAPTER 1

THE KEMYELL INHERITANCE

Another son of Guy was Geoffrey —
from whence, downwards, we look
upon this family as Cornish.

Thomas Wotton

The Calendar of Patent Rolls for October 1331, the year before Margaret de Raleigh had married into the St Aubyn family, contains the following entry:

> Ralph de Bloyou, knight, going beyond seas on the king's service has letters nominating Peter Kemyell and Guy de Sancto Albino his attorneys in England for one year.[1]

Sir Ralph was the baronial overlord of one of Guy's manors in Lugdvan. He belonged to a senior Breton family, on whom the Conqueror had bestowed substantial estates in Cornwall. The choice of Peter Kemyell as an attorney made sense, because he represented another of the old Cornish families who, like the Tretherfs, had weathered the changing face of their overlord after the Conquest. But out of the many candidates who served Sir Ralph in feudal tenure, it was surely the Breton connection that directed de Bloyou to entrust his affairs to Guy de Sancto Albino, alongside Peter Kemyell. In 1334, impressed by Guy's growing standing in Cornwall, who was by now married to Margaret, Edward III appointed him as one of the Collectors of the Lay Subsidy.[2]

After their marriage and settling near Ladock, Margaret de Raleigh bore Guy de Sancto Albino a third son, Geoffrey. As well as English, he grew up speaking Latin in his schoolroom and the Cornish tongue – so close to that of his ancestors – within the household. While his elder brothers were drawn to Devon, this last son to Guy and Margaret was becoming 'proper Cornish'. Meanwhile, Peter Kemyell, sometime after he and Guy had managed Ralph de Bloyou's estates together, married Sibil Hallegan. She was the heiress to Hallegan, a manor in the west of the county, whose Cornish name meant 'the hall on the hill'.[3] Small rooms with fireplaces were replacing the open hearth in great halls across England at this time. Hallegan likewise was soon converted by the Kemyells into their family home and adopted the name of Clowance.

This 'valley of echoes', as this name meant in Cornish, had belonged to the Kemyells since at least 1209, when 'Henry de Kemyell, knight, in pure and perpetual alms' had granted to the priory of St Michael's Mount 'a cartload of wood each week from his grove at Clowance, pannage for ten pigs there, and pasture for the oxen when they come for the wood'. In 1232, he gave timber to repair 'and twigs for covering' the houses on the Mount; and in 1241 he witnessed an endowment to the priory by his neighbour Alan Basset, heir to the lords de Dunstanville at Tehidy.[4]

Peter and Sibil Kemyell had a daughter and heiress, Elizabeth, who was probably born ten years after Guy and Margaret's son, Geoffrey. Their betrothal sealed the tight Breton circle which had settled in the west.[5] Reconnecting through this marriage with their ancestral roots, Clowance would provide the seat of the St Aubyn family for the next five centuries.

The Black Death spread to Cornwall in 1349. Unlike his son John in Devon, Guy survived, but it felled a third of the population. Tin production collapsed and half the farm holdings in some manors were left vacant.[6] The ensuing labour shortage across England prompted the Ordinance of Labourers, which bound workers to their level of wages in 1346, and tied them to their lord – the first serious attempt by national government to freeze prices and wages. With parliament's blessing, commissioners were appointed in February 1352 across the country, 'to levy and collect any outstanding fines, ransoms, issues forfeit and amercements of workmen, servants and artificers made and adjudged in accordance with the statute touching the wages of workmen'.

Guy was one of those appointed in Cornwall, each year from 1352 to 1354.[7] But soon workers simply rejected the statutory wages and by the 1390s, their rates of pay would double. Guy was appointed again in 1357, the same time that Sir Richard Sergeaux, Alice's grandfather, also served. But a month later: 'William Bodrugan is appointed to act in the county of Cornwall in the room of Guy de Sancto Albino'.[8] Guy had finally died of old age.

By now, the marriage of Geoffrey St Aubyn to Elizabeth Kemyell had prospered with the arrival of two daughters, whose marriages were further proof of the St Aubyns' absorption into Cornish society. Elizabeth married Richard Boscawen of Tregothnan; then Margery (named after her St Aubyn grandmother) wed John Penrose of Penrose. After Geoffrey had sailed back from his abortive naval mission to Lisbon, Elizabeth bore him two sons as well, called Geoffrey and Peter.

In 1393, Geoffrey was County Coroner[9] and was one of those charged with collecting the two subsidies in March and October. They were ordered 'to go from town to town and the place to place, and cause to come before them two men and the reeve from every town and the mayor, bailiffs and four men from every city and borough … the money to be levied and delivered without delay'.

Geoffrey's civic role attained its peak, when appointed High Sheriff in 1399,[10] in charge of the Crown's Duchy estate as well as the regular duties of his office. This included handling the estate of William, 1st Baron Botreaux, a former mining partner of Geoffrey and one of the Crown's most important tenants-in-chief.[11] His widow was left with a grandson, also called William, now 10 years old. Geoffrey was joined by William's uncle, Sir Ralph Botreaux, and one other executor to handle the estate's affairs.

The duties of High Sheriff were indeed onerous and Geoffrey sometimes found it hard to keep up to the mark. In June 1402, he sought 'a Writ of *supersedeas omnino*' from Henry IV, in respect of 'any process against Geoffrey Seintaubyn late sheriff of Cornwall, by the late king appointed'.[12] It appears that the late King Richard II had issued instructions to Geoffrey and others to enquire into certain 'evildoers and breakers of the peace' but 'the same was never delivered to the said sheriff, as he has made oath in chancery'.

Soon after being granted this absolution, Geoffrey died. William Botreaux's inheritance was left in the hands of his jealous uncle, Sir Ralph. But after coming of age, young Botreaux became an attendant to King Henry V at court, before joining the war against France. He would soon meet the two sons of his former executor, Geoffrey and Peter St Aubyn, who had also been inspired by Henry V's military prowess.

In April of 1418, while John St Aubyn was in Normandy, 'Commissions of Array' were issued to each county, 'for the defence of the realm while the king is in foreign parts for the recovery of the inheritance and rights of the Crown'.[13] Twelve men-at-arms were appointed to raise troops from Cornwall, to defend the coast. They included Sir William Lord Botreaux, his uncle Sir Ralph and young Geoffrey St Aubyn. According to the muster roll in May, his brother Peter was enlisted by Geoffrey and a cousin from Parracombe also joined them.[14,15]

By early July, there were repeated warnings of a French attack on the royal fleet lying in dock. Along the coast, watches were ordered to be kept. Eight balingers and barges were sent out to patrol the southern and western parts of the English Channel for three months.[16] They would provide extra security from raids and attacks on the coast, while the nation's naval resources remained focused on supporting the siege of Rouen.

No detailed reports of this task force survive, but a vivid account by the chronicler of *Gesta Henrici Quinti* of a dawn engagement in the Channel with an enemy carrack the previous summer, conveys the perils of the sort of naval duty to which these three St Aubyn men were now suborned.[17] The deck of the carrack 'was more than a spear's length higher' than the English balinger, but still they grappled the sides, and re-engaged time and time again until it was nearly dark:

> …at long last, having run out of missiles and other weapons of offence, and with great number of those on the carrack killed on this side and that, and with some of our own men also killed, and with many of both parties seriously wounded, just when our men were on the point of taking possession of the carrack they had to break off further attacks on her because of the lack of missiles, boarding-ladders, and weapons of offence, and she made off at speed…

It was not only enemy weapons that the combatants had to fear in such skirmishes:

> '…Thomas West, an agreeable and handsome young knight, had been killed aboard his own ship before the engagement … a stone which was being hurriedly hoisted to the top of the mast fell from its sling on to his bare head and in so doing inflicted a wound and a fatal one. He reached England, however, on

the day before he breathed his last. His death, because of the gallantry and valour expected in the future of one so young, brought sorrow to many.

Naval battle was both primitive and deadly and it was little short of a miracle that all three St Aubyns returned to dry land physically unscathed, although the brutality of their tour of duty was a portent of future trouble. On their return, they were also greeted with the news about the senior member of their family – John – who had not been so lucky in France.

CHAPTER 2

CORNISH GENTRY

Both with spear, bill and brand,—
'Twas a mighty sight to see;
Hardier men both of heart nor hand
Were not in Christianitie
The Ballad of Chevy Chase c.1430

The absence of so many of England's barons, overlords and liegemen engaged in war on French soil, made all the harder the task of quelling lawlessness at home. Disorder gathered momentum as troops, returning from the trauma of the battlefield, stoked the propensity for violence throughout the country.

One wartime survivor was Sir William Plumpton, a member of the Yorkshire gentry, who had earned his spurs in France. In 1441, he led twenty-four members of his household and a cohort of followers, to protect the villagers of Knaresborough from raiders sent by the Archbishop of York. After a rout, the Plumpton men killed prisoners they had taken in cold blood; others were maimed and left for dead on the moor, while those not beaten or stabbed '…were robbed and terrorised … gentlemen, yeomen, artisans and labourers alike'.[1] After this show of brutality, Sir William's Lancastrian overlords helped him become steward of Knaresborough Castle, then Sheriff of Nottingham and later of Derbyshire, as his power and influence grew.

This rampant culture was to be found in Cornwall, as in any other part of the realm.[2] William Botreaux, the titular head of his family, had returned equally unharmed from the coastal defence, during which he had captained the St Aubyn men. But in August 1426, powerful commissioners were appointed to investigate complaints by William about his uncle Ralph Botreaux, 'knight', who had acted along with 'William Langkelly, yeoman, and other malefactors of their covin and assent, unmindful of the salvation of their souls and not having God before their eyes'.[3] They had procured John Alwode of Trudoxhill, Somerset, Hugh Bowet of Kilmington, Somerset, chaplain, and John Neuport 'who are said to practise soothsaying, necromancy and art magic, to weaken and annihilate, subtly consume and altogether destroy by the said arts, the body of the said William Botreaux'.

As a result of the investigation, Sir Ralph was imprisoned in the Tower, only to be released after two months on the surety of £1000. A later agreement drawn up between the Botreaux uncle and his nephew, in February 1433, reveals the cause of the trouble: under pain of £1000, Sir Ralph (who had no children) was required not to prevent his lands from descending to his nephew, and undertook not to 'implead' Lord Botreaux or any of his tenants.

While under Botreaux's command at sea, Geoffrey and Peter St Aubyn may not have been wounded, but they were certainly among the many who returned from their naval duties battle-hardened. It is otherwise hard to square Hals' description of this 'genteel and knightly family'[4] with two accusations of misdemeanour, levelled against the St Aubyn brothers a decade apart.[5] The cases were heard by commissions of Oyer and Terminer, that is before several local justices and a jury, the first of which was appointed in February 1422:

> …on complaint by John Wybbury of the county of Cornwall, esquire, that Geoffrey Seyntaubyn of Clowens, co. Cornwall, and other evildoers went armed to Northleigh, co. Cornwall, by night, broke his closes and houses there, lay in ambush to kill him and inflicted great injuries and grievances, killed forty sheep of his worth 100s., carried off two horses of his worth 100s. and assaulted, wounded and ill-treated his men and servants.

The second, appointed in October 1431, reads no better:

> … on complaint by William Antron of the county of Cornwall, esquire, that John Penras Methle of Penros Vyen, co. Cornwall, 'gentleman', Peter Seyntaubyn of Clowens, co. Cornwall, 'gentleman', and Geoffrey Seyntaubyn of Clowens, 'gentleman', having gathered to themselves many malefactors, names unknown, lay in wait to slay the said William at Helstonburgh, and there assaulted, wounded and ill-treated him.

It should be noted first, in the brothers' defence, that these allegations led nowhere. Whether or not their former captain Lord Botreaux, as the county's leading baron, could afford the St Aubyn brothers some protection when these disputes were heard, a presumption of innocence should always be weighed heavily against allegations of assault at this time. Gratuitous claims of violence were often added to a case, in order to elevate its judicial treatment to higher authority and circumvent the influence of local supporters of the accused.

The authorities only accepted these two complaints because each of them was made, on payment of 'one mark in the hanaper', by an 'esquire'; that is someone with an income from land of £10 or more a year, as against 'gentlemen' with an income of only £3. Further, the intent to murder and so forth does seem to be included merely to bolster the charge sheet; the only complaints which could be based on factual evidence were of being 'ill-treated' and the taking of the horses. This suggests that in reality, each of these grievous allegations probably arose out of an unpaid debt, for which other means of redress had run their course.

In 1427, one Richard Trevynsyn of Redruth sought a pardon for not appearing before justices 'touching a plea of debt of 40s' owed to Geoffrey St Aubyn.[6] In 1430, a steward, Warin Kelly, sought a pardon 'touching two pleas, one of debt of £40 and the other of trespass', in which Geoffrey was the aggrieved plaintiff.[7]

The safest conclusion to be drawn from all these cases is that unlike the senior branch of the family, which had simply collected the dues from their tenants, Geoffrey was in the reduced situation of managing his land and business for profit, a far more precarious existence. This was along with his brother Peter, who was recorded as living with him at Clowance in 1431. Not only did they lack those inheritances, which their Devon cousins had enjoyed from their advantageous marriages, but the dower owing to the young Guy's widow Alice Sergeaux, since 1404, continued to burden the family estate for decades. Her £10 a year, extracted from three of the family's remaining Cornish manors, dwarfed the income of Geoffrey and Peter combined.[8]

Alice's second husband, the Earl of Oxford, had fought at Agincourt with distinction, only to be killed in the Normandy campaign two years later. His widowed countess, now with two dowers, was soon wed to Sir Nicholas Thorley, another hero of Agincourt, who had happily survived. But in October 1421,[9] Thorley was hauled before the Council, to whom he admitted that he had married Alice without royal consent. The Chancellor took into the king's hands all the lands of his Oxford widow until Thorley could pay the fine for their recovery, being a full year's rent. He was sent to the Tower in irons, where he remained until February 1424, when Alice managed at last to raise the money. She also obtained a papal indult for plenary remission in 1426, after which they were fully pardoned for having married without royal licence.

Alice had not only lost two husbands to the Crown's vaulting ambitions in France but had also been penalised for finding love again. After that, she had no reserves of sympathy to give to Guy's remote Cornish cousins, whose impoverished state arose from her dower, an income for life after just four years' marriage three decades before.

Still, it was tactless for her and Thorley to be presented to the parish of St Erme in 1332.[10] This was where in 1405, she had probably appeared in the place of her dying husband Guy, at the installation of a chaplain. It was also inconsiderate of Alice to live until 1452, when the combined rents of Geoffrey and Peter,[11] nearing their seventies, was still only £7; that is £3 less than her St Aubyn dower alone – never mind her far larger income from both Oxford and Thorley, who had also by now departed.

Yet for all the financial discomfort she caused the St Aubyns, Alice Sergeaux, Countess of Oxford, earns admiration for the way she asserted her rights as a woman in a world steeped in patriarchy. She achieved both financial independence and the freedom to love whom she chose. While skirting the norms of society, she had parlayed her childhood inheritance worth £20 a year into a dower income of several hundred pounds. Her effigy rests in St Stephen's Chapel, Bures, next to the earl to whom she gave a son, and whose title she insisted on retaining, even after marrying Sir Nicholas. She wears an elaborate headdress which was fashionable in the day, but drew harsh criticism from the clergy, who likened its eye-catching form to devils' horns, prophesying damnation for those vain enough to wear it. The two small dogs frisking about the feet of Alice's bejewelled effigy hint at her disdain for such prudery.

In 1453, the surrender of Bordeaux marked the end of England's war with France, leaving Calais as her only remaining prize. A century of military overreach, expended in order to prove the Crown's God-given right to rule, had ravaged the number and the fortunes of the old social order. In 1399, for example, Geoffrey St Aubyn had enjoyed an income from land of at least £20 a year, in order to qualify as High Sheriff. In 1451, only seventy-five barons, knights or esquires in the whole of Cornwall reported an income of over £20 and his battle-weary sons, Geoffrey and Peter, did not count among them.[12]

This younger Geoffrey had married Alice Tremere, the daughter of venerable Cornish stock. They had four sons and four daughters, but the record survives of only two sons, Thomas and Peter. They first appear as young men during the 'War of the Roses'. England's failure in France, combined with the unrelenting culture of violence at home, had proved the recipe for another thirty years of conflict between the competing York and Lancastrian factions at Court. In October 1473, this rivalry even reached Cornwall, when the following commission was issued by the Yorkist King Edward IV. This was two years after his Lancastrian opponent and predecessor Henry VI had been captured and murdered in the Tower of London:

> To John Arundell, knight, John Colshyll, knight, Robert Willoughby, knight, John Crocker, knight, John Fortescue, Henry Bodrugan, John Sturgeon, Thomas Whalisburgh, John Trenowth ... to array the king's lieges of the county of Cornwall, and of other counties adjacent if necessary, to conquer John, late Earl of Oxford, and other rebels who have entered St Michael's Mount, co. Cornwall, and to bring back the Mount into the king's hands.[13]

John de Vere, 13th Earl of Oxford, was the grandson of Alice Sergeaux and one of the ablest soldiers in the Lancastrian cause. His seizure of the Mount a month earlier had been in open defiance of the Yorkists. Those commissioned by the king – whose names ran to a further fourteen Cornish gentlemen – was a roll call of Edward IV's most trustworthy supporters. No St Aubyn was included, a sign of the family's reduced circumstances at this time, rather than support for Oxford's rebels. But Thomas St Aubyn was now married to the daughter of John Trenowth, one of those on the king's summons. He no doubt arrayed Thomas and his brother Peter St Aubyn, living just ten miles away at Clowance, to join 'the king's lieges' and besiege the man whose grandmother they recalled as the bane of their childhood.

Oxford held out on the Mount for a remarkable six months, but after many followers had deserted the island stronghold and Oxford himself had been shot in the face by an arrow, he was, in February 1474, compelled to surrender. Escaping imprisonment and joining Henry Tudor in exile, he would later play a crucial role in winning the Battle of Bosworth and become one of the great men of the new Tudor order.

Several of 'the king's lieges' fared rather less well. Years earlier, having been warned that 'upon the yellow sand, thou shalt die by human hand', Sir John Arundell had moved inland to live at Trerice. But during the siege, in a skirmish on Marazion beach, he was slain by the rebels.[14] Sir Henry Bodrugan, another veteran of the French wars, later paid a heavy price for his brutal support of the Yorkist faction of King Richard III. After Bosworth, his arrest was ordered and his enemies pursued him over the Cornish cliffs, from a point ever after known as 'Bodrugan's Leap'.[15] He landed safely in the water, but his escape in a boat to Ireland marked the end of his line. Peter St Aubyn, the younger son of Geoffrey and Alice, would soon find that misplaced loyalty to the House of York led to his own cliff-edge on several occasions.

This Peter St Aubyn was born in about 1440 and later entered into the service of the Arundells of Lanherne. In 1479, the widowed Lady Arundell's will left him nearly £10 and 'his colt that I have given him at Isle Brewers'.[16] But like Henry Bodrugan, four years later he became ensnared in the machinations of Richard III, even after unsavoury rumours swirled around the new king after his brother Edward IV had died and his two sons then vanished. Richard went on the offensive, to secure his crown against Henry Tudor and his rebel supporters.

In November 1483, Peter St Aubyn was commissioned with others 'to arrest and imprison all rebels in the counties of Devon and Cornwall, to take their castles, lordships, manors, lands, chattels and possessions into the king's hands'.[17] An inquisition by Peter and these other Ricardians, held on 3 December 1483 in Bodmin, came six weeks after a plot for a general rising in the West had begun, by publicly proclaiming Henry Tudor king in Exeter. But the plot was bound to fail, as its leader, the Duke of Buckingham, had already been betrayed and executed.

The rebels indicted at this Bodmin inquisition included Courtenay, the future Earl of Devon, and Sir Thomas Arundell. On 3 November, it was said they had 'arrayed in warlike manner … with swords, clubs, bows and arrows, rebels and traitors to the king [Richard III], conspired together, and collecting a great multitude of people, incited them to murder, slay, and utterly overthrow the king himself'.[18] In the smokescreen thus created, the rebels slipped away to Brittany to join Henry, until a better chance to defeat Richard might arise.

The following August, although the ringleaders had escaped, 'the king's servant Peter Seyntaubyn' was granted 'for his good service against the rebels' the manor of Trenay with a yearly value of over £23, 'to hold with knights' fees, wards, marriages, etc ... by knight-service and a rent of 18 shillings yearly'.[19]

This was a very valuable reward and Peter seemed well trusted by Richard. In November 1484, Richard III commanded 'his well-beloved servant Piers St Aubyn' to ensure that Sir James Tyrell – another loyalist – received the Cornish rents due to him from the rebel estates.[20] But the usurper who had stolen the crown from the unlucky Princes in the Tower, was not to last.

A year later, Richard III's demise at the Battle of Bosworth, at the hands of Henry VII, spelt disaster for Peter. The Act of Resumption ensured that within months all these gifts to Ricardian supporters, like Peter and Bodrugan, had been rescinded by Henry VII, to be parcelled out to the new king's favourites.

As an example, Henry issued a Charter in December 1487 '... granting from special favour and mere impulse, to the beloved and faithful John Trelawny, of Mahenest, co. Cornwall (and his heirs)' a licence to a market every Friday in his manor, also 'a court-leet and view of frankpledge ... with correction and punishment ... the goods and chattels of felons and fugitives to be confiscated ... and without account or any other thing to be rendered, paid or done, to the king, his heirs and successors'.[21]

Henry's men were the masters now. The resentment of the Arundells, Peter's former employers, and others whose rents he had seized on the usurper's behalf, can only be imagined. Not only were the Arundells well entrenched with the new Tudor regime, but they also owned the 'Right of Wreck' along the Cornish coast. That cannot have helped Peter when he was charged along with a yeoman, Thomas Polgrene, with stealing goods from a wreck at Looe Bar, at the 1494 Winnianton Manor Court near Helston.[22]

The luckless Peter fell on mining ventures to earn a living. But then Henry VII invented new taxes and penal restrictions, which crippled the profits of the Cornish trade, leading to two Cornish rebellions by the tinners in 1497. Peter's fellow wrecker, Polgrene, was attainted and hung at Tyburn,[23] for his part as a ringleader in the first of those rebellions, led by Michael Joseph; the second was inspired by Perkin Warbeck, claiming to be one of the missing Princes in the Tower.

As a die-hard Ricardian, as well as trading in tin himself, Peter lent the Cornish rebels of 1497 his wholesome support and was one of the residents of St Michael's Mount who lined the causeway when Perkin made a theatrical entrance to the island stronghold.[24] When Perkin's gimcrack army was defeated, Peter managed to avoid Polgrene's fate. But the St Aubyn family still paid heavily for his exploits, suffering along with the whole county from Henry's retribution – a massive penalty levied across Cornwall of twenty thousand pounds. Peter was named as a manucaptor – one of the men of substance tainted by the revolt – liable for the share of the fines levied on Helston, Sidney and Crowan 'for their contempt against the King perpetrated, made and committed'.[25]

According to W.C. Borlase's *History*, the repercussions of the rebellion on Cornish land holdings was startling: 'Estates changed hands by wholesale, and there can scarcely be a collection of old Cornish records in the county which does not bear traces of some forced conveyance or compromise effected at this period by a captor on the lands of his captive'. Jane, the daughter of John Pendyne, conveyed all the land she owned, so as to have her father released by his captor, one of Henry VII's sergeant-at-arms.[26]

In *The King's Book* of 1501, Peter's elder brother, Thomas, was listed as one of thirteen Cornish squires with a knight's income of £40 a year, but no knighthood.[27] Debt and dishonour within their families would weigh sorely on the Cornish gentry for decades to come. In his *Tudor Cornwall,* John Chynoweth estimated that 'half the families resident in 1501 had become extinct or had left by 1603'.[28] But as we shall see, surviving gentry from 1501 could also rise above those newly arrived, spurred in this case, by the mercurial recovery in St Aubyn fortunes from the nadir of the mid-1400s.

Shaken after the rebellions, Henry VII dared not to poke the hornets' nest and an entire cross-section of Cornish society treated his tin mining regulations with contempt. Matters came to a head in 1508, when Henry agreed to rescind his regulations and restore self-rule under the Stannaries, on payment of a fine of eight thousand pounds levied across the industry.[29] Those he pardoned reads almost as a roll call of honour. Robert Willoughby, Lord of Broke and John Godolphin headed the list, before 'Peter Seintaubyn of Helston-borough "gentleman"' and many other esquires and gentlemen, along with a general number of 'merchants, tinners, bounders or possessors of tin-works'.

Along with this political resolution, in 1508 Peter succeeded Sir Richard Nanfan as the 'Firmarius' (or Lessee) of St Michael's Mount and in 1511, he was appointed as a commissioner of array, just as war against France was declared.[30] Two years into this conflict, an enemy fleet entered Mount's Bay and landed just east of Marazion, its objective to seize the island castle. But while they could not prevent the town from being plundered and burnt to the ground, the garrison under Peter deterred the attack on the island. The prodigal son had returned and his Compotus rolls, giving an account of the farm of the Mount, are preserved for the years 1508 and 1512.[31]

Peter's elder brother, Thomas St Aubyn, who was decidedly the good son, had also been born to Geoffrey and Alice in about 1440. Thomas married Matilda, the daughter of John Trenowth of Fentongollan, who had called him and his brother Peter to arms in 1473. Matilda Trenowth's sister and co-heiress married Thomas' neighbour and close friend, Sir John Godolphin.

Since the early 1200s, the Trenowths had acted as one of the leading Cornish barons. That several generations represented the county in parliament did not moderate their baronial behaviour. The official record of Michael Trenowth, MP for Cornwall in 1331, puts modern political misconduct in the shade:

> … his lawful business operations included ownership of tin mines and loaning money; his criminal activities included smuggling, wrecking, fraud and coercion.[32]

But Michael owned the finest tin mine in Cornwall. The suit of armour he fashioned for the Black Prince, first Duke of Cornwall, earned him 'a pardon for all his offences'.

By the time of Thomas' marriage to Matilda, the Trenowth lands were somewhat dissipated, not least when an uncle was arraigned for murder and his inheritance seized by the Crown. In 1529, instead of granting it back to the St Aubyns, as they might have hoped, they would learn that it was going to some new man in favour at court.

Yet by diligent application, Thomas restored the dignity of the family, despite his brother's escapades. The family's omission from the roll call to arms against the Earl of Oxford was not repeated in 1490, when Thomas was among the fourteen local landowners commissioned by the king 'to array the fencible men of [Cornwall] and to place beacons for warning the people of the king's enemies'.[33] Every year between 1492 to 1502, he was appointed as one of the county's magistrates, often along with his father-in-law, John Trenowth.[34]

In 1494, the very same year that his brother was arraigned for wrecking before the manor court near Helston, Thomas, together with the leading men in the county, was one of the magistrates tasked 'to deliver the gaol to

Launceston'. A prison inspector's report from centuries later suggests this would have been grim work:

> This gaol though built in the large green belonging to the old ruinous castle, is very small, house and court measuring only 52 feet by 44 feet, and the house not covering half that ground. The prison is a room or passage 23½ feet by 7½ feet, with only one window 2 feet by 1½ feet, and three dungeons or cages on the side opposite the window.... Their provision was put down to them through a hole (9 inches by 8) in the floor of the room above (used as a chapel), and those who served them there often caught the fatal fever.[35]

Thomas also acted that year as a Justice of the Peace in the Lostwithiel Assizes, sitting with Richard Vivyan, his near neighbour on the Lizard Peninsula. They heard many cases of assault, forcible entry and robbery with violence, led by bands of 'gentlemen' numbering from a dozen to a couple of hundred. Peter St Aubyn was hardly alone in his misdemeanours and the following cases heard by his brother give some idea of the lawlessness still running throughout Cornwall,[36] following Henry Tudor's troubled accession to the throne:

- In July 1492, a band of men led by a yeoman and five tinners forced their way into the house of the minor friars at Bodmin.
- In 1494, Stephen Tregassowe, 'gentleman', with two yeoman and the holy water clerk of St Probus, carried off six silver cups worth £40 belonging to the parishioners.
- Another 'gentleman' with many others 'unknown' robbed Henry Wulcock and later carried off his wife Johanna and kept her at Manahan for the space of five years.

Another twenty-six complaints concerned a certain Roger Whalley, a yeoman from Egloshayle, who harassed his neighbours over three years. One case would have especially caught Thomas' notice:

> John Trenowth complaineth that the said Roger the xxiii day of April, the sixth year of the reign of our sovereign lord the king that now is, with force and arms came to the place of the

said John Trenowth at Trewen and there made assault upon his wife and beat her and shot in at his windows and put him in despair of his life.

Declarations of interest played no part in Tudor justice and no doubt Whalley was meted his deserts.

On a lighter note, friendship with Thomas' brother-in-law and neighbour at Godolphin House blossomed. The story goes that one afternoon the two of them staked their farms on the outcome of a snails' race.[37] As the St Aubyn snail raced ahead, Sir John Godolphin vented his frustration with his own champion by pricking it with a pin. At this, the mollusc expired, leaving his rival a clear run to the finishing line.

There was no question of the bet being literally enforced. But every spring, Thomas sent his bailiff round to Godolphin House to collect a token rent. According to Dr Borlase, writing three centuries later, 'The Manor of Godolphin is still held of Sir John St Aubyn, as of his manor of Lambourne, by the payment of a gammon of bacon'.[38]

As well as maintaining the family's position, Thomas and Matilda also redressed the impending shortage of St Aubyn men. They produced three sons as well as daughters. The twilight of the Middle Ages promised a new dawn for the family name.

CHAPTER 3

STAR CHAMBER

The Court acts as the curious eye of the State and the King's
Council prying into the inconveniences and mischiefs which
abound in the Commonwealth...[and] which otherwise
might prove dangerous and infectious diseases.

William Hudson, *Treatise on the Court*
of Star Chamber

John and Peter, the first two sons of Thomas and Matilda, sadly died young
and so the Clowance estate passed to the third brother Thomas, who was
born in 1487. He was sent to London, in the coming fashion for the offspring
of the gentry, to learn the law.

At the age of 20, he passed out of the Strand, one of the junior Inns of
Court, and entered Inner Temple.[1] Thomas, who was one of the first entries
in the Black Book which has since recorded every student, would have
learned his craft by attending court sessions, sharing accommodation and
taking part in moots – those verbal jousts on points of law which comprised
his formal instruction. Attending the many festive ceremonies and paying
one's bills were the other prerequisites of being called to the Bar in 1507.

Yet legal knowledge was useful in the West Country. One in seven cases
before Star Chamber – the highest court in the land – came from Devon and
Cornwall in Henry VII's reign and out of 716 cases in his son's reign, 65
referred to Devon and 64 to Cornwall.

By 1525, Thomas was well established as a local magistrate in succession
to his father, with a modest income of £50 a year and six children. He
had married Mary Grenville, one of the eligible daughters of Sir Thomas
Grenville, the head of the far more powerful Cornish family based at Stowe,
in North Cornwall. Mary's sister, Honor Grenville had married Thomas'
neighbour, Sir John Basset of Tehidy, whose estate was rich in tin and who
had another estate, Umberleigh, in Devon. The Grenvilles claimed descent
from Rollo, first Duke of Normandy,[2] and many of them retained a streak of
the Viking warrior's disposition.

Thomas had also kept on excellent terms with his cousin and nearest neighbour, William Godolphin, who had succeeded his father and was enjoying the wealth of the tin under Godolphin Hill. None could guess how fate was about to hurl all these families into the vortex of a struggle between the most powerful men in Europe, as the Portuguese flagship the *San Antonio* hit the Cornish rocks.

In West Cornwall, shipwrecks were once so common that thousands of lives and limitless treasure were lost time and again over the centuries. Here, the bounty washed ashore was christened 'God's grace', but the drowned on the foreshore were left unburied out of fear and superstition. This was especially true in Mount's Bay, which had been forged by a freak of nature, a prehistoric fusing of two land masses into a pair of pincers.

There are so many recorded wrecks in Mount's Bay that the chart runs out of space. Before steam, any ship which sought close shelter in the Bay ran the risk of a change in the wind to leeward. This would force her bows relentlessly towards the deceptive sands, until the moment when her hull struck the rocks hidden below. Sometimes, a battle between man and nature would last for days, as the ship's captain tacked to and fro in a play for time and a fresh direction for the wind, while Cornish wreckers watched in anticipation from the cliffs. The wreckers had no reason to lure such ships onto the rocks – as they have sometimes been accused in the past – but when disaster struck, despair and poverty often drove them to ruthless measures.

The Portuguese fleet of the 1520s boasted the most proficient sea farers in Europe, with trading outposts as far flung as Japan and Brazil. But the heart of her trading empire was Antwerp and it was from here, in January 1427, that the *San Antonio* and her flotilla collected treasure worth £100,000 and began the voyage to Lisbon. This was the dowry due to Juan III of Portugal, on his marriage to Catherine, sister of the all-powerful Spanish Emperor Charles V. According to the ship's manifest, which is still preserved, the portion of the dowry on board the *San Antonio* was worth £18,880 – mostly in copper, silver, jewels and ready money – and a sum equivalent to well in excess of £50 million today.

The carrack carried a ship's crew of 80 men and weighed 300 tons. As she sailed past Land's End, in a storm that had raged into the night, she was blown into Mount's Bay and onto the rocks. Half of the men drowned under a moonless January sky, along with the admiral of the fleet. Only a fraction of the treasure – just a few thousand ducats – was recovered to shore. Or so the Cornish claimed. Yet the *San Antonio* had sunk in barely two fathoms of water.

A typical wreck in 1527 might be laden with tin coming out of Helston, or cod returning from Newfoundland. With a ship's crew of about a dozen, these wrecks could be worth £500 to £1000. Any cargo recovered to the shore was governed by the 'Right of Wreck'. Along most of the Cornish coast, this right was held by the Crown; but in Mount's Bay, Henry II had granted the Right of Wreck to the Arundells, Cornwall's leading family. They in turn employed Officers of Wreck to guard their interest and prevent the wreckers' thieving, as Peter St Aubyn had learnt to his cost in 1494. Sometimes, officers and wreckers worked hand in glove to share the spoils, at the expense of any survivors from the ship. At other times, rival gangs of henchmen led to riots and writs.

By any measure, the size and value of the vessel put this wreck in a league of its own. Yet James Chynoweth, Arundell's Officer of Wreck in 1527, was beaten to the scene by the three local magistrates: Thomas St Aubyn, William Godolphin and John Milliton. Their knowledge of the law – William as well as Thomas had studied at the Inner Temple – drove them to work this advantage to their own ends. But in so doing, they stepped unwittingly into a European intrigue.

1527 was a turning point in history. As the *San Antonio* foundered, so did the marriage of Henry VIII to Catherine of Aragon. Catherine was aunt to Charles V of Spain and his sister, who had betrothed Juan III. But her years of marriage to Henry had produced only one child, Mary. Spain was expecting Mary's eventual succession to the English throne to reinforce the all-embracing creed of Charles V's Grand Chancellor, Mercurino Gattinara, that 'a universal peace requires a universal monarch'. But Henry wanted a boy. A year earlier and it is hard to believe Henry would have tolerated the insurgent Cornish stealing the prized dowry of a royal relative. Now he found himself at odds with the most powerful throne in Europe.

There was more. By the terms of the Treaty of London (1359), the king was bound to return stolen Portuguese property or make good the loss himself within six months. But this claim faced its own complication. At the same time as Charles V had redeemed the £100,000 dowry promised to his new Portuguese brother-in-law, he had defaulted on the even heavier debt he owed to Henry.[3] Whatever the legal niceties, it cannot have helped Henry's mood to learn that his long-standing loan demand has been passed over in favour of the Portuguese king, who now wrote demanding reparations from his purse.[4]

Juan III sought a local settlement of his dispute through his consul in Flanders, Roderick Fernandes, both businessman and spymaster, who ran Portugal's trading empire from a vast storehouse in the heart of Antwerp. His claim suggests that his agents had surmised how much was at stake.

On 12 May 1527, Cardinal Wolsey appointed a local Commission of Enquiry under John Chamond, who happened to be Thomas' brother-in-law.[5] The Portuguese case was given short shrift.

Juan III followed up his letter by sending one of his most nefarious courtiers, Francisco Pessoa, to petition the English Crown and on 18 April 1528, Wolsey – one of whose clerks was Sir John Arundell's younger son – appointed a second commission.[6] This surviving record of the writ petitioned by Pessoa, the king of Portugal's factor, summarises the Portuguese position succinctly:

> ...the wreck occurred on Saturday, 20 Jan. 1527 near Gunwalloe, in the hundred of [Penwith], Cornwall. The ship had merchandise to the value of £16,000. Most of the people in her were saved, and with the aid of the inhabitants recovered goods to the value of 1,000 ducats the same afternoon; but in the evening they were attacked by John Wylliam, miller, servant to William Godolphin, and two servants of John Milliton, captain of the Mount, who robbed them in their masters' names.
>
> Next day, being urged to sell the ship's goods, the Portuguese replied that they belonged entirely to the King of Portugal. When they complained of the robbery before certain justices of the peace, they were told they could have no redress, as it was 'the custom of the country'. After the house where they took refuge was broken into, and themselves put in great danger, Diogo Alvares was induced to sell the goods for fear of worse consequences. After this, he was treated as a prisoner by the purchasers, Thomas St Aubyn, William Godolphin and others, who carried him behind them on their horses, and rode about the country with him. On one occasion they made him break in upon his former comrades, and help to rob them of all they had, except their apparel.[7]

The county was certainly no stranger to violent crime involving Cornish gentlemen. But at this point, there were particularly desperate circumstances.

'In the winter season of this year', Holinshed tells us, 'fell great abundance of raine'.[8] It started in September 1526, poured throughout November and December and '...on the sixteenth of January [1527] it rained so abundantly that great flouds thereby ensuing destroyed corne fields, pastures, and drowned manie sheep and beasts'. The tempest which blew the *San Antonio* off her course was the zenith of this first deluge. 'Then it was dry till the twelfe of April and from thence it rained every day or night till the third of June, and in Maie it rained thirtie hours continualie without ceasing, which caused great flouds, and did much harm...'.

Crop failures led to a national scarcity of bread. In the Capital, the Inner Temple's Christmas feast was 'not kept as accustomed for the scarcity of corn'.[9] Elsewhere, the poor 'were fayne to sell for very need for bread corne their peauter, their bras and bedding with such other as they had to their utter undoing'.[10] A landowner like Godolphin, with about 500 acres, found forty tenants and their families pleading a stay of rent. But for Thomas St Aubyn – who appears to have farmed his own land to make ends meet – the loss of crops and cattle was devastating. For both gentry and pauper, 'God's grace' cannot have landed in Gunwalloe cove at a more opportune moment.

Despite this dire predicament, far from being the Cornish villains of Francisco Pessoa's petition, a different complexion is given to the affair by the account sworn by Thomas St Aubyn himself:

> In this he states that being in the neighbourhood of Gunwallo he heard of the wreck, rode to it and assisted in saving the men; Godolphin and Milliton afterwards joining him with the same object; and in endeavouring to save part of the cargo, one of the men was drowned.
>
> They found that very little could be rescued, and seeing that the men were destitute, without money to buy meat or drink, they bought the goods of the ship in lawful bargain with the captain.
>
> They further deny any assault, or that they took goods to the value of ten thousand pounds from the sailors, in fact they only saved about £20 worth altogether, the bulk lying in the ship still, and although they tried to recover more, they failed even to pay for the cost of the labour they employed.[11]

Thomas and his two associates faced a Portuguese claim for £10,000, a sum far greater than their combined wealth. With a crisis on their farms, defeat on such a scale would destroy them all. The two sides were so at odds that mediation by the Cornish commissioners was doomed to failure and on 3 September 1528, Sir John Arundell referred the suit back to Westminster.[12] He summarised the Cornish version of events, with a reminder that the first commission had already found in their favour.

The Cornish defendants were now required to appear before the Star Chamber. In these proceedings, 'answer was exhibited on oath ... the defendant was then examined on any questions of fact arising'. Whereas the devious Pessoa could lodge his claim without swearing on his Bible, St Aubyn would be affirming falsehoods at his peril:

> Should perjury be discovered in the examination, the defendant
> would be punished by being made to wear humiliating papers
> in Westminster hall or by imprisonment in the Fleet. Under
> Wolsey, the council in star chamber punished perjury wherever
> it was detected.[13]

As they moved from the dependable judgements of their kinsmen to that of the cardinal, Juan III wrote another letter.[14] On 24 September 1528, he again demanded that Henry VIII make good the loss of his cargo, but with the sweetener that 'when an opportunity arises we shall repay you with equal kindness in any business of yours'. Juan III's penchant for resolving disputes by bribery was notorious, a reputation which Pessoa would know how to play to advantage.

The famine which had struck London in 1527 was followed by an outbreak of plague in 1528. Thousands died, lawyers escaped the Inns of Court to the country and the legal process ground to a halt. By Christmas 1528, Thomas St Aubyn could cheerfully perform his role of steward at the Inner Temple festivities, knowing that delay had been the defendants' friend.

Meanwhile, the 'King's Great Matter' – as Henry's divorce suit against Catherine became known – had led the Spanish to plot his overthrow. They sought to place his daughter Mary on the throne before her succession could be denied by a Boleyn bastard. In July 1527, Ambassador Mendosa had written to his Emperor: '...Should six or seven thousand men land on the coast of Cornwall to espouse the cause of both mother and daughter, forty thousand Englishmen would at once join them'.[15]

Wolsey dispatched Silvester Darius, the 'protonotary' of the Pope in England and so a neutral party, to parlay with the Spanish.[16] In November

1528, Darius reported back an alarming exchange with the Emperor's Grand Chancellor Gattinara: 'The Chancellor answered, why do you talk of the king of England? If we wished, we could expel him from his kingdom … he would be driven out by his own [subjects] in three months'.[17]

Who were these insurgent subjects? Wolsey could not be sure, but an obvious threat surely came from Cornwall; the more so if Portuguese gold, money and artillery was now stashed ashore by potential rebels. This was no time to alienate either Godolphin, who had succeeded his father as the leading force among her archers and wrestlers; nor Milliton, governor of St Michael's Mount, a notorious starting point for rebellion. Meanwhile their confederate, St Aubyn, was dealt a trump card of his own.

Mary, Thomas St Aubyn' wife, was one of four Grenville sisters. Of the others, Jane was married to Sir John Arundell of Lanherne, with whom there was the recurring friction over his Right of Wreck; while Honor was wife to the elderly Sir John Basset, the close neighbour at Tehidy. In January 1529, Basset died and Honor swiftly remarried to Arthur Plantagenet, Lord Lisle. Arthur was the childhood friend of Henry VIII, a Knight of the Garter, a member of the king's council (of which Star Chamber proceedings were a part) and above all, the Vice Admiral of the fleet (where he dealt with piracy).

Honor and Lisle were genuinely in love – 'ye be both but one soul though you be two bodies', as Lisle's friend, Sir Francis Bryan remarked[18] – which suggests the love affair started some time before old Basset was cold in the ground. Also evident from their correspondence is their affection for Thomas. In the 1530s, when they were posted to Calais, he would be trusted to become their agent for the Tehidy estate. For now, their alliance in marriage surely stretched to their St Aubyn brother-in-law, facing ruin at Cardinal Wolsey's hands.

While Lisle could hardly dictate terms to the cardinal, as Vice Admiral he would have expected to join his friends on the king's council when they sat in Star Chamber on a case of alleged piracy. His partiality would be no barrier to deciding a case in Tudor times, as we have seen before.

Further, in cases before Star Chamber, defendants were put in the hands of leading attorneys.[19] One of these was John Densell, who also acted for Lisle as his legal counsel. He was a Cornishman and it was later said of Densell that he 'was no corrupt or griping lawyer, for he made no improvement at all of his estate'.[20] He was also a leading authority on the law of wreck, ideally placed to take up the Cornish suit on their behalf.[21]

Purely civil cases could wait many years for any decision from Star Chamber. In this instance, the three magistrates were accused of violence and theft, which gave their hearing a criminal urgency. Yet even such a case, on being referred back to Westminster, could take a year to reach judgement. In 1529, not only was there the backlog created by the plague, but Wolsey now found himself embroiled in hearings over the King's Great Matter. His Star Chamber cases dragged on, just as his power ebbed away.

Then, at the end of the summer sessions of 1529, the hearings for Henry's divorce from Queen Catherine collapsed in confusion. The king could not forgive Wolsey for this humiliation. By the time the San Antonio case reached him, there was a new Lord Chancellor presiding. Sir Thomas More was not only another upright lawyer, like Densell, who abhorred the disreputable tactics of men like Pessoa. He was also a close friend of Lisle.

So while the Star Chamber record was lost in a fire in the next century, we can divine the outcome, especially given that neither Thomas nor the other two magistrates appeared to have suffered at all. William Godolphin's daughter married John Milliton's son shortly afterwards, at the same time as two wings were added to Godolphin House, its ceilings decorated with a plaster motif of tulips, which come out of Antwerp – a sly tribute, perhaps, to the ill-fated *San Antonio*.

The Portuguese were probably offered about £600 to settle the case, based on the amount they could prove was taken to shore. This would have satisfied Juan III. With an income of £1 million a year from his seafaring empire, it was not the financial cost of the wreck which he counted, but his pride and principle. Sir John Arundell's Right of Wreck entitled him to half of anything taken ashore, which would have been only £300, in proportion to the Portuguese. Thus he might have been squared by the magistrates, if not too happily.

As for finding the money to make such offers in settlement, the magistrates may have secured its value on paper – the ship's manifest listed precious metals and jewels alone to a value of £12,000. But how to sell 8000 cakes of copper, for example, without the truth being discovered? A report fifteen years later provides a clue. One St Clere complained to the Privy Council that 'in Devon and Cornwall certain gold is ignorantly molten with the tin, and so unawares conveyed abroad to the profit of strangers'. He was granted letters, 'to permit him "to put his cunning in ure" for one month and to certify the result'.[22] In Cornwall, he was to work through 'Mr St. Aubyne and John Militon'. Nothing came of his enquiries.

Quite apart from Godolphin's regular trade in metal, from Helston to Brittany, there was Milliton's harbour on St Michael's Mount as a collection point, to provide alternative avenues of disposal; while Honour and Arthur Lisle, posted to Calais in the 1530s, were to be regular recipients of Cornish gifts from Thomas St Aubyn, their brother-in-law and land agent.

The three magistrates would surely maintain that their conduct had been exemplary – quite distinct from the dispossessed gentry who were arraigned before their bench, at their regular assizes. For as Thomas' witness statement made clear, they had a defence in law for the whole *San Antonio* episode. The survivors of the wreck would almost certainly have been murdered on the foreshore, by the tinners who first came upon them, if Thomas and the other magistrates had not intervened to save their lives. The Portuguese accepted the bargain shrewdly offered, £50 for the right of salvage. The magistrates in Helston could then dismiss their complaint, as it was 'the custom of the country' – a direct reference to the Rules of Oleron, the international maritime law at that time, which governed the treatment of sailors and cargo washed ashore.[23]

Balzac may have observed that behind every great fortune, 'is a crime forgotten because it was properly executed'.[24] But with their knowledge of the law of wreck, sharpened both by training and experience, it was precisely because Thomas and Godolphin executed their plan properly that it was not a crime at all.

CHAPTER 4

THE KING'S MERCY

For here every man shifteth for himself.[1]
John Borough to Lord Lisle

Whatever proved to be Thomas' share of the spoils, when the *San Antonio* dispute was resolved, the 1530s certainly marked a distinct change in fortune for the St Aubyn family, social as well as financial, as reflected in the warm relations between Thomas, Mary and the courtly Lisles. This is obvious from Honour and Arthur Lisle's letters to their wide circle of friends, as well as their business at court. The letters have been preserved as one of the most notable records of the period, skilfully edited in Muriel St Clare Byrne's fifty-year-long work of scholarship, *The Lisle Letters* (1981).

The wilful side to Thomas St Aubyn did not desert him entirely after the *San Antonio* escapade. In 1530, Thomas was named in the tussle over a silver cross found at Gunwalloe and, more seriously, in 1544 he was named as one of those involved in a violent dispute over the recovery of two shiploads of Newfoundland cod.[2] Again, it was the Arundells – Thomas' long-suffering in-laws – on whose ground he was treading.

Among his entries in the 'Black Book' of the Inner Temple, Thomas' financial problems feature with several demands to pay fines and other dues.[3] Thus in February 1527, a month after the sinking of the *San Antonio*, there was the following entry: 'St Aubyn and Vyvyan amerced £10 each because, after being elected stewards, they did not come'. But for Christmas 1528, he was given another chance as steward, so three weeks later the senior benchers relented: 'Thomas St Aubyn pardoned all offices and vacations, for a fine of £4'.[4]

It therefore comes as a pleasant surprise to find how St Clare Byrne chooses to describe Thomas in the succinct introduction to her work:

> Thomas St Aubyn settles himself in the imagination as one of those delightful, friendly, simple, generous and useful people who are relied upon by everybody, are of good reputation in the world, kindly and sympathetic, and the most desirable of

acquaintances, though perhaps lacking in that extra ounce of drive and toughness which pushes a man to the front and brings worldly success.[5]

St Clare Byrne is writing about the Thomas of the 1530s, a time when his wife wrote of him to her sister 'Though youth hath ruled him before this, yet now ... he is well amended and intendeth to be more diligent than ever he hath been'.[6] This was some time after Thomas had written to Honor Lisle, accepting her invitation to become the agent for the Basset estate of Tehidy, less than seven miles from Clowance. Honor was by now in Calais, where her husband Lisle had been appointed Deputy.

The following extract from Thomas' letter of February 1533 is a fine example of the qualities St Clare Byrne identifies:

> My bedfellow and I have sent to my good lord and you a dozen of puffins, which Boswarthogga or John Keagwyn of Mount's bay shall deliver you. If it may do you any pleasure I would be glad, as our Lord knoweth, who ever preserve you, Amen. Written on St Blaise his day, with very little leisure, with the rude hand of me, your old knave,
>
> Thomas Seyntaubyn.[7]

A dish of puffins was a regular gift from the St Aubyns to the Lisles, who by return sent venison from Umberleigh. Carew reports that the puffin hatched in holes in the cliff, whence young ones could be fetched out and kept salted. They were 'reputed for fish, as coming nearest thereto in their taste'.[8]

Over the next three centuries, such were the ties which grew between the St Aubyns and the Bassets, by marriage, property and politics, as to render them branches of the same Cornish family.[9] But at this point, Thomas walked a fine line as Honor's agent and in this first report to Lady Lisle on the Basset estates in 1533, he portrays several features of daily life with some formality:

> ...concerning the Barton place of Tehidy, there is none willing to take it at fifteen pounds to my knowledge, as Richard Harris this bearer can shew you, and how much may be had for it, and what cases the hedges and the outhouses lieth in decay. Also, as for the hedges that Harry Manse made, it is now abroad like the feathers of a goose new pollyd with a hungry fox.

He ends with the good news that:

> Also, good Madame, all the works at Carnkey and Carnbrea been all in good peace, thanks to God Almighty … and at every wash I have been at it, both early and right late, and have seen to the uttermost of your profit as it had been to mine own, and have done my diligence about in your courts and at your audit.[10]

For centuries, tin was one of England's most valuable exports; that extracted from the Basset estate at Tehidy would prove of the highest grade once mechanised processes were later developed. But Thomas was observing the ancient practice of tin streaming – tinstones brought to the surface by the action of streams wearing the main lode, which then had to be washed to separate out the clay. Once highly prised nuggets, by Tudor times according to Carew, '…low grounds, beforetime fruitful, having herethrough their wrong side turned outwards, accurse the tinners injury by their succeeding barrenness'.

These were harsh times for the tinners, the price of the metal not keeping pace with rising costs thanks to Tudor debasement of the currency. Credit also squeezed their rewards, as they habitually borrowed to survive until they could sell at market.[11] So when in 1538, the Lisles sent a ship laden with wheat to Thomas, his thanks were as effusive, as the generosity his reply reveals:

> My duty unto your good ladyship done, in the right heartiest recommendation I recommend me to you and so I would I might be to my good lord your loving and most gentle bedfellow, and so to your loving sister my wife to you both: in likewise with most loving thanks for your great reward and gift ye sent to your nieces my daughters, and for your cloneys, gulls and other pleasures, and for your ship of wheat, and for other manifold goodness; and, high thanks to Almighty God and you, I shall not lack wheat while your ship wheat endureth.[12]

Thomas shared this windfall with the Godolphins and 'all other gentlemen and women about me, with other divers substantial men and many poor men… I would every other ship and boat might have such grace!' He ends by sending 'a dozen of good puffins' and promising to do 'the best of my diligence therein, to your most profit'.

Yet Cornwall and Calais could not forever ignore Henry VIII's tyrannical rule, as the religious convulsions of his break from Rome reverberated into every corner of his kingdom. Arthur and Honor Lisle had been two of the six honoured guests at Henry's marriage to Anne Boleyn in Calais. His appointment as Deputy had come soon afterwards, as the apogee of his courtly career. Yet within three years, Anne had been executed for treason, while to suppress the Pilgrimage of Grace, Thomas Cromwell had more than 200 lords, knights and priests hung by the neck, some also drawn and quartered. One Margaret Cheney, 'a very fair creature and a beautiful', was drawn from the Tower to Smithfield and there burnt at the stake.

One after another, noble men and women suspected of treachery or heresy had also met their fate on the scaffold at the Tower of London. Finally, the terror which Cromwell had unleashed threatened to devour him. In a last and desperate attempt to confound his enemies, he seized on a popish plot to hand the keys of Calais to the French. Its instigator was Gregory Botolf, a wayward priest; 'the most mischievous knave that was ever born', known as 'sweet-lips' for his way with words. Cromwell convinced the king that Arthur Lisle, Deputy of Calais, was at the heart of Botolf's conspiracy. In April 1540, Lisle was summoned to London.

Mary St Aubyn's two nieces, Anne and Katherine Basset, had by now enjoyed serving as young ladies at Henry VIII's Court for three years. These greatly sought after positions, a brilliant first step on the social ladder for an eligible daughter of 16, were won through the combined intrigues of their tenacious mother Honor and John Hussey – the likeable courtier who was known to the king, as to all others, as 'my Lord Lisle's man'.

Then in September 1537, Anne Basset was 'sworn the Queen's maid', as a 'yeoman-usher' to the newly crowned Jane Seymour, the king's third wife.[13] This must have come as a great comfort to Honor, whose hopes of providing Lisle with an heir were being cruelly dashed. John Hussey now cautioned Anne not to wear the 'French apparel', as the queen disdained the foreign fashions promoted by her predecessor Anne Boleyn, whose trial and execution a year before, organised by Cromwell, had been followed by Jane Seymour's marriage to Henry VIII just a day later.

Anne Basset was granted an income of £10 a year, out of which she was to pay for a servant. Her 'livery' – her accommodation, food and formal costumes – were all provided for her as well. But as Hussey wrote to her mother, daily court clothes must come from her own wardrobe:

> ...the Queen's pleasure is that Mrs Anne shall wear no more her French apparel. So that she must have provided a bonnet or two, with frontlets and an edge of pearl, and a gown of black satin, and another of velvet, and this must be done before the Queen's grace's churching. And further, she must have cloth for smocks and sleeves, for there is fault found that their smocks are too coarse; and also they must have chests ...[14]

Hussey's endearing list becomes exhaustive, ending with 'All this stuff is taken of Christopher Campion, but it is nothing so good as that which is bought for ready money'. This touches on a perennial problem for the family – they were living well beyond their means. Since the war between England and France a decade before, trade through Calais had been redirected to Antwerp. A drastic fall in customs duties was leaving both the upkeep of the town and its Deputy short of the income, which had previously supported the town's defences and made Arthur's post a prized appointment. As it was, the walls of Calais were crumbling as fast as Arthur's finances.

In Henry's louche Court, 'the prettiest and wittiest, the beauty of the family' (St Clare Byrne), polished by a French education, was soon being touted as a candidate for the king's attentions herself. Chapuys, the Spanish ambassador, reported: 'Within eight days after publication of his marriage, having twice met two beautiful young ladies, he said and showed himself somewhat sorry that he had not seen them before he was married'.[15] Peter Mewtas, a gentleman of the privy chamber, wrote to Lisle that '...the King's Grace, not two days past, talked of you and your children ... his Grace thought Mistress Anne Basset to be the fairest'.[16] This gossip gained new currency when Henry's third queen died suddenly, only a month after Anne's appointment, and twelve days after giving birth to a son. Had Arthur Plantagenet the drive and guile of a Norfolk, which along with proximity at court were prerequisites of success in the royal matrimonial stakes, history at this point might well have turned.

But as well as being in Calais, Lisle was preoccupied with Honor's recurring symptoms of pregnancy. He was put in touch with Dr Le Coup, who observed 'many or diverse cold and slemysh humours within your body', for which he prescribed strict adherence to a complicated diet.[17]

Honor's friends commiserated with her, none more touchingly than Thomas, whose letter in January 1538 promised:

> I am not your pricklouse nor knave, but mercy ever cry to have. Moreover, good madame, high thanks to Almighty God, my wife and I been right glad of your good recovery and that ye have your health, and also that my lord is so gentle, loving and kind, and your most comfort at all times, and most at your uttermost grievance.[18]

Thomas was at the same time tending to Mary St Aubyn, for as he added as a postscript: 'your old servant my daughter Philippa is departed on Christmas Day, Almighty pardon her soul; and my wife hath taken great discomfort thereby'.

A gift of another dozen Cornish puffins were sent to bolster Honor. But Thomas and Mary were surely beyond knowing how to support her daughter Anne, now the object of the king's attentions. Given the fate of his wives, it is doubtful Anne welcomed these advances, whatever her parents' ambitions and much as she was duty bound to comfort Henry, for his loss of his queen. For a lively young girl, the old king with an ulcerated leg could not hope to compete with the attractions of the young men at court. The most handsome and promising of these was Thomas Culpeper, who was only six years older than Anne.

In 1535, Culpeper had informed Honor that he had 'written to my Lord for a spaniel in Calais, which I hear good report of, werein I desire your ladyship's furthereance'. By postscript, he added: 'Madam, by my servant I have sent you a buck … let me hear from you if there be anything to do for you a' this side the sea for yourself or your friends. Send to me as sure as you would your own son: so shall you find me during my life'.[19]

Two years later, we find another correspondence from Culpeper to Honor, who replied: 'Good Master Culpeper, I do send you by this bearer two bracelets of my colours according to your desire. They be of no value to be esteemed, but only that it was your gentle request to have them; praying you accept them for they be the first that ever I sent to a man'.[20] This singular gift should not be misconstrued, for Honor was prompt in also 'sending your token mine embracelett' to her brother-in-law Thomas, which as he wrote to thank her, 'I wear according as ye wrote, and shall as long as it endureth'.[21]

Then in October 1537, just as Anne was taking up her role as 'the Queen's maid', Culpeper wrote to Honor: 'In my lowliest manner, I humbly salute your good ladyship, trusting in Jesu that your ladyship be in good health, which I pray Jesu long to continue to his pleasure and your heart's desire. Good madam, I heartily thank your ladyship for the hawks that you sent me, which kindness I can never deserve; but any pleasure of service that in me shall lie, at all times you shall find it ready'.[22]

These exchanges and tokens, from hawks to cap-rings, show Honor at her most artful. She was well aware that the young and highly eligible Culpeper had purchased Higham Park in Kent. This was a substantial estate on the road from Canterbury to Dover, a staging post not only for the Lisles on their way to Calais, but also perhaps for her daughter Anne, on her way to a suitable husband.

The dead Queen Jane's entourage were all dismissed from service, but alone among them Henry promised Anne a place as maid of honour under his next wife, whom he had decided would be a European princess. Over the next two years, many royal houses disdained his unwelcome advances, while Anne tarried as a maid in the household of her cousin, the Countess of Sussex, where Lady Wallop reported she continued to attract admirers:

> Mistress Anne I have seen divers times, and is as fair a gentlewoman, and as well made, as any that I know, and as gentle, and as well she behaveth herself that everybody praiseth her that seeth her; and there is no doubt but she shall come to some great marriage.[23]

Meanwhile Culpeper, as another of the king's favourites, was promoted to 'Master of the Armoury' in June 1538 and granted extensive monastic lands by Henry. The proximity of these youthful favourites, in the orbit of an egotistical king to whom alone they dared show affection, was no doubt tantalising. 'I durst not be so bold to move his Grace for it no other wise', Anne wrote to Honor of several maternal requests, 'for fear lest how his Grace would a'takyt it'.[24] Anne might accept the king's gift of a horse and saddle, or his arranging her stay in the country to enjoy fresh air and country walks,[25] but she avoided being beholden to Henry, in any way which might make his advances unstoppable.

In the spring of 1540, Cromwell found his power over the king in jeopardy. He had at last succeeded in procuring a Protestant princess for his master, but Henry took an instant dislike to the dull, Lutheran Anne of Cleves and was furious with Cromwell as a result. Then, while the virtuous Anne Basset became one of her maids of honour, as the king had promised, so did the flirtatious Katherine Howard, a childhood playmate of Culpeper and the niece of the Duke of Norfolk.

The king's attentions quickly turned to Katherine, relieving Anne Basset, but catching Cromwell on the horns of a dilemma. If he failed to arrange a swift divorce from Anne of Cleves, Henry would dismiss him. But if he succeeded, Henry would be released to the spell of this new love interest, marry her and so fall into the hands of the Norfolk faction.

Norfolk was now his deadly enemy, at this very moment gathering evidence in Calais of Protestant heretics, to whom he suspected Cromwell had been treacherously lenient. At the same time, the faction in the town aligned to the Pope were brewing the Botolf Conspiracy. In the confusion of this power struggle, Lisle as Deputy refused to take sides, with the result that he could count on no one to support him except the king, with whom he urgently sought an audience. But the king's summons, when it came, spoke nothing of the danger that awaited:

> Right trusty and right wellbeloved cousin and councillor, ...
> as by your letters you have desired to repair hither ... we be
> now therefore desirous to hear your advice therein and to
> consider and declare our mind and pleasure unto yourself in
> that behalf.[26]

Arthur's friends assumed he would come to England to be promoted; the most recent Earl of Oxford had just died, creating a promising vacancy. On 4 March, Lisle's long acquaintance, the Earl of Southampton, had written to him: 'I trust much to your comforts'.[27]

Lisle set off for England upon receipt of the king's invitation, attending a chapter meeting of the Order of the Garter a week later in Westminster. At this point, it so happened that William St Aubyn, Thomas' younger son, was due to start his studies at the Inns of Court.[28] It may well have been Lisle who had sponsored his nephew to forsake the Inner Temple, scene of his father's youthful escapades, in favour of Lincoln's Inn, to which Lisle had been admitted in 1510. While Lisle attended eight sittings of the House of Lords, until it rose on 11 May,[29] he certainly had every opportunity to meet his Cornish nephew and give William some advice at the start of his career. In any event, it was surely from this son, for the next few years ensconced in this hub of gossip and rumour, that Cornwall first learnt the news, as a tragedy unfolded for Mary St Aubyn's sister and her family.

A month proved a long time for Lisle in the mercurial world of Henry's court. By the Feast of St George, according to the chronicler Gruffudd, '... none of the great men of the Council looked at him save askanced, for they saw that he was besmutted in some way or other'.[30] Then, on 19 May, the king's council summoned Lisle to a meeting. Present were Norfolk and Suffolk, Cromwell '... and others of the Council. Some say the King was there in person; but such witnesses spoke against [Lisle] that he was unable to go against them, for he went down on his knees and appealed to the King to help him in his righteousness. The King retorted: "Doth thou not ask for righteousness! For I shall trouble to hear this matter myself"'.

Marillac, the French Ambassador, tells us that Lisle was delivered to the Tower that very evening, 'a very straight prison, and from the which none escape save by a miracle'.[31] Meanwhile, in Calais, Honor and her daughters were held captive. All their letters and papers were seized, to seek proof of their complicity in Botolf's treason.

From the alleged lovers of Anne Boleyn in 1536, to the circle of the Poles and Courtenays beheaded in 1538, Cromwell's interrogators had mastered the art of incriminating innocent victims. Thomas Wyatt, recalling his own examination, described how cunning charges were 'weaved in and out to persuade you and trouble me here and there to seek to answer that is in the one afore and in the other behind'.[32] Honor and their daughters in Calais were now interrogated in this fashion. Suspicion was cast, by the discovery of concealed love letters. These revealed the secret betrothal of Mary Basset to a French nobleman, without the king's consent. As for Thomas St Aubyn's genial correspondence with these suspects, at the very least we know his proposed candidature for High Sheriff was tainted, year after year.

Lisle's fate and that of his family now depended on the decision of Henry to 'hear this matter myself'. Yet by his side remained Anne Basset, the queen's maid of honour. She had comforted him for two years with her beauty, intelligence and sophistication, until Cromwell had chosen him a wife, but one in whom all such qualities were wanting.

For the Lord Privy Seal, this error now proved fatal. On 10 June, three weeks after Lisle's fall, he was arrested. The king was persuaded that Cromwell had been 'a fauter, maintainer, and supporter' of 'great and detestable heresies committed and sprung in many places of this your realm'.[33] There was enough evidence of Cromwell's indulgence of the

Calais heretics to hoist him with his own petard, the same interrogation of witnesses now used to convict the man who had perfected the art. On 28 July, his botched execution on Tower Hill took three blows of the axe.

————◆————

Cromwell's demise not only removed the impetus behind Lisle's trial for treason, but also the main obstacle to dissolving Henry's marriage to the 'Flanders Mare', on grounds of non-consummation. Henry wed Katherine Howard two days later, with Anne Basset again appointed the queen's maid, while Thomas Culpeper remained as one of Henry's closest attendants.

Ten years earlier, Cromwell's vocal defence of Wolsey, even after the Cardinal had been charged with treason, had recommended him to Henry, as the one man of integrity at court. Her father at this point being in the Tower, also on a charge of treason, and with her mother and her sisters captive in Calais, it would have marked out Culpeper to the king as one to trust, had he boldly sought at this point to seek Anne's hand. It would not only have furthered his career, but also saved his life.

Instead, Anne now discovered that the man who had pledged himself to her mother, five years before, as 'your own son: so shall you find me during my life', was neither trustworthy, nor shrewd. Dazzled by his childhood playmate Katherine, he began a reckless love affair with the queen, one which both betrayed the king and wounded her maid of honour.

Katherine was charged with adultery in November 1541 and her fate and that of Thomas Culpeper was soon sealed. United by their grief, if ever there was a time, this was when Anne may have become Henry's mistress. The Council wrote[34]: 'Order must be also taken with the Maidens that they repair each of them to their friends there to remain, saving Mistress Basset, whom the King's Majesty, in consideration of the calamity of her friends, will, at his charges, specially provide for'.

The St Aubyns could only lend moral support to their niece, caught in this precarious situation, let alone help her father. Thomas communicated directly with Hussey,[35] but their letters do not survive and from the point of his master's arrest, he ceased to be 'my Lord Lisle's man'. Yet William's studies at Lincoln's Inn gave Thomas, quite apart from constant news, a pretext for London visits; while his role as agent for Tehidy gave him sufficient excuse to visit Lisle in the Tower to make report.

As 1542 wore on, matters improved. We learn from a letter Chapuys wrote to his Spanish Emperor that '… it is also rumoured that the King has taken a fancy for … a daughter by the first marriage of the wife of Lord Lisle. This last attachment of the King, as the report goes, is founded on the fact that the above-mentioned official, who has been nearly two years in close prison in the Tower, goes at liberty within it, and his arms, which were removed from the chapel of the Order, are ordered to be restored'.[36] A fortnight later, the king's secretary visited Arthur in the Tower to impart the formal decision, bearing the king's diamond ring as a mark of absolution. Lisle was declared 'nothing guilty to the matter' and 'void of all offence', the king's 'most true and faithful kinsman'.[37]

But Lisle had spent two years in a fortress where old age had wearied him. From his cell, he had seen innocent friends and kinsfolk beheaded on Tower Green, while the king who had ordered their execution toyed with his daughter. Arthur's cousin, the elderly Margaret Pole, had been executed by a henchman 'who literally hacked her head and shoulders to pieces in the most pitiful manner'.[38] Heart and mind strained beyond endurance, within days of receiving the news of his release, in the words of the Tower record Arthur Plantagenet 'died from joy'; without ever again tasting his freedom or seeing his beloved Honor. As Sandford later remarked, 'this King's mercy was as fatal as his judgements'.[39]

CHAPTER 5

A PERILOUS COUNTRY

*This is a perilous country, for God's love
let the King's grace look to it in time.*
Simon Haynes to Thomas Cromwell[1]

The disruption caused by the break with Rome did not abate with the death of Thomas Cromwell; nor did absolving Arthur Plantagenet mark an end to the terror fed by the insecurities of the Tudor throne. As for the new reign of Edward VI, the child king crowned in 1547, it would lead to a culmination of the Cornish grievances about Tudor rule which the county had nursed for fifty years.

Within weeks of Arthur's death, Honor and the daughters in Calais were released. They sailed back to England, with a helpful £100 grant from State coffers to settle their affairs. According to Foxe's *Actes and Monuments*, Honor then 'fell distraught of mind and so continued many years after',[2] living for another twenty-four years but never to marry again. She retired to her Cornish roots and to the comforting embrace of her family, not least that of her sister Mary and Honor's 'old knave', Thomas St Aubyn.

At Tehidy and Clowance, they no doubt viewed the unending convulsions of English policy with a jaundiced eye. Their cousin Roger Grenville was second in command on the *Mary Rose*, the flagship which in 1545 sunk in Portsmouth harbour on her way to support the costly siege of Boulogne, drowning all her crew. Their neighbour William Godolphin, the son of Sir William and a protégé of Cromwell, in the same campaign (says Carew) 'demeaned himself very valiantly ... as appeared by the scars he brought home, no less to the beautifying of his fame, than the disfiguring of his face.'[3]

Anne Basset successfully navigated the treacherous waters of the court, through the reign of Edward VI and into that of Queen Mary, being richly rewarded by the Crown and rising to the position of Lady of the Privy Chamber.

But the trauma of these years had evidently coloured the judgement of the innocent girl of 16 who had arrived in 1537. For Anne chose late in life, with a generous dowry from Queen Mary, to marry into the unhappy family of the much younger Walter Hungerford. His grandfather had been accused of poisoning his wife and his father had treated his wife with brutal cruelty before he was executed in 1540 for 'the abominable vice of buggery ... of sodomy, of having forced his own daughter, and having practiced magic and invocation of devils'.[4] Anne died three years after this ill-advised marriage to Walter, who evinced familial traits when he later accused his next wife of adultery and even of trying to poison him.

Meanwhile, cleared of any lingering suspicion as the Lisle's agent, and his role in the Portuguese wreck long forgotten, Thomas St Aubyn in 1545 had at last been chosen as High Sheriff of Cornwall for the coming year.[5] Recognised as one of the twenty-five leading men in the county, he again served as a magistrate in 1547.[6] His eldest son, John, was also now well established. He had followed his father's path to the Inner Temple as a young man, where the senior bencher, a cousin of Arthur Lisle, had written to Honor in 1533 to describe John as 'Master St Aubyn, your ladyship's nephew ... a sad, wise and discreet gentleman, which heartily recommendeth him'.[7]

By the late 1540s, John had children of his own, having married outside the county to Blanche Whittington, a member of a wealthy Gloucestershire family,[8] whose forebear, Richard, had been the worthy Mayor of London, later immortalised by the legend of his cat. Blanche's sister was married to Thomas Throckmorton, a committed supporter at court of the Lord Protector, the role secured by the Duke of Somerset during the regency of his young nephew, Edward VI.

Somerset was an arch reformer, determined to use Henry VIII's political break with Rome to achieve religious upheaval as well. He drew up plans for an English prayer book, to supplant the hallowed Mass in churches across the country. But while the studious John St Aubyn may have supported the Crown's reforms, the loyalty of the Cornish populace still lay with the Church of the old religion, its Latin verses and Cornish sermons. For West Cornwall especially, English was the foreign language.[9]

The dissolution and loss of the monasteries, which had been the main instrument of poor relief since time immemorial, had created a more practical grievance. Compounding this problem, as Chapuys wrote in July 1536, were the 'legion of monks and nuns who have been chased from their monasteries wandering miserably hither and thither ... there are over 20,000 who know not how to live'.[10]

The Protector responded to this with Calvinist fervour. By the 1547 Vagabonds Act, able-bodied vagrants were to be treated as criminals, branded with a 'V' and sentenced to two years' servitude.[11] A second offence could even earn the death penalty, although local magistrates like Thomas often balked at imposing it.

It was in Helston that the seeds of conflict first erupted. The catalyst was William Body, a notorious follower of Cromwell, who had wormed his way into the Archdeaconry of Cornwall ten years before and had been ruthlessly exploiting this posting ever since.[12] In December 1546, he was charged by the Privy Council to make an account of the jewels, plates and images which adorned Cornish churches. The purported aim was to secure them from pilfering, but as Body went about West Cornwall with reformist zeal, suspicions as to his true intentions quickly spread.

Body summoned representatives from across Penwith to explain his purpose. His orders were to reassure them that the aim was 'the preservation of the church jewels', but somehow they took his words – spoken in English – to mean that the church goods were to be seized by the Crown.[13] They may well have recalled how a decade earlier, an inventory had been made of the jewels, gold and silver candlesticks and goblets on St Michael's Mount, treasures accrued through the ages by the beneficence of pilgrims. Then the commissioners – of doubtful character – had swiftly hoisted the entire haul up to London, their plunder of the church only legalised by an Act of Dissolution a year later.[14]

Riot now ensued and the local justices, Sir William Godolphin, Thomas St Aubyn and John Milliton – the last newly appointed as High Sheriff – had to intervene to calm matters. The Council in London thanked the three magistrates for 'their pains taken in appeasing the tumultuous assembly' and Body was punished with a week's imprisonment, before being sent to London to answer for 'handling himself after such a manner as … much contrary to the Council's intent.'[15]

Yet by February, Somerset and the Council had resolved to support those like Body who had taken their earlier directive to the extreme. They sent a letter instructing bishops across the kingdom to 'order that all the images remaining in any church … within your diocese be removed and taken away'. Soon, Body was back in West Cornwall with a new commission and began flagrantly removing precious emblems of the old faith. Then on Easter Day, 1 April 1548, the new 'order of communion' service was performed, just as Body and his henchmen 'had cut down and broken the crucifix of a church, which the people had insisted should be left'.[16] The torch paper was lit.

An enraged populace, summoned to Helston in their hundreds by church bell ringing, broke down the doors of Body's lodgings in the town and tore him to pieces. Thousands more now swelled to the rebels' rallying call, defying the local magistrates to punish those who had committed the crime. Godolphin, St Aubyn and Milliton reluctantly resolved that the Helston assizes, which were due to start a week later, must be moved to Launceston.

So it says much for the bond which still held between them and the magistrates that 'afterwards the commons were pacified by the gentlemen of the country with small trouble'.[17] Although Godolphin was known as a reformer, the 'commons' found themselves caught in a symbiotic relationship with him; some mined his family's tin on Godolphin Hill, others sold it in Helston, while the strongest among them were plucked for his corps of archers. Behind Godolphin's authority stood both the courage he had displayed at Boulogne (now 'beautifying' his face) and his men-at-arms in the town square.

As for the other two, apart from dividing with tinners and farm hands the spoils of 'God's grace' from the occasional wreck, Milliton and St Aubyn were conformers, not reformers. The fury of the people was reserved for that minority of Protestants who dared to advertise their sacrilegious beliefs.

Nevertheless, it had required the assistance of many other Cornish gentry and their entourage to cower the protestors into submission. On 17 April, Somerset and the Council wrote to Godolphin, Milliton and St Aubyn along with seven other 'very loving friends' with 'our most hearty commendations, understanding by your letters of the 13th of this instant your good diligence and wise and earnest proceeding in the stay of that seditious commotion lately stirred up'.[18]

In May, Godolphin, St Aubyn and four others, headed by Sir Richard Grenville, were commissioned to try the ringleaders, who had been rounded up and held in Launceston jail.[19] Suspected sympathisers were placed on the jury to test their loyalties. At the same time, a general pardon to the people of Cornwall was granted by the king 'of his inestimable goodness, replenished with most godly pity and mercy'.[20] This leniency was eventually extended to many of the ringleaders, as only seven of them were hung for Body's murder.[21]

This betrayed the nervousness of the regime towards the common mood, a nervousness shared by the West Cornwall justices. Thomas' prosperous nephew, Peter St Aubyn, who lived in Helston where he continued his father's tin trading business,[22] would no doubt have shared his intelligence of the feelings on the ground. On 3 July, Godolphin and St Aubyn, along with three others, summoned a meeting of 'all the constables, the gentlemen and 2 or 3 of the head men of every parish within the hundred of Penwith', to meet at eight o'clock the next day on the village green opposite St Michael's Mount, with a further meeting on the following Friday at Redruth. The purpose was 'to know what number of trusty men may be in a readiness upon a sudden warning to serve the king'.[23] The fear of further disturbances in the county ran into the autumn.

In December 1548, John Milliton's year as High Sheriff came to an end. He remained captain of St Michael's Mount, having acquired a new thirty-year lease in 1533 from the Abbey of Sion, twelve years after he first took the post. But following the dissolution of the abbey, in 1539 the Crown had become his landlord and promptly sold its interest to Humphrey Arundell, a cadet member of Cornwall's most powerful family.[24] Arundell lived near Bodmin and was an experienced soldier who had led a troop of ten men at the siege of Boulogne.[25] Like the rest of his family, he was also a devout Catholic; on his mother's side, his grandfather had been attainted in 1497 for supporting Perkin Warbeck.[26]

By July 1549, word had reached Bodmin of a startling development in Stamford Courtenay, forty-five miles across the Devon border. Local parishioners had obliged their priest to don 'his old popish attire' and perform the Latin Mass, an affront to the new order which was rapidly copied by neighbouring parishes. As in Helston a year before, when a crowd began to swell in Stamford Courtenay, it fell to local magistrates to restore calm. But lacking the awesome authority and stern resolution of Godolphin and with no murder to solve, they chose to withdraw when 'the small company of commoners' proved unwilling to disperse.

At this point William Hellyons, an arch reformer, took it upon himself to come and remonstrate with the crowd. They carried him by force into the church house. Once there Hellyons 'so sharply threatened them with an evil success that they all fell in a rage with him'. Like Body the year before, as a symbol of the hated policy to eradicate the last remnants of the old faith, Hellyons had made himself a target. As he was leaving, one of the crowd struck him in the neck with the flash of a hedger's billhook; then 'a number of the rest fell upon him, slew him and cut him into small pieces'.[27] The angry and burgeoning crowd, unimpeded by the weak Devon justices, now marched towards Exeter.

Meanwhile as word spread, rebels began to flock together in Bodmin from all parts of the county, pitching their camp on Castle Kynock, the hilly mound half a mile south-west of the town, where five decades before Perkin Warbeck had gathered his army. Any gentleman who resisted their demands for support was threatened with being imprisoned. But Arundell, drawn from his house nearby, saw that his moment had come and was appointed General of the rebel host. According to their later indictment, Arundell and the other leaders of the rebellion 'for six weeks' following, at Bodmin and elsewhere in the county of Cornwall, by ringing of bells, hue and cry and otherwise, raise[d] a multitude of malefactors to an amount of 1,000 persons and upwards ... to levy war against the king'.[28] Rebels were accused of parading the Bodmin streets shouting, 'Kill the gentlemen!'

Across the county, with the rebels 'feloniously and traitorously despoiling the lieges of the king of their goods and chattels by force of arms', those opposed to rebellion sought refuge.[29] Sir Richard Grenville sheltered a band of loyalists behind the thick walls of Trematon Castle, near Saltash; John Killigrew holed up with over a hundred soldiers at the mouth of the Fal in Pendennis Castle; while in the far west, loyalist families fled to St Michael's Mount. Arundell, wounded by this affront to his own freehold, ordered a detachment to assail the island fortress. Carew records a rapid surrender '... to those rascals' mercy who, nothing guilty of the effeminate virtue, spoiled their goods, imprisoned their bodies, and were rather by God's gracious providence, than any want or will or purpose ... restrained from murdering the principal persons'.

That the resolute trio of Godolphin, St Aubyn and Milliton could lose control of West Cornwall speaks to the unbridled forces which the rebellion had unleashed. It is doubtful whether the justices placed their families among those 'principal persons' on the Mount, but we do know that William Trewinnard, living just a few miles away in St Erth, had fled there. He was fatally 'hurt with gunpowder at the assault by the rebels ... being of the king's party then defending and resisting the said rebels ... for which thereupon his house was by the rebels afterwards spoiled'.[30] Trewinnard had been one of the gentlemen who had joined William Godolphin in suppressing the protest the year before. Yet again, a vocal supporter of the king's policy had become an object of hate.

There is no record of such despoiling at Tehidy or Clowance, perhaps because it was recognised that the Bassets and St Aubyns bore the new iconoclasm under sufferance. While Godolphin and Milliton were in the reformist camp, Godolphin's fortress of a house and Milliton's Pengersick Castle remained impregnable, even if as captain of the Mount he was personally caught defending the island. Pendennis Castle, with its coastal access for supplies, held firm for John Killigrew.

But not so Trematon, where Mary St Aubyn's brother, Sir Richard Grenville – another proponent of the new faith – was persuaded 'by mingling humble entreaties with rude menaces ... to issue forth at a postern gate for parley'.[31] In a moment, his 'aged unwieldy body' was in the rebels' hands and soon so was the castle. Its defenders were treated with 'barbarous cruelty ... gentlewomen, without regard of sex or shame, were stripped of their apparel to their very smocks, and some of their fingers broken, to pluck away their rings'. Sir Richard and his wife were hauled off from Saltash to Launceston jail, the very place where he had put the men condemned to death a year before.

With the rebel base in the county secured, albeit with thousands of them tied down to contain pockets of resistance, Arundell now led the main part of his army over the border and towards the prize of Exeter, inspired by news that insurgency had spread to fourteen counties across the realm. The Council in London was slow to react, not at first realising how much more dangerous was the West Country revolt compared to all these others. But if Lord John Russell, their appointed commander, could marshal his local soldiers and foreign mercenaries in time, better trained and more heavily equipped, they would put the outcome beyond doubt.

The first decisive encounter took place at Fenny Bridges, on 29 July, in a field thereafter known as Blood Meadow, where the Devonians, supported by the first Cornish contingent, were roundly beaten. After a second encounter a few days later, a total of more than 400 rebels had been slain for minimal loss on the loyalist side. Then Lord Grey, 'the best soldier in England', arrived to support Russell with a troop of 1500 hardened mercenaries on horse and on foot.[32] The tide had turned.

After the next two engagements at Woodbury and Clyst St Mary, another 2000 rebels had been slain, compared to several hundred loyalists wounded and a few lost. On 5 August, another assault by 2000 rebels was repelled, where a loyalist reckoned another hundred of them fell, to the loss on his own side 'not above 3 or 4'. The next day, Sir William Herbert, 'a mad fighting young fellow' as recalled by John Aubrey,[33] arrived with a thousand Welsh foot soldiers. The contest was over and those besieging Exeter fled. But the slaughter of the rebels continued unabated.

St Michael's Mount was relieved by 20 August and Grenville was freed from jail. But he was a broken man after a month in a cell where, as an inspector's report would later put it, 'those who served them there often caught the fatal fever'. He died a few months later, his wife surviving only another five weeks.[34] Yet such treatment of two leading county figures can barely justify the extreme cruelty with which Sir Antony Kingston, appointed provost marshall in the field, now set about punishing the Cornish rebels. Kingston proved a man so steeped in viciousness and cruelty as to eclipse the memory of William Body.[35]

Having already decided that the Mayor of Bodmin was guilty, Kingston invited himself to lunch and so the mayor prepared a lavish meal. Just before they sat down, Kingston took him aside and told him there had to be an execution, so could he please arrange for gallows to be constructed. This was done and at the end of the meal, Kingston asked to see it and enquired: 'Are the gallows strong enough, do you think?' After assuring the provost marshall that they were, the mayor was told: 'Then climb up to them, for you have been a busy rebel'.

Kingston enjoyed this trick so much that he played it again on the Portreeve of St Ives, hung from the George and Dragon Inn. On another occasion, told that he had hung a miller's servant by mistake, rather than the guilty rebel himself, Kingston retorted: 'And so? Could he ever have done his master a better service than to hang for him?' Another time, he found a crowd gathered around a grave, while the parson waited for some dues to be paid before committing the body to burial. Kingston had the priest himself thrown into the grave and buried alive.

Kingston's father Sir William, who had long served the Tudors as Keeper of the Tower of London, had been one of Arthur Lisle's closest friends.[36] But the widowed Honor had to sue the son for £1200, a debt he contested for ten years.[37] At other times, Sir Anthony was arraigned on charges of adultery, consorting with coiners and trying to rob the Tower. Finally, he was under escort there on a charge of treason against Queen Mary, when he brutally forced his horse to leap over the parapet at Henley Bridge and died before he could meet the traitor's fate he had perhaps spied as a boy and so richly deserved himself.

Throughout this turmoil, the members of the leading gentry of West Cornwall had keenly felt the loss of their authority. They had also received strong evidence that the religious grievances of the 'commons' had been exploited by the Arundells for their personal political ends. For 'in the midst of the hottest stirs', Humphrey Arundell's secretary, Kestell, had 'sent his secret advertisement to Mr Godolphin and other gentlemen of so much as he knew of Arundell's proceedings and the rest'.[38] It seemed Humphrey

Arundell had been playing the stooge for his family's higher ambition, to topple Protector Somerset and to install the senior Tudor Mary as queen regent.

Evidence of conspiracy is circumstantial. At a critical point in the uprising, the Council considered appeasing the 'commons' by mooting that in Cornwall, the new service would be held in the native tongue. But Humphrey Arundell, fixed on the political prize, would not be interested in this balm for the rebels' fury.[39] There was also Sir Thomas Arundell's notable absence from the county during the 'commotions' and his failure to respond to Russell's pleas for help. He had stayed at his estate in Dorset, where on hearing of the first rising in Devon, he had 'caused two masses to be said'. Several of the rebel ringleaders were later named as servants of the Lanherne household.[40] Suspicions of Sir John of Lanherne were also fuelled by his allies' connection to Kett, the man who in Suffolk had led the other major uprising of 1549.[41]

In any event, at the height of the rebellions, Sir John had been sent for by the Council, kept in custody and then examined. He was later released, but bound over with his brother, Sir Thomas, in a large sum to remain in the City, a restriction only removed in November.

The Arundells of Lanherne had been fatally compromised by the rebellion and this had consequences for all three of the West Country justices. Milliton would be released from Humphrey Arundell's interfering freehold of the Mount, which he was sure to forfeit as a traitor. For John and Blanche St Aubyn, there was relief that their brother-in-law's faction at court had survived, with the promise of favours to come. As for Sir William Godolphin, he had been summoned to London, having been appointed High Sheriff for the coming year. He burned with desire for retribution against Cornwall's leading family for its part in the rebellion. And where one house fell, he saw that another might rise.

Godolphin came across Sir John on the London street and challenged him, presumably with the evidence of collusion between Sir John and his nephew, as supplied by Kestell. There was a fierce row and on 14 December 1549, Sir John Arundell and Sir William Godolphin were bound in £1000 each to keep the peace 'and neither by themselves, friends, nor servants or others, procure displeasure the one to the other', and to appear daily before the Council until the causes at variance between them were settled.[42] Soon enough, Godolphin was on his way back to his duties as the new Sheriff of Cornwall, while Sir John was returned to the Tower, followed on January 30 by his brother Sir Thomas.

By now Humphrey Arundell and the others had pleaded their last desperate testimony, which probably implicated his uncles as well. In any event, Sir Thomas was beheaded in 1552 for allegedly plotting against Dudley, who had replaced Somerset as leader of the Council.

Sir John survived his release that year long enough to enjoy the restoration of his fortunes, which followed Queen Mary's accession to the throne in 1553. Yet her bloody counter-reformation was doomed by her deeply resented and childless marriage to Philip of Spain. With the succession of Elizabeth, the Anglican religion was secure and Sir John's descendants at Lanherne found their wealth and power drained by their devotion to their faith.

CHAPTER 6

COUSINS

The inhabitants of Belerium are especially hospitable
to strangers and have adopted a civilized manner of life
because of their intercourse with merchants of other peoples.
Diodorus Siculus, *c*.40 BCE[1]

Five influences have been identified as 'the ties which bind the natural
units of history and integral elements of the human experience'.[2] The
powerful combination of language, territory, religion, race and ethnicity
created the differences that pitted ancient Egyptians against the Hittites,
medieval Franks against the Visigoths, just as on a greater scale, the same
five elements distinguish the nation states of today. Seen in these terms, it
is beyond doubt that Cornwall itself comprised a 'natural unit of history'
from time immemorial.

The Conquest had simply replaced indigenous Cornwall's Anglo-
Saxon Thanes with Norman Barons.[3] So it fell to the Tudors to be the
first rulers since the Saxon invasions of the Dark Ages to threaten this
profound Cornish identity and in the process, reawaken its cultural
awareness. A series of disruptive interventions, from the attempt to
abolish the Stannaries in the 1490s, to the suppression of the monasteries
in the 1530s, to the English prayer book of 1549, aroused latent Cornish
passions to the point of violence. Defeat and suppression only served to
embed a renewed Cornish 'sense of difference', feeding a resentment of
the rest of the kingdom.

Mathew Parris, the thirteenth-century chronicler, had written of the
Welsh and Cornish 'that they always regard the nation of the Angles, even
to this very day, with mortal hatred, as if it were owing to them that they
were banished from their proper country, and they are not more willing
to associate with them than with dogs'. Writing in 1602, Richard Carew
could still comment that 'one point of their former roughness, some of the
Western people do yet still retain, & therethrough, in some measure, verify
that testimony which Matthew of Westminster giveth of them'.[4] Norden
also observed '… a kind of concealed envy against the English, whom they

yet affect with kind of desire for revenge for their fathers' sakes, by whom their fathers received the repulse'.[5]

Yet this Cornish sense of difference was one which nevertheless contained two conflicting strands.

The first was that far from being insular, the Cornish were in so many ways the most open and internationally minded of people. They took pride in their mining tradition, a heritage stretching back to biblical times. Their trade with the Phoenicians was held to be the earliest record of Britain's commerce with the outside world.[6] In this Tudor era, as well as the active tin trade with the Bretons and Germans, the Cornish sailor journeyed further than any British crew had done before, whether following the Portuguese trade route to Southern America, or establishing the first fishing colonies in Newfoundland, after its discovery in 1497.

It is no coincidence that the parish of St Keverne near Helston proved the flashpoint of revolt in every Cornish uprising of this time,[7] for it contained not only one of the largest contingents of miners, but also of fishermen and sailors. Travel broadens the mind and their contempt for London authority was nurtured on many a voyage to the world's furthest reaches and its fabulous revelations.

The second conflict was that on another plane, the Cornish were inclined to intense loyalty to the Crown. The county's long shoreline being prone to attack, the security of their families was bound up with the defence of the realm, which at the same time provided ample employment in the expanding Navy, Falmouth becoming a significant royal port. Above all stood the ties of fealty to the Duchy, albeit less so in the far west where it held little sway.

From the perspective of the throne, feelings towards the Cornish were equally conflicted. On the one hand, tin was one of the major exports in the national economy and the balance of trade, ranking alongside wool and lead.[8] Great hoards of Newfoundland cod now added to the pilchards, which Cornish fishermen drew from the sea to nourish English tastes.[9] The Duchy not only provided the Crown with a crucial source of income, but its produce such as corn was exported both across the Tamar and into Europe. Until surpassed by seventeenth-century advances in gunfire, Cornish archers remained a strategic military asset. Lately there was also piracy, or state endorsed 'privateering', as richly laden galleons offered irresistible rewards.[10]

On the other hand, remote from the centre, many instinctively saw Cornwall as culturally backward, hidebound by its own language and pastimes – such as wrestling, hurling and miracle plays.[11] It was also regarded as poverty stricken, not least given the destitute living conditions of the miners,[12] or measured by the low level of collections from Tudor taxes, which were often deflated by Cornish methods of account.[13]

Yet to acknowledge the existence of a separate Cornish identity begs the question of its scope, intensity, salience, and political importance. In the hands of Michael Joseph, Perkin Warbeck or Humphrey Arundell, it rose to play a fleeting part on the national stage. But for most of the time and for most Cornish families, the wisest course was to mull it over while leaving its latent ambiguities unresolved, unless or until some new state intervention provoked another violent reckoning. After the 1549 Western Rising, in and after which so many Cornishmen suffered,[14] it would be ninety years before a challenge arrived which was to divide family loyalties and exploit unbridled passions, with a greater intensity than ever before.

———————

For the St Aubyn, Basset and Godolphin families, the most obvious aspect of their Cornish identity was geography. As members of the emerging 'gentry' class, their experience was in stark contrast to those living in the typical English county, where territorial threats from competing families fed a constant insecurity.

A good example is the Plumptons of West Yorkshire, whom we have already met at their zenith; in 1441, Sir William's brutal methods had been richly rewarded by the House of Lancaster, to which he was beholden. But twenty years later, his Yorkist neighbours had seized the upper hand in the Wars of the Roses:

> Deprived of his offices and their income, kept away from his own lands in the north, Plumpton found himself exposed to his enemies. Arms were stolen from his house at Plumpton, precious household goods and even a surplice from his chapel was taken. The monks of a monastery sieved his fishponds for bream, tench, roach, perch and dentices.

His woods were stripped of timber, his oxen stolen and his hay harvested by others. By 1520, Plumpton's heirs had been reduced to penury, their estates dispersed and their name soon lost in time, in a story repeated across England.[15]

The Plumptons of this time lived surrounded by enemies. The triumvirate of West Cornwall, on the other hand, were surrounded by sea. Instinctively bound together against foreign incursions, the bonds of kinship underpinned the advantages of hanging together to resolve internal threats as well. Unlike other parts of the country, land changed hands in West Cornwall between these three families only by marriage, or, as we have seen, by the token of a snail's race or some other friendly exchange.

When the Millitons, with rumours of their dubious past,[16] came into possession of the strategic outpost of Pengersick Castle, the instinct was nevertheless to embrace them. Nor was this confined to joint wrecking ventures and promotion to the Bench at Helston. Honor Godolphin, sister of the younger William, was pledged in marriage to John Milliton's son William, who succeeded to Pengersick Castle on his father's death following the Mount assault of 1549.[17]

Honor was the second Godolphin lady to cross its portals – in the eleventh century, a previous Godolphin wife had been brutally murdered there by a monk, her ghost still said to haunt the ruins.[18] Sadly, Honor's experience was not a great deal happier. There was even a story that one night she and William, fuelled by mutual loathing, tried to poison each other over dinner.[19] But they produced six daughters who married local gentry. Following William's death at sea in 1571,[20] Honor remarried William Harris, who succeeded to the Milliton lease of St Michael's Mount, while Pengersick castle was acquired from the Milliton heiresses by the family of Hals, the scurrilous chronicler.

During the later Tudor reigns, another feature special to Cornwall was the remarkable expansion in the county's representation in the House of Commons.[21] Eight boroughs were invested with the elective franchise under Edward VI, one under Mary and a further six under Elizabeth, each returning two MPs and doubling Cornish representation in the Commons to forty-two seats. By comparison, Wales was kept to only eighteen seats and even by 1600, Cornish representation was over nine times its share of the country's population as a whole. The simplest explanation for this policy is that in craving absolute rule, Tudor monarchs sought to tame the power of the nobility by calling upon that of the Commons. It also made sense for these new MPs to come from a county where the most powerful noble family was the Crown itself; this was even if the Duchy's role was limited to neutralising Cornish factions, rather than to create its own.

Henry VIII's parliament of 1528 had already transformed the relationship between the Crown, the people and the Church, making parliament the supreme legislative body, over and above the executive. But in the words of Sir Geoffrey Elton, the distinguished sixteenth-century historian, 'by apparently imposing a limitation upon the Crown they in fact greatly elevated monarchical power provided it was associated with the Lords and the Commons in the making of laws'.[22] Then following the dissolution of the monasteries, the Commons moved to St Stephen's Chapel within the Palace of Westminster, where they now sat alongside the Lords. From 1547, their daily business was recorded – and by the Crown monitored.

The 'invasion of the gentry' into parliament had a variety of motives – base, political, or religious for some, but also merely social for others. Parliamentary seats created an orderly hierarchy of local influence in the choosing of candidates. The duly elected members of the Tudor gentry were flattered but enjoyed the mere illusion of power. For '... the House was to be repeatedly taught and warned, especially by Elizabeth, that the Royal will must prevail, that members were to be complacent and submissive in registering the Sovereign's decrees and in voting the sums which the crown required for State or personal purposes'.[23]

This is not to discount the opportunities for advancement which a seat in parliament offered; nor its use as a platform for deeply held beliefs. Others had more nefarious purposes. John Killigrew represented Falmouth as MP in the 1570s purely to bolster his lucrative appointment as the piracy commissioner. Exerting control both from his home at Arwennack and from Pendennis Castle, he worked in open connivance with the pirates and smugglers who frequented the Cornish coast.

But for the St Aubyns and for others, their 'novel desire to enter parliament' began more as a symbol of their place in society and as a mark of their professional standing.[24]

John St Aubyn's younger brother William was a religious traditionalist, who combined his legal career with a seat in Queen Mary's parliaments. Supported by Sir Thomas Arundell, who had held sway during his time at Lincoln's Inn, William was elected twice for Helston in 1554, just four miles from his home on the Lizard. He was elected again, for West Looe in 1555 and for Camelford in the parliament of 1558.[25] Lanherne's return to royal favour under Mary was marked by Sir John's own election as one of the two county members before he died.

His death was perhaps just as well because Elizabeth's reign marked the turning of the political tide. Sir John was the last of the Lanherne Arundells to feature in any parliament at all. As county members, it was now the staunch Protestants, the Godolphins and the Grenvilles, along with the Arundells of Trerice, who monopolised the hustings. These years marked the start of the Grenville ascendancy in the county, the Godolphins not far behind, as Sir Richard sought to avenge his grandparents' fatal imprisonment in

Launceston with an unrelenting campaign against Catholic recusants. His victims included Francis Tregian, Sir John Arundell's grandson, whose vast estates were forfeited after Grenville discovered the priest and Catholic martyr, Cuthbert Maine, hiding in Golden, the Tregian mansion, with an incriminating Papal bull and devotional items in his room.

The St Aubyns stayed out of this conflict. William, who had married Elizabeth Borlase, died soon after his last election when he was still in his thirties. He may have been a victim of the epidemic which swept Cornwall in 1558–9, his wife surviving another twenty-five years. His father, owing to whose marriage to Mary Grenville the St Aubyn family line had revived, was reappointed as a JP in 1555,[26] but he may well have been taken by the same epidemic; so this is where we bid him a fond farewell. Mary's redoubtable sister Honor lived on until 1566, when she too was laid to rest, in a lost grave at Illogan, near Tehidy.[27]

According to Carew, 'in a long and peaceable date of years', Thomas' son John and his wife Blanche 'exercised a kind, liberal, and never-discontinued hospitality', as well as playing their part in county affairs, John spending an uneventful year as High Sheriff in 1568. Carew's description of the Cornish gentleman's way of life gives an apt description of the Cornish society which the St Aubyns now inhabited:

> They keep liberal, but not costly built or furnished houses, give kind entertainment to strangers, make even at the year's end with the profits of their living, are reverenced and beloved of their neighbours, live void of factions amongst themselves (at leastwise such as break out into any dangerous excess) and delight not in bravery of apparel: yet the women would be very loth to come behind the fashion, in newfangledness of the manner, if not in costliness of the matter, which perhaps might over-empty their husbands' purses.
>
> They converse familiarly together, & often visit one another. A Gentleman and his wife will ride to make merry with his next neighbour; and after a day or twain, those two couples go to a third: in which progress they increase like snowballs, till through their burdensome weight they break again.[28]

A less subjective account, by John Norden the mapmaker in 1581, is no less fulsome:

> The gentlemen and such as have tasted civil education are very
> kind, affable, full of humanity and courteous entertainment.
> And in causes of equity, stout.[29]

While not sitting on tin deposits to rival the Godolphins or the Bassets, John
St Aubyn took up his Uncle Peter's connection to the trade. This was through
a venture at Binnerton, lying midway between Clowance and Godolphin, with
William Carnsew. He was a Puritan friend of Blanche, as well as being married
to yet another Grenville cousin, Honor, named after the Basset matriarch.

The tin streaming that John's grandfather had overseen for Honor Basset
was now making way for tin mining, as far as fifty fathoms into the lode,
opening up new opportunities. John's other cousin, Francis Godolphin, who
had succeeded to the family estates from his uncle, was developing these
new mining techniques (some learnt from Germany) with such success that
Carew says:

> By his labours and inventions in tin matters, not only the whole
> county hath felt a general benefit, so as the several owners
> have thereby gotten very great profit out of such refuse works
> as they before had given over for unprofitable, but her Majesty
> hath also received great increase of her customs by the same,
> at least to the value of £10,000.[30]

Godolphin's services to mining were, in Carew's view, 'perchance not to be
matched again by any of his sort and condition in the whole realm'.

After Godolphin, the most active of the Cornish gentry was this St Aubyn
partner Carnsew, who is described by Carew as having a 'well qualified and
sweete pleasing sufficiency'.[31] He embraced the opportunities presented
by the new technology and worked with City financiers to develop a host
of mines in Cornwall and smelting works in Wales. He disdained the
importation of foreign labour, however, declaring that 'our countrymen …
out of all peradventure be as skilful in mining, as hard and diligent labourers
… in that kind of travail as are any to be found in Europe'. The Cornish
miner proved cheaper too, as he preferred the chance to be paid by results,[32]
to the certainty of a day rate.

The copper mines at St Just produced fifty tons in four months – the
captain who employed twenty lucky miners remarking on this result to
Carnsew, 'I would to God we had a dozen such mines as St Just's ore'.[33]
The copper was taken to St Ives by boat, from there freighted to South

Wales to be smelted, anticipating the industrial trade of two centuries later. But at many mines, horse-drawn water pumps and candlelight failed, before reaching the deeper lodes that the steam engine and the Davey light would one day make profitable. The miners, as well as the investors, felt the loss.

Carnsew's diary, transcribed by N.J.G. Pounds, gives us another glimpse of this late sixteenth-century Cornwall.[34] In the month of February 1576 for example, after visiting his Catholic friends the Roscarrocks in wild weather, Carnsew came home to find his wife on her way to admire a friend's newborn. On their return, he journeyed westward to see to his affairs, stopping on the Monday night with the Protestant Arundells at Trerice, where he heard that the Bishop of Exeter was to be removed to Salisbury.

Tuesday night he slept at Roscrow, then Wednesday with the St Aubyns at Clowance; meanwhile 'at home Jane Penkivell's boy ran away with her money'. On Thursday, John St Aubyn and he rode to see the mine at Binnerton and to oversee the working of it, after which he rode on to Lelant near St Ives, where he spent Friday. Then back to Clowance for Saturday and at Binnerton again on the Sunday:

> Bargained with Roger Tregantallon for to work the work. Viz. he to work the hole and to take that only which he can make tin of, and blow it then being blown, and not coigned, to deliver one-third to Mr St Aubyn for his portion and to deliver me clear of eight parts three and to keep to his own use the other five. JSA must find wood and coal for the work in Binnerton.

In the treeless far west, 'JSA' would no doubt look to his grove at Clowance, from which Sir Henry Kemyell had once supplied the monks. Otherwise, the terms of this partnership with Carnsew seem clear enough. Tregantallon was their manager and once he had smelted the tin into slabs, he was to make sure they were not 'coigned' (a chip taken off the block and tested for purity).[35]

On leaving the St Aubyns, Carnsew visited John Nance, where one Richardson 'delivered unto me a Book of Discipline, I think put forth by Cartwright, *incerto authore sine nomine*'. Carnsew corresponded copiously about religious matters with fellow Protestants, such as John's wife Blanche, and two months later, he would hand this book over to Ford, the preacher. Thus was spread their faith.

In his diaries, we glean a contemporary love of reading, from puritan epistles and philosophical tracts to medical science, history and current affairs; the broad social circle from the knights and gentry of the county to village priests and the players of quoits and bowls and above all the interest in family, sons studying at Oxford, Cambridge or the Inns of Court and daughters getting wed. Puritan, patriarchal and parochial certainly; but also inventive, enterprising and full of life.

In Carew's words, John's son, Thomas, 'took to wife the daughter of Mallet; and with ripe knowledge, and sound judgment, dischargeth the place which he beareth in his country'.[36] Zenobia Mallet's father was descended from one of the Conqueror's closest companions, entrusted with the dead body of King Harold after Hastings; but as well on his mother's side, from Honor Lisle. Zenobia's mother was a Monck, another ancient family claiming Norman origins, into which Arthur Lisle's daughter, Frances, had been drawn.[37]

Marriage had once again proved the safer way to advance. By the time he inherited from his father in 1590, Thomas St Aubyn owned over a thousand acres stretching from Land's End to the Devon border.[38]

Zenobia bore her husband eleven children, although we only have a record of three of them: John, Thomas and Anne.[39] This was the thirteenth generation of St Aubyns, beginning with Mauger the foot soldier in William's invading army. The family had barely survived the deadly toll of war in the middle ages, which had wrought the extinction of thousands of knightly dynasties. But the favourable environs of West Cornwall had regenerated the family line.

It now held as good a position in society as its Devon forefathers had ever enjoyed, through loyal public service and happy marriages. While they had witnessed the perils of so doing, the first St Aubyn member to make an impact on the national stage had yet to come. The family's ambivalent position during the commotions of 1548–9 had precluded them from the rich rewards for the Crown's champions, while averting the heavy penalties which Peter's support of the Yorkist cause had cost the family fifty years earlier.

Surviving as a family into the seventeenth century would mean adjusting to a whole new framework of society. A Stuart king, intensely at odds with his parliament, would cause a pivotal moment for the St Aubyn family, as it faced its most momentous decision since Mauger de Sancto Albino crossed the English Channel in 1066.

PART THREE

PRIZE POSSESSION

CHAPTER 1

THE JEWEL IN THE SEA

'A school of Mars...the temple of peace.'

Carew

As you make your way into the far west of Cornwall, through the parish of Lugdvan, before the sea finally hoves into view you often catch a glimpse of the waves in Mount's Bay; and of the captivating feature which makes this seascape so enchanting.

Likewise in the preceding chapters we have caught glimpses of this jewel, as the moment nears where it almost seems that fate itself has decided that the descendants of a Breton born in the shadow of *Mont Saint-Michel* should one day assume possession of the Norman monastery's one-time Cornish priory.

This westernmost of the castles of the British Isles is in many ways the most interesting and picturesque of them all. A fortress girded on all sides by a natural moat, it differs from all others because this moat is the sea. More than a fortress on an island – like Beaumaris or the Marisco's castle on Lundy – the island is a fortress in itself, a cliff-edged rock accessible only where steps to reach the summit have been etched by man. A seabound rock can appear shapeless and unattractive – like the outer island of Tintagel – but St Michael's Mount rises gracefully into a majestic pyramid, its apex crowned by a splendid array of granite buildings, both spiritual and secular.

The Mount is at its most serene at high tide, when the causeway is closed. Then it floats on the water, even more so at evening, its black outline and crown of towers silhouetted against the glories of the sunset. It was not always so. This granite mound once belonged to the mainland, separated by a cataclysm lost in the midst of time.[1] Later, it was almost certainly Ictis, the island where the Phoenicians traded with the Cornish for tin:

> For at the time of ebb-tide the space between this island and the mainland becomes dry and they can take the tin in large quantities over to the island on their wagons (*Diodorus*).[2]

The island has been a centre of pilgrimage since Christianity first came to Cornwall 1500 years ago and St Michael appeared there to local fishermen. Edward the Confessor founded an island priory of Benedictine monks in 1044, which Count Robert – first Earl of Cornwall – later gave to Mont Saint-Michel as a daughter house, so that for 300 years it was an 'alien priory', often put in the charge of those sent over from Normandy with names like de Carteret and de Gerenon.[3] Then in 1346, war with France provoked the Commons in parliament to 'pray that all alien monks quit the realm, and their priories, etc be bestowed on Englishmen'.[4]

The church dates from 1135, with many later alterations. The first were by Henry de Pomeroy, an earlier wanton member of his line who in 1194 seized the Mount by disguising his soldiers as visiting monks.[5] As a desperate refuge from justice, he rapidly built up the island fortifications, in a vain attempt to avoid his fate as a traitor to Richard I. The king restored the prior and monks to their home, but seeing the military importance of the island, appointed a castellan and put him in charge of the Mount as a royal castle. St Michael's thus became at once sanctuary and fortress, and so remained until the dissolution of the monasteries.

Henry de Pomeroy's escapade was spun into legend. It was his descendant Joan who married Sir John St Aubyn and bore him Guy; his widow Alice being the grandmother of the 13th Earl of Oxford, who was inspired by Pomeroy's trick to repeat it in 1473. It is tempting to think that this is how the story was passed down to him and certainly this second seizure of the castle proved better planned, if ultimately just as hopeless. That Pomeroy and Oxford were connected in this way, through the family that would eventually capture the Mount on a more permanent basis, is a very Cornish coincidence.

In 1497, Perkin Warbeck did not so much seize the Mount as charm his way into it, so by the time the gentry fleeing the rebels of 1549 sought refuge there, its defences had not been tested for eighty years. Meanwhile, gunshot had shifted the balance in favour of attack, giving rise to the need for further defensive building works, once the Millitons – and then the Harris family – were restored as tenants of the Crown.

By now, the castles of Tregony, Liskeard, Bottreaux, Tregothnan, Lanihorne and Binomy (near Stratton) – all either destroyed or rebuilt out of recognition – bore witness to the extinction of the baronial families who had once ruled Cornwall.[6] As their lines died out and their estates reverted to the Duchy, in the name of the Crown, their castles had been dismantled or allowed to fall into decay. Thus Leland's journal of 1538 had recorded that Lanihorne had become 'decaying, for want of coverture', Bottreaux was now 'a thing of small reputation', Liskeard was 'all in ruin'. As for the Duchy's own castles – Launceston, Trematon and Restormel – they were still standing, but also in decline; after 1547, for six decades there was no Duke of Cornwall to live in them, even had he so wanted. It would take the ravages of the Civil War of 1642–46 to finish other Cornish castles as places of residence, but already by the turn of the century, there were few fortified dwellings in private hands, and none measured in importance with St Michael's Mount.[7]

In 1584, the rising religious tensions with Catholic Spain spilt over into war. That year, Captain Arthur Harris petitioned the Crown for new fortifications, including cannon and shot. The commissioners 'appointed for viewing that place have certified that the queen has only two pieces of iron ordinance there', but that 'eight or nine men will serve for continual guard if 200 or 150 of the inhabitants of the adjoining parishes may always be at command to serve'.[8]

The south-west coast was now very exposed and it appears that Harris' requests were granted. When after several false alarms the Spanish Armada of 130 ships was spotted off the Lizard on 7 July 1588, the first beacon to warn the country was lit on top of the Mount. Drake's brave victory against the enemy fleet would enter folklore, but the threat of further invasion persisted, along with audacious forays by either side.

The most famous of these came with Sir Richard Grenville's command of the *Revenge*, a faster and more agile design of galleon. When the English fleet were surprised by the Spanish off the Azores, in 1591, Admiral Howard signalled a retreat. But Sir Richard, the former scourge of Catholics in Cornwall, 'utterly refused to turn from the enemy … he would rather choose to die than dishonour himself'.[9]

After twelve hours, inflicting heavy damage on fifteen galleons, the *Revenge* was at last subdued, but not Sir Richard. Before he expired of his wounds, he cursed his sailors as 'traitors and dogs' for at last submitting to the enemy. His curse lingered, for another fifteen Spanish warships with the captured *Revenge* in tow were caught by a cyclone and sunk without trace during a week-long storm.

His St Aubyn and Basset cousins mourned his loss, but their own reckoning with the Spanish now hung over them. The gentry of West Cornwall were called to the defence of their coast, which required trained men, ready to be summoned from each parish. But Queen Elizabeth's mission to subdue Ireland had drawn away a constant stream of the ablest and best, with their munitions, to support her campaign. This left a poorly equipped and motley crew to man the home front.

Sir Francis Godolphin, the mining engineer, had acquired the lease of the Scilly Isles, a strategic outpost whose defences he was working to reinforce against the Spanish threat. So the need to drill these volunteers fell upon Thomas St Aubyn and three others, whose correspondence on their commission survives, between 1592 and 1600.[10] By then a typical muster order, issued when 'the time of year now is like to be fair and the days long', rather than in the testing conditions more favoured by military minds, portrays their sense of weariness with this business of war.

Captains of companies were to 'come before us with your company complete and armed at Helston Downe on Tuesday in the Whitsun week next by nine of the clock in the forenoon', which was hardly a demanding hour. The men would be 'viewed mustered and trained' until Wednesday afternoon, but only 'if we see occasion'; they were advised to bring powder for every caliver and musket, 'with match proportionable and some bullets'. Thomas St Aubyn adds in his own hand that this is a copy of the order he has sent to his cousin Basset and that he has franked it 'Clowance, April 28th, 1600'. Job done, again.

But this was five years on from the startling events of 23 July 1595, when four Spanish galleys had appeared out of the mist off Mousehole, the little fishing village just west of Penzance. Two hundred of the enemy landed and swiftly burnt the village and its surrounding hamlets to the ground, an echo of the French attack on Marazion eighty years before.[11]

The terrified inhabitants, fleeing towards Penzance, came across Godolphin. It is fortunate that the most capable of the local gentry happened to be on his way to the Scilly Isles that morning. He feared this raid – and reports of enemy ships in Falmouth Bay – to be the prelude to a full-scale invasion and quickly sent word to Drake at Plymouth: 'consider what is to be done for your own safety and our defence … here is assembled 200 naked men'.

Unarmed, the local populace now faced the full force of the Spanish contingent, as they sailed on to Newlyn, next to Penzance, and 400 soldiers disembarked, their galleys continuing to fire on the native defenders. The Cornishmen panicked and not even Godolphin's drawn rapier could persuade them to hold their ground in the market square. A dozen of his own men stood with him as the mob retreated, but they were forced to leave Penzance to a blaze of destruction by the Spanish, who then returned to their galleys.[12]

Marazion and the Mount were now in peril. At last, great numbers flocked to Godolphin's side, Thomas St Aubyn and his fellow commissioners having been prodded into action, with tinners and farm hands drawn from Godolphin Hill, Clowance and Tehidy. Hannibal Vivyan, in charge of Pendennis Castle, also sent word to Drake in Plymouth, to send down some battle-hardened captains and to put his ships in readiness.[13] The next day, the swelled ranks of defenders saw off a Spanish attempt to land on the west side of Mount's Bay and the day after, support from Plymouth arrived by both land and sea. At this point, the wind shifted north-westerly and the enemy galleys seized their chance to sail away.

This episode administered a salutary shock to the Council in London, who still failed to grasp the true position in the county. Since 1585, Sir Walter Raleigh had been both Lord Lieutenant and Lord Warden of the Stannaries, to avoid any conflict of authority. He warned the Council:

> … there is no part of England so dangerously seated, so thinly
> manned, so little defenced and so easily invaded, having the
> sea on both sides, which no other county of England hath, and
> is withal so narrow that if an enemy possess any of the two or
> three straits, neither can those of the west repair eastward nor
> those of the east westward.[14]

The campaign in Ireland had drained the queen's treasure as well as her men, so the Crown hawked the residue of its monastic lands. Robert Cecil, Earl of Salisbury, was one of the most avaricious bargain hunters, even borrowing money from London aldermen to speculate on purchasing £30,000 of Crown property.[15] On 19 March 1602, he wrote to the Mayor of Marazion:

> I have purchased of the Queen's Majesty the manor of
> St Michael's Mount in Cornwall whereof the town of Markasue
> is a member. I would be glad to have some particulars…[16]

It took two years for Salisbury to have sight of the deeds and it was only in 1612 – the year of his death – that the Crown finally confirmed his acquisition of the Mount freehold and its possessions. But the lease to Arthur Harris still held good and in 1627 we find him again importuning the king's secretary to address the need for reparations. When Arthur died the following year, the Mount lost a true and faithful servant, to which his monument in Gulval church testifies.

Salisbury had covenanted with the Crown to defend the Mount with a captain on £50 a year, a gunner at £12 and eight soldiers costing £8 each. But part of this obligation was passed on to his tenant, Captain Harris, in his lease agreeing to supply five of the men out of his own pocket, as well as rent. The captaincy had more than paid for itself, as well as being in good hands.

But Salisbury's son and heir, William, soon discovered the true cost of managing such a remote property, when Hannibal Newman succeeded Harris as captain. He proved a poor choice, as we shall see, and the castle rapidly fell into decline. By 1640, this second Cecil earl was looking to sell and offering to set £200 against the price, towards remedial repairs.[17] A willing buyer proved to be Sir Francis Basset of Tehidy, not least since ownership of the Mount would bring with it relief from the tithes of Tehidy, a burden on the estate confirmed by a Church commission of enquiry as long ago as 1365.[18] Fortunately, mining their lodes for tin had by now propelled the Basset fortunes; they could easily find the £2150 purchase price agreed in April 1640, with the Cecils retaining a third of the Mount's original endowment for its income.[19]

This was the month of the Short Parliament, a disastrous attempt by Charles I to reverse the deep dissatisfaction which eleven years of his absolute rule and arbitrary taxes had spread among the gentry. One of the new MPs vocal in his opposition to the king was Salisbury's son, Charles Cecil, and the earl's efforts to remain above the conflict soon failed.

In 1642, the Crown confiscated those Cornish manors which the Cecils had retained, citing their opposition to the king. These properties were handed over to the Bassets. Sir Francis was an ardent royalist and with a value of over £1000, this grant was vital to him. His family's loyal support for Charles I was about to be tested to the limit, in the Civil War whose coming storm would pound through Cornwall.

CHAPTER 2

CROWN AND PARLIAMENT

The state of monarchy is the supremest thing upon earth,
for kings are ...God's lieutenants upon earth.
King James I to Parliament, 1610[1]

While Robert Cecil was securing his acquisition of the Mount from his queen, he was also secretly securing her throne for his future king. In 1603, as Elizabeth I lay dying, Cecil sent James V of Scotland a draft proclamation of his accession, which was published within hours of the old queen's death on 24 March. For the first time since the Conquest, a new royal house was installed without the shedding of blood. This smooth transition to James I was a remarkable political achievement. But from the very first, there were portents of future trouble.

Whereas Elizabeth had been miserly in her granting of honours, James showered knighthoods like confetti.[2] On his progress from Edinburgh to London, forty-six new knights were created at Belvoir castle before breakfast. By Christmas 1604, over 1000 new creations had trebled the ranks. Such largesse quickly devalued the currency of the honour, just when James sorely needed his powers of patronage. The Scottish king believed that he was 'swapping a stony couch for a deep feathered bed', but the courtly extravagance which now followed his arrival provoked a rising militancy in his parliament.

Peter Wentworth, the scourge of Elizabeth's parliaments, probably never even visited the Cornish seats which launched his parliamentary career. When he had died in the Tower, refusing to renounce his attacks on the monarchy, he was still an embarrassment to the gentry members of the Commons, who remained in awe of the queen's majesty.[3] Yet in the very first parliament of his reign, James I discovered that the spirit of Wentworth had come alive in the chamber.

One of those who had attended the last parliament of Elizabeth's reign was Thomas and Zenobia's younger son, another Thomas, who was returned for St Ives[4] while he was still studying for a legal career at the Middle Temple. He probably then missed James' first parliament in 1604, because he was about to be called to the Bar. It marked an abrupt end to the honeymoon between the new king and his people, as the Commons refused his request for a subsidy and James declared 'I am not of such stock as to praise fools'.

In November that year, the discovery of the Gunpowder Plot at the opening of parliament inspired a rare mood of loyalty, which Cecil exploited to obtain a subsidy greater than all but one of those ever granted to Elizabeth.[5] But by the time of the third Stuart parliament, in 1614, the mood among the gentry had changed irrevocably.

Thomas had pursued a successful career as a barrister and he was now elected for Grampound, near where his father owned property.[6] His elder brother, John, had married Katherine,[7] a daughter of the Arundells of Trerice, who had succeeded their recusant cousins at Lanherne as one of the County's main power brokers. In the same parliament, John St Aubyn was also elected, to represent the County as one of the knights of the shire.[8] He was the first member of the family to enjoy such a distinction, since Devonshire had been represented by his namesake exactly 200 years before.

Unfortunately, the only parliament in which two St Aubyn brothers would ever sit together, was also the least productive in history. By 1614, James had succeeded in offending every sensibility of the gentry class, at the same time as his need for their co-operation had grown ever more pressing. Apart from his monumental errors of statecraft, for families like the St Aubyns it was probably James' disregard for their knightly heritage which was really galling. In order to perpetuate the feudal bedrock of monarchy, their ancestors had sacrificed their lives and inheritances. Now the coats of arms which their descendants bore with pride were being trivialised by the king's gratuitous gifts and mercenary dealings in 'honours'.

His most heinous offence was his invention in 1611 of the baronetcy, a brilliantly logical piece of cultural vandalism.[9] It built upon his even earlier monetisation of knighthoods. James had reasoned that just as a knight could forgo military service for a year by paying scutage, so could he forgo such service for life by paying a life subscription of £30. Likewise, the king now decreed that if his subjects paid the capital sum of £1000, they could secure the privilege of the knightly title without performing the military obligation, in perpetuity for their heirs.

These sums were supposedly used to fund the monarch's military expenses, in particular to support the Protestants in Ulster. But by now the demands on the Crown's purse were as diverse as some of the recipients of this new honour. Feudal obligation had originated as a recuring test of loyalty; so every time James sold the obligation, he dissipated adherence to the ancient ties upon which rested his authority.

The single session of 1614 became known as the 'Addled Parliament', because as soon as James could not bend it to his will, it was dissolved before any laws could be passed. Thomas St Aubyn was reconciled to this fruitless experience by his happy marriage to Katherine Bonython, one of the granddaughters of William Milliton, in April 1615.[10]

Meanwhile, the sale of honours, monopolies and other devices enabled the king to avoid calling another parliament until 1621. One of those sales granted a Scottish peer, the Earl of Tullibardine, a patent monopoly of packing, drying and salting fish in Devon and Cornwall, a thriving local industry owing to new methods of curing.[11,12] This grant provides a classic example of how the crass dealings of James' courtly ministers spurred the growth of an organised opposition in parliament.

This monopoly caused such huge protests in the West Country, that in 1619 some of the local gentry sent a delegation to London. But John Arundell, Katherine St Aubyn's brother, was not satisfied by the compromise which the delegates reached with the Privy Council. He resolved to use his position as a local power broker to form a Cornish faction in parliament, including his brother-in-law John St Aubyn. This would force the complete surrender of the fish-packing patent.

At the 1620 general election, he persuaded William Coryton and Sir Reginald Mohun to stand aside so that he might attend the Commons with all the authority of a Cornish knight of the shire. He facilitated his electoral path by providing seats at Mitchell for the two previous knights, Richard Carew and John St Aubyn.[13]

Mitchell, the town bordering the St Aubyn's ancestral tenures, was now one of more than ten Cornish manors in the hands of the Arundells of Trerice. They appointed the town portreeve, who was the returning officer, while the only other local landowners with influence were the Cosworths,[14] into whose family John St Aubyn's Aunt Agnes had married some years before.

Two other seats controlled by Arundell were Tregony and Grampound, the latter going to John Hampden, the wealthy Buckingham squire whose later opposition to Ship Money – one of the Crown's notorious impositions – would secure his place in history. It says much for the talent of this modest Cornish faction that they succeeded in getting a bill to cancel the reviled patent onto the floor of the House. But the Commons was so taken up with suppressing other patents and pursuing cases of bribery and corruption against the king's favourites, that their bill ran out of time[15] before parliament was yet again dissolved.

This experience drew Arundell into a wider local gentry grouping led by William Coryton, which also included such prominent local figures as Charles Trevanion and Jonathan Rashleigh. This circle shared their electoral favours wisely. Thus in 1624, John St Aubyn stood aside and Arundell arranged the return of Rashleigh's nephew, John Sawle, as MP for Mitchell to further this wider alliance.

By now, the younger brother, Thomas St Aubyn, had settled permanently at Helston, having surrendered his Middle Temple chambers in 1621. As town mayor in 1624, he presided over the borough's parliamentary election, where he helped Sir Francis Godolphin to challenge the Duchy for control. They secured one of the two seats for Trevanion's brother-in-law, Thomas Carey.[16] Despite the parliament lasting only six weeks, this time Arundell's measure to abolish the fish patent passed into law.

The following year, Charles I succeeded his father and almost immediately, the poor relations between Crown and parliament sunk to new depths. However, after Thomas' election to Grampound in 1626 was reversed over a technicality,[17] both St Aubyn brothers lost interest in further hustings, although they remained loyal to the Cornish faction which the Arundells had formed with Coryton.

One whose election in 1626 had been successful was Bulstrode Whitelocke, a precocious young barrister who kept a copious and entertaining diary throughout his life.[18] Forsaking an ambition to go on a grand tour, he chose instead to follow the judge's circuits and in 1627 this took him to the West Country. He eventually reached 'Launceston, the shire town where the judges then kept the Assises for Cornwall ... Here, at the judges' table, I became acquainted with a worthy gentleman, Mr Arundell of Trerice'.

After a day at Trerice, 'hindered in my journey by tempestuousness of the weather', Whitelocke was introduced by John Arundell to the St Aubyns. 'Of my treatment with him and with Mr St Aubyn of the same county I shall only say with Diodorus Siculus, that they are *especially hospitable to strangers.*'[19] Whitelocke was a Middle Temple man, like Thomas St Aubyn, who now arranged Cornish guides for his tour:

> The captain sent his man with me to the lands end, by the way
> we went up to St Buryan steeple, whence in a clear day, the
> Isles of Scilly, 20 leagues from the shore (as they informed

me) may easily be discovered, but the weather did not favour us, yet some of the company affirmed, that they saw plainly the white sands of the islands. This Isles of Scilly in former times, paid 300 puffins yearly, for a rent to the D[uchy] of Cornwall, by which they held their land, and these puffins are accounted a kind of fowl, but in taste, so like to fish, that the Pope allows them to be eaten on fish days.

After visiting Carn Brea and peering at 'divers notorious rocks, as the Armed Knight, which is a tall straight rock, with many lesser after it, joining to the lands end', Whitelocke remarks that:

> ... the common people speak altogether the Cornish language, but little of it in other places, it hath a great affinity with the Welsh tongue, ... both were the language of the Britains, before the Saxony scattered them... The Cornish pronounce their language smoother than the Welsh.

Dinner in Penzance involved a 'variety of good fish, and at so cheap a rate, that what here cost me but twopence, could scarce be had in London under 5(?) shillings' before Thomas St Aubyn settled him at Clowance for the night. The next morning, 'We came together to St Michael's Mount'.

> At the foot of the Mount, one met us, whom they styled Lieut. Newman, and though near drunk made a shift to lead us up the Mount into the fort. At the entrance, whereof in the foremost place, stood one in a red waistcoat, without a doublet, holding his warlike hand upon his rusty sword, and looked just like the picture of one quarrelling, with him stood 3 or 4 more, unlike soldiers, yet in being almost drunk, were all like their Lieutenant. These with an undaunted courage, charged us to render up our weapons, before we entered the fort, we obeyed, but marvelled how these day Labourers, learnt this custom, it being doubtful, whether any of them ever talked with a soldier.
> They showed me all the fort and the Chapel in it where I saw a few pikes and an old cross bow, which (as they related) was with many others, taken from the Earle of Oxford, who fortified this place against K[ing] E[dward]. In the Hall were

some pieces, and about the fort, some few ordinance mounted, the place is nowhere well kept, nor of consequence, here being no good siding for ships, about it, and Penzance too far, to be commanded by it.

Without the Mount, is St Michael's Chair, a seat in the rock, and near it, the stone, about which, if one goes thrice round without touching it, he shall have remission of all his sins, which may be questioned, unless he come very well prepared, for his is sure to break his neck down the nook, if he save not himself by holding on that stone. In a hole like an oven on the side of the rock, is a fresh water spring, though the rock be encompassed by the sea, and it is called St Michael's Well.

The touring party returned to Clowance, where Whitelocke was given 'noble entertainment':

Here I was informed of great fishes, called seals, of 11 or 12 foot in length, which in high tides come upon the rocks, and lie there with their calluses, till the next high tide fetch them off again, and being pursued with guns or staves, to kill them, a sport usual here, the seals will cast a stone backwards with great strength, against those that follow them.

After discourse of this, and of the tin working, Mr St Aubyn bestowed on me pieces of tin ore, and powder ready for the blowing house, pieces of tin cast, Cornish diamonds, and a guilt and silver Hurling Ball.

The next morning, after visiting 'Men Amber, a famous stone geometrically poised, and remembered by all our Geographies in the description of this Country', they rode to Thomas' house in Helston, 'a town of much report, and a great market'. After seeing the ruins of a priory and a Duchy castle nearby, they '...thence went to Pendennis Castle, which by the favour of Mr St Aubyn, we were permitted to enter, and were showed the rooms and ammunition in it'. He found a stark contrast to the defence of the Mount:

This castle is the best fortified and kept of any that I have seen in England, here were 50 good pieces of ordinance mounted, and store of powder, shot, and armoury in it with a competent number of Soldiers doing duty constantly.

Whitelocke was also impressed by the haven besides Penryn, 'very safe, and so convenient, by reason of the largeness of it, that ships may go out thence, with any wind, except full South'. After that, 'we rode to Penryn market town, … and here with many thanks for his civility and good company, I parted with Mr St Aubyn'.

One day Whitelocke would repay this instinctive hospitality many times over. He was to prove one of the most versatile politicians of his age, first as counsellor to Oliver Cromwell and the Commonwealth. Later, having narrowly avoided the fate of those executed under the Act of Oblivion in 1660, he would become a private adviser to Charles II, for his legal expertise on the Constitution.

Wisely omitted from his record of dinner at Clowance, may well have been a discussion of the lawfulness of Charles I's new tax raising ruses. In 1627, in any event, the St Aubyn brothers refused to contribute to the Forced Loan; and they declined to 'compound for knighthood' in 1629, a retrospective fine for not appearing at the new king's coronation, on the Whitelockian grounds that their father Thomas had still been alive at the time.[20] He had only died in March 1626, having attained the age of 83.[21]

In 1635, John St Aubyn was appointed High Sheriff. Given his opposition to Stuart taxes, this appears to have been a cynical choice by the Privy Council.[22] For the role had become a poisoned chalice, owing to its revenue collecting duties; while in Cornwall John's predecessor, Hugh Boscawen, had left £704 of Ship Money for him to extract from a recalcitrant county.

By tradition, Ship Money was a levy to pay for defending Britain's coastline; and with one of the longest, Cornwall had few grounds for complaint, unlike the landlocked counties of middle England But in 1635, the Privy Council had almost doubled the amount to be raised in Cornwall and in seeking the balance due, John encountered the same stiff resistance as his counterparts were finding elsewhere.

In December 1635, shortly after his appointment, John asked the government to write off the amount or else to relieve him from office. Then to alleviate the problem, he attempted to amend local assessments; as collection was already underway, this only managed to upset all sides. By June 1636, the Privy Council was accusing John of 'supine neglect' of his duties and warning of the serious consequences of further delay.[23] He paid in £340 shortly afterwards and finally cleared the account in November, 'with much trouble, extraordinary charge and great opposition'; it had left him £50 to £60 out of pocket.[24]

Taking note of his difficulties, the Privy Council moderated their next demand on Cornwall for Ship Money, from £6700 to £5500. This was also eventually collected in full, whereas in July 1637, the Privy Council sent a letter to two out of three of the High Sheriffs across all England, admonishing them for their 'slackness and remissness' in collecting their quota.[25] By 1640, less than a quarter of the Ship Money demanded was being paid and the Crown gave up on this most notorious of all its tax raising devices.[26]

The St Aubyn brothers had witnessed the growing divide between Crown and country, but neither would live to see its deadly culmination. John drew up his will in December 1638, 'in some indifferent manner and measure of health', but confident that in the life to come he would receive 'an incorruptible, immortal, strong and perfect body'. He left £500 to each of his five unmarried daughters – a going rate at this time for girls from well-to-do families – and £600 with property to his three younger sons. A personal bequest of only £10 to the parish of Crowan, for both church repairs and poor relief, suggests that the family estate at Clowance was already making regular provision.

Thomas' will, in February 1637, testified to his strong Protestant beliefs. The preamble affirmed his assurance of salvation, envisaging him in 'the company of archangels and angels, the holy martyrs and prophets and the rest of the holy choir of heaven'. He requested a simple interment, leaving money for a funeral sermon and for any tithes he may have overlooked. His sons were dead and his one daughter, Zenobia, unmarried; she would receive no benefit from his entailed estate. Along with his law books, this was left to his nephew, another John, when Thomas died shortly afterwards.

Five years later, when civil war broke out, this John St Aubyn would have little use for those law books. He would soon find himself in conflict, not just with his family's closest friends and neighbours, but even with his younger brother, Thomas. The two would face each other as officers, in the armies preparing for battle, on either side of the Cornish 'mousetrap'.

CHAPTER 3

THE SPOILS OF WAR

'They pretend that they fight for the King,
but they would cut his throat if they could
and so they would ours.'
Sir Bevil Grenville, September 1642[1]

Charles I was merely the second son of a Scottish king when he was born in Dumfermline Palace on 19 November 1600. He was a sickly baby, a 'weak and backward child', unlike his elder brother Henry, who teased him mercilessly. Thought to suffer from rickets, weak joints and a debilitating stammer, at 4 years old he could still barely walk or talk.

But at this point he was put into the care of a redoubtable Cornishwoman, Elizabeth Trevanion, who had married an ambitious courtier, Robert Carey. A descendant of Mary Boleyn, Carey had ridden to Scotland in 1603 to be the first to break the news of the old queen's death, to the new King James.

Elizabeth wrought a transformation in 'baby Charles', as King James still termed him well into manhood; away from the strictures of the royal household, the young prince began to thrive. Charles left the Careys when his formal eduction began, at the age of 11. A year later, his brother's death from typhoid brought the shy young man, not much more than five foot tall, into the spotlight. On ascending the throne at the age of 25, he would acknowledge his debt to Elizabeth's family by the grant of titles, land and income.

The Trevanions had owned the manor of Caerhays since 1379 and by dint of his family's shrewd support of the Reformation, Elizabeth's nephew, Charles Trevanion, had inherited 8000 Cornish acres from her brother, a power base for Trevanion influence in local politics for the next thirty years.[2]

A leading member of the county faction, to which the Arundells and St Aubyns belonged in the 1620s, Trevanion shared their hostility to the king's rapacious taxes. He oversaw the collection of the Forced Loan during 1627, but only in order to recover his position as Deputy Lieutenant, once his faction's attack on the ill-advised royal fish patent had succeeded.

For at the 1628 general election, Trevanion confirmed his political loyalties. He arrived at the poll for the knights of the shire, with Arundell and Bevill Grenville, at the head of a large band of followers. They secured the election of the two parliamentary champions, Coryton and Eliot. Trevanion did not settle his £200 fine for composition of the knighthood until July 1633; the burden of becoming High Sheriff later that year may well have been designed as a punishment, as in the case of John St Aubyn two years later. Trevanion again ignored the government's request in 1639, when they sought a contribution for the First Bishops' War.

Yet when King Charles finally raised his standard against his opponents in parliament, in Nottingham on 22 August 1642, Trevanion came down emphatically on the royalist side, selling his plate and mortgaging his estates to raise funds, and using his local influence to rally support for the Crown.[3]

So it was with the heads of nearly every other major family in Cornwall, including the Grenvilles, the Arundells of Trerice, the Godolphins and the Bassets. The parliamentary faction, on the other hand, was predominantly made up of lesser gentry or the cadet branches of these major families. Yet now joining them was the new head of the St Aubyn family, breaking the alliance with his grander Godolphin and Basset neighbours, which his forbears had nurtured for six generations.

When this John St Aubyn succeeded to his inheritance, in 1640, he was 30 years old. He would have been at the dinner in 1627 with Bulstrode Whitelocke, the Middle Temple radical, and was himself admitted to that nest of lawyers in 1631. Five years later, John's father negotiated his union with 'the sole only daughter and heir apparent of the said Francis Godolphin of Trevaneage', as the draughtsman to the marriage settlement described her. Or rather, to anyone with a pulse, the 'virtuous and beautiful' Catherine.[4]

Charles Trevanion was one of the trustees to this happy couple, who wed in March 1637. Then in the Short Parliament of 1640, John joined his uncle, John Arundell, as the MP for Tregony. So he remained well in with the major opposition faction, to which his father had belonged. But their adherence to the Crown now revealed their overriding priority: to preserve the elevated position in Cornwall, which the convulsions of the previous century had gifted to their families.

As a cadet member of his family, however, Francis Godolphin was for parliament. So his son-in-law followed suit, both out of love and conviction, a choice which threatened to come at a heavy price for both of them. Cornwall was in royalist hands and the two parliamentarians soon became refugees over the border in Plymouth.[5]

The commander of the royalist forces, Sir Ralph Hopton, wasted little time in mounting his first assault on the port that December. But the fleet carrying the men of a Scottish colonel, William Ruthven, had fortuitously been driven by a storm into Plymouth harbour and their assistance proved decisive in driving Hopton back to Launceston. His first invasion of Devon had ended in ignominious failure.[6]

The next month, Hopton resolved to re-engage Ruthven before he gained reinforcements and a decisive battle was fought at Braddock Down. This time the parliamentary forces fled, with 1250 taken prisoner and about 200 killed. But the Cornish bands under Hopton balked at crossing the Tamar, while the Plymouth garrison under seige was resupplied by sea. After further skirmishes, an uneasy truce was agreed in March and extended to the end of April 1643.

During this truce, from the royalist stronghold at Oxford, came Charles' command to his commissioners in Cornwall: for 'the preservation and keeping of our Isle of Scilly … our pleasure is that you sequester the Estates of Francis Godolphin of Treveneage, of John Seyntaubin (except the Barton of Clowance), of John Trefusis, William Cooly and Richard Erisey'. From those properties 'belonging to the Delinquents' was to be given 'the sum of [£]2,473 to the hands of our trusty and well beloved Sir Francis Godolphin Esquire, Governor of our said Island'.[7]

Parliament responded by appointing John St Aubyn to various assessment and sequestration commissions of their own, although these were mere tokens while he remained in Plymouth. But John also became captain of a troop of horse, in the regiment of Lord Robartes, holding steadfast in the city while hostilities raged between a succession of royalist and parliamentary forces across the West Country.

———

Both Charles Trevanion and his son John, who was married to a St Aubyn cousin, formed regiments of foot in November 1642. Sir Charles' trained band was assigned to local defence duties throughout the war. But young John Trevanion's Old Cornish regiment fought for the king in all the western campaigns that followed. Thomas St Aubyn, the younger brother, joined John Trevanion as his second in command.

At Braddock Down, the two St Aubyn brothers may have faced each other for the first time and Hopton's complaint, that the Cornish deliberately spared many of the fugitives because of kinship, was no doubt aimed at the likes of Thomas.[8] Then a month later, it was the royalist forces of Godolphin and Trevanion, including Thomas, who had to slip away in the night, from a parliamentary ambush at Modbury.

The royalists marked the end of the truce, which eventually followed, with a lavish dinner party in Launceston, before engaging the enemy the very next day. Musket fire was exchanged, until the Trevanion and Slanning regiments arrived in the evening, to mount a charge. This time it was the parliamentary force who beat a skilfull retreat to Okehampton.

By mid-May, the parliamentary army had gained sufficient strength to march back into Cornwall and breach Hopton's defensive line, strung along the Devon border. Their troops encamped on a broad hilltop near Stratton, not far from the regiments of Trevanion and Grenville.

The two sides engaged and just as the royalists were about to run out of powder for their muskets, they made a decisive advance up the hill. The best of the parliamentary troops were captured in an ill-timed counter-move and the rest fled the field in a crushing defeat. The victory inspired Sir Francis Basset to write to his wife: 'Dearest Soul, Oh, Dear Soul, praise God everlastingly. Read the enclosed: Ring out your bells, Raise Bonfires, publish the Joyful Tidings, believe these truths...'[9]

By June, Okehampton, Crediton and then Tiverton had fallen to the royalists and they prepared to meet the parliamentary army coming from Bristol under General Waller. He attempted an ambush, which was foiled by the Trevanion, Godolphin and Grenville regiments under Hopton, forcing Waller to retreat to Bath. A skirmish at Chewton Mendip, costing both sides forty or fifty men, was followed by a two-week lull, during which Hopton wrote to Waller, before the war a professional colleague, to suggest a meeting.

Waller's reply dated 16 June 1643, is one of the most moving letters of the conflict:

> The experience I have had of your Worth, and the happiness I have enjoyed in your friendship are wounding considerations when I look at the present distance between us. Certainly, my affections to you are so unchangeable, that hostility itself cannot violate my friendship to your person; but I must be true to the cause wherein I serve ... with what a sad sense I go upon this service, and with what hatred I detest this war without an enemy.[10]

Three days later, all sentiment cast aside, defeating Waller became the prime objective of the royalist council of war. More skirmishes followed, until the royalists found Waller, 'the best shifter and chooser of ground', ideally placed in a defensive position on Lansdown Hill, 225 feet high above Bath and preempting Hopton's own moves.

In the battle that followed, the great Cornish leader, Bevil Grenville, was fatally hurt. In all, Cornish losses amounted to 200 dead and 300 badly wounded, against a loss on Waller's side of just 20 men. Then the next day, a carelessly struck match blew up an amunition cart, taking its prisoners with it and half blinding Hopton, who was standing nearby.

Yet a week later, at Roundway Down, the royalists inflicted another decisive defeat, Waller losing 600 dead and 800 wounded. His army was destroyed and the way to Bristol for the royalists was now clear. But the assault on the city in July proved one of the most closely fought and bloodiest of the war.[11] Two hundred Cornishmen were killed, including the young colonels John Trevanion and Sir Nicholas Slanning, who in the same moment were both 'shot in the thigh with musket bullet'.

Grenville, Trevanion and Slanning had all been inspirational leaders, in their king's own words, 'Eminent persons, who shall never be forgotten by us'.[12] Along with the poet, Sidney Godolphin, who had died for the cause in February, this sad couplet written sixty years later captures the lingering sense of their loss:

> *[Gone] the four wheels of Charles' Wain,*
> *Grenvile, Godolphin, Trevanion, Slanning slain*

Yet Thomas St Aubyn now became colonel of the Trevanion regiment, while John Basset – the son and heir to Sir Francis – took command of Slanning's. Under this new leadership, the royalist regiments followed through their taking of Bristol with that of Exeter in September and Dartmouth in October. The king published an effusive letter to 'his Loving subjects in Cornwall', thanking them for 'their great and eminent Courage and patience in their indefagitable Prosecution of their great Work against so potent an Enemy'.[13] The letter was displayed in churches throughout the county.

Meanwhile, naval support ensured that Plymouth remained impregnable, where the St Aubyn brother, with Catherine his wife, was safely embedded. So Thomas, along with the rest of the royalist army, retired for the winter.

Today, Thomas St Aubyn still stands proud in his cavalier costume, sword in its scabard and pike in hand, in his full length portrait which greets visitors to Pencarrow, the home near Bodmin of the Molesworth-St Aubyns. Booted and spurred, he cuts an inspiring figure and it is not hard to imagine how he might have developed into another leader who captured the heart and soul of a Cornish army.

But there were two obstacles which stood in his way. The first was his brother's 'delinquency', which probably raised suspicions over his own loyalties, given the bitter rivalries which plagued the royalist camp, without whose endorsement he remained marginal. The second was the welcome into that camp, in March 1644, of Richard Grenville, Beville's duplicitous younger brother with an outsized faith in his own abilities.

Playing on his brother's memory, with the king's blessing, this younger Grenville quickly imposed himself as the leading commander of what remained of the Cornish army. In July 1644, he was forced to retreat to mid-Cornwall, as parliamentary forces under Essex entered the county. Between Truro and Penryn, Grenville vainly sought to build new battalions under his command; Thomas St Aubyn among those regimental commanders supporting him, while others faltered. Then Charles I himself arrived in Cornwall, in pursuit of Essex, at the head of 10,000 seasoned troops. Cornwall's royalist sympathies reasserted themselves.

Essex, encouraged by Lord Robartes, had overestimated the support he would find in the county, and mistreatment by his troops further alienated the local populace. He moved south towards Lostwithiel and Fowey, to maintain contact with the parliamentary fleet, but in the process found himself caught in a Cornish 'mousetrap', set by the armies of both Charles and Grenville, who advanced in a pincer movement on his position.

By mid-August, the two armies had combined into a force of 18,000 men, facing only 10,000 troops under Essex's command. Yet Charles dithered as to how to secure a decisive victory, which gave the Roundheads time to hatch an escape. Essex and his generals resolved to desert their army by slipping down to the river at Fowey during the night, thence by ship to Plymouth, arriving the next day. Hals takes up the story:

> On the same day Sir William Balfour, with two thousand five hundred of the Parliament horse, with divers officers, viz., Colonel Nicholas Boscawen, his Lieutenant Colonel James Hals, of Merther, Henry Courtenay, of St. Bennet's in Lanyvet, Colonel John Seyntaubyn, of Clowns, and his Lieutenant Colonel Braddon, Colonel Carter, and several other officers and gentlemen of quality, early in the morning forced their

passage over St. Winnow, Boconnock, and Braddock Downs,
though the body of the King's army, which lay encamped on the
heath in those places, maugre all opposition to the contrary.[14]

From there they rode to Plymouth, arriving 'safely the same day, amidst
their own garrison and confederates'. The most vulnerable point in the
royalist line, on the road from Lostwithiel to Boconnoc, had been defended
by just fifty musketeers, garrisoned in the grounds of a cottage. Whether
they simply slept through until daylight, or consciously chose to let their
Cornish cousins depart without bloodshed, confusion and recrimination
washed over the royalist camp at this debacle.

Those abandoned by Essex were left with no choice but to surrender to
the mercy of the king. The upcountry footsoldiers, who had looted Cornish
homes only weeks earlier, felt the full force of Cornish hostility, as under
escort they headed back to Portsmouth. In the first few days, as many as
a thousand died from hardship or violence, revenge taken for their own
earlier brutality. In retreat, only one in six would make it to the safety of the
Roundhead stronghold.[15]

Parliament's pamphleteers soon seized on this mistreatment of its
soldiers to demonise the Cornish with old tropes; as early as March 1644,
one pamphlet had lamented that 'the men of Cornwall are very heathens, a
corner of ignorants and atheists, drained from the mines'.[16] Now they were
disparaged in the Roundhead press as bestial 'choughs', 'cormorants' and
'bloodhounds', who as one account reported in October 1644, 'so coursed
and harried our soldiers that many fell down under their merciless hands'.[17]

The royalist command saw in the latent Cornish 'sense of difference'
their own opportunity, to stem the desertion of the Cornish regiments.
Support was reenergised by the presence of King Charles' son in July 1645,
who styled himself 'Prince of Great Britain [and] Duke of Cornwall'. But
these efforts were contradicted by their prejudiced western commander
Goring, who openly regarded his Irish soldiers as 'worth ten Cornish
cowards'.[18] Once again, the talisman of Cornish identity was providing a
host of contradictions.

No one illustrates this better than Sir Richard Grenville, who inspired
in his followers unswerving devotion. When a sniper shot him in the groin
before the siege of Taunton in April 1645, his soldiers responded with
unusual savagery, reportedly 'stringing up every man, woman and child
who came voluntarily out of the garrison'.[19] Having recovered by midsummer, he was met by the young Prince Charles at Liskeard. With the

prince's blessing, he was able to gather the disparate strands of his New Cornish Militia once more.

But as Cavalier fortunes waned, he depended increasingly on his troops' loyalty to the county, rather than to the Crown. This culminated in his wild suggestion, in November 1645, that the Duke of Cornwall should declare a separate kingdom and make his own peace with parliament. He wrote:

> ... yet the whole county seeing ... that his Highness's labour tends only to the preservation of these parts from utter ruin and destruction: I am most confident, that upon a general meeting of the chief gentry of this country, the whole body of this country, then finding how far the preservation of their persons and estates are concerned, will unanimously join in the defence thereof .[20]

This suggestion was treated with ridicule by the Roundhead press, and with disdain by the royalist high command.[21] But it did not stop them from exploiting separatist sentiment themselves, to rally the county's men to cross the Devon border yet again, only to be routed in an attack on 8 January 1646. This forced a retreat back across the Tamar.

The tensions in the royalist position were now fully exposed, with Grenville refusing to let his men out of the county, or Goring's troops into it; a stance which the prince's council regarded as a 'senseless pretence'. His courage and ability in the field could no longer absolve his zealous self-regard and violent temper. On 19 to 20 January, Grenville was dismissed from his command and imprisoned. The partisan spirit was broken and without it, Cornish support for the Crown soon drained away.

The Cavalier leadership's contempt for their own Cornish troops sits oddly however with the success of one Cornish colonel in maintaining regimental discipline. Thomas St Aubyn's men loyally melded into the main Cavalier force, taking part at Newbury and the seige of Taunton, before ending the war in the garrison at Exeter. The royalist campaign might have been a great deal less chaotic if they had promoted the role of this second son from a modest Cornish estate, rather than the self-serving Sir Richard from Stowe, who later fled abroad and never returned.

Yet whatever strategy they chose, royalist strength in Cornwall was never going to count against the loss of the north of England, following the defeat at Marston Moor in July 1644; while the reorganisation of Roundhead forces into the New Model Army, tilted the balance decisively in favour of parliament from 1645 onwards.

Preserved in the St Aubyn records on St Michael's Mount is *The Jubilee of England*, a pamphlet printed in June 1646 to celebrate the litany of Roundhead victories, 'From Naseby to the Mount in Cornwall', which now followed. Thus it recorded through the summer of 1645, 'Taunton the second time mightily relieved … Victory at Langport against Goring … Bridgewater stormed and taken; a mighty piece'. (This last, with its arsenal of forty-four barrels of gunpowder, was a real body blow to royalist morale.) The list continues on to: 'September 11, 1645. Bristol stormed and surrendered to the Parliament; Think how great strength and wealth; and what a mercy, not easily dived into: Oh, Love the Lord…' There then follows three pages of *The Jubilee* consumed by God's righteous cause and expressed with Protestant fervour; from which we can deduce that in joining the Roundheads, religious faith had inspired the support of Godolphin and St Aubyn, as much as their political creed.

By January 1646, Plymouth had been relieved and John St Aubyn was able to assume an increasingly important role in Cornwall, as an acceptable face of the victors. As well as becoming a colonel in his own regiment, he had been appointed Vice Admiral of South Cornwall in 1644 and High Sheriff of the county in 1645 (for the coming year). He now took part in the delicate negotiations to persuade the Cornish gentry to accept that parliament had won.

Secret communiation began between the leading gentry of East Cornwall and the parliamentary command in Devon. In February, as the New Model Army forced its way across the Tamar, Sir Ralph Hopton ordered all royalist forces to retreat. But his divisions in East Cornwall refused to obey and instead entered formal negotiations with Sir Thomas Fairfax,[22] culminating with their surrender on 5 March, St Piran's Day. This marked the end of royalist hopes and in Truro ten days later, Hopton himself laid down his arms. Colonel John St Aubyn was one who signed his articles of surrender.[23]

As High Sheriff, he was also party to the articles agreed with the garrison at Pendennis Castle, where Colonel John Arundell of Truthal finally surrendered the following August, but not before putting up the stoutest resistance. Given two hours to accept Fairfax's summons to deliver up the castle, the 70-year-old Arundell had replied that:

> … if I should render, I brand myself and my posterity with the
> indelible character of treason. And having taken less than *two*

minutes resolution, I resolve that I will here bury myself before
I deliver up this Castle to such as fight against His Majesty...[24]

The siege lasted five months, only ending when Arundell's proud band of
men, now half starved and eating horsemeat, were allowed to leave with
the honours of war, 'Drums beating, Colours flying, Trumpets sounding'.[25]

At St Michael's Mount, Sir Francis Basset had died the previous year,
having exhausted his finances on its defence. His brother Arthur, after
succeeding in command, also surrendered to Fairfax and in March 1647,
John St Aubyn was nominated as captain of the Mount, an order confirmed
by both houses of parliament in June. He may have enjoyed a wry smile
at the thought that he was the first St Aubyn to hold this post since Peter
St Aubyn in 1508, who had also been a rebel against the Crown. But
his pleasure was shortlived, when the following order suddenly arrived,
addressed to Colonel Robert Bennett:

> By virtue of the power and authority given me by both houses
> of parliament to command all ye land forces within the
> Kingdom... I do hereby authorise you to command the forces
> belonging to the garrison of St Michael's Mount in the County
> of Cornwall and do require you immediately to take the said
> garrison into your possession and safely to keep the same till
> further order from me to the contrary And hereof you may not
> fail. Given under my hand and seal this 3rd of August 1647
> Fairfax.[26]

Colonel Bennett was a Cornish gentleman with a house called Hexworthy,
just south of Launceston. Captain of a local militia since 1629, Bennett was
involved in some of parliament's least glorious episodes, during the western
campaigns of 1643–4. He had also lost his wife when, left at home and
'being frightened by a troop of cavaliers', she had miscarried and died. But
attached to the New Model Army under Fairfax, his administrative skills
quickly elevated him to the rank of colonel and by 1646, he was playing host
to Oliver Cromwell, on his visit to Launceston. As an Anabaptist, in August
1647 Bennett was more in favour than John St Aubyn, a Presbyterian with
royalist relations, whose replacement would appease the Levellers, at this
point attaining the zenith of their influence.

Bennett's family had started as Sussex lawyers. It must have rankled to
hand this command to a Tudor 'newcomer', one coming from the opposite

end of the county as well. But St Aubyn and Bennett had been serving closely since 1642; thus in July 1644, parliament had nominated the two of them to be commissioners for Cornwall, 'for raising moneys for the maintenance of the army'.[27] Bennett had also appeared alongside the High Sheriff in signing the surrender of Pendennis Castle, although he had not been present at Truro for the signing of Hopton's capitulation.

His appointment as governor could be seen as merely an orderly sharing out of the duties burdening the Vice Admiral of the Fleet, who a few months later would play a critical role in maintaining order in West Cornwall, just as Bennett was quelling renewed unrest in Pendennis Castle. Both of them were only too aware of the precarious position they held; they could not allow petty jealousy to divide them at this stage.

The year 1648 started badly for England's parliamentary rulers, with the Scots threatening to invade, recalcitrant royalists stirring and the captive Charles intransigent, in the live hope of festering old divisions between the 'Presbyterians' and 'Independents' among his foes.[28] In the West Country, Colonel Sir Hardress Waller was given command of a task force to quell disaffection among the local militiamen, who had been ordered to retire before they had received all their wages. At Pendennis Castle, Bennett negotiated with Colonel Richard Fortescue over his men's four months' arrears, without which they refused to disband. He just managed to borrow enough money to pay them to leave the castle on 29 April.

But on 16 May, a fresh threat of disorder came to the attention of the Cornish County Committee meeting in Launceston, attended by St Aubyn and Bennett. A Penzance merchant called Gubbs informed them of a planned uprising, led, he claimed, by former royalist officers, including John Arundell, Sir Arthur Basset and Charles Trevanion. The insurgents marched from Penzance the very next day, to confront the unpopular garrison under Bennett's command on the Mount; but the island castle was already in a state of readiness and on arriving in Marazion, they were met by John St Aubyn and a couple of the other committee members.

St Aubyn now played for time, by proposing a meeting to hear the rebels' complaints, while he sent word to the east for reinforcements. The rebels returned to Penzance, hoping for more time to garner support. But on 19 May, St Aubyn rode across rebel-held territory to St Ives, 'to quiet them who were suspected to have a hand in the confederacy'.[29] Thirty parliamentary soldiers rode into Helston and stayed to quell a group of disaffected townsmen there, followed by 400 horse and 200 foot on 20 May led by Bennett and Herle, who had succeeded John St Aubyn as High Sheriff. With superior arms, they managed to supress the revolt over the next few days and on 24 May, Colonel Waller was able to assure parliament in a message from Truro, that the insurgents had been dispersed with the taking of 200 prisoners.

But many more had been killed and tragically, 'some of the principal firebrands', pursued by Bennett and Herle's men along the Lizard coast, 'were so desperate, that scorning mercy, they joined hand in hand and violently run themselves into the ocean, where they perished in the waters'.[30] Dreams of Cornish independence may be said to have drowned with them.

A Committee for Troubles was appointed and after St Aubyn and Bennett had examined the captured rebels, they were both thanked by the Commons.[31] The evidence revealed a familiar picture: the royalist devotion of the rebel leaders had formed a combustible alliance with the deep sense of alienation felt by many of their followers, given the barely concealed contempt shown by their new Roundhead overlords, for their Cornish ways and local customs. This point was driven home, when some mocking Roundheads paraded around Penryn, burnishing three silver hurling balls impaled on the ends of their swords.[32]

John St Aubyn must have been only too aware of how this cultural divide would make it all the harder to reconcile him and his family with his recently subdued neighbours. In quelling a West Cornwall rebellion, he had usurped the leading role that in previous times would have been assumed by a Godolphin or a Grenville. Some moderates, notably Sir Thomas Fairfax, retired in protest at the execution of their former king in January 1649. Yet over the next decade, John would become one of the leading men in his county to support Cromwell. He was named to the assessment commissions appointed in April and December 1649; by early 1650, added to the Cornwall commission of the peace; and continued to serve as Vice Admiral until at least August 1650.

Overlordship had its advantages. In 1652–3, John was busy with a legal suit to gain compensation for horses seized from him by the 'delinquent' Warwick, 2nd Baron Mohun, during the early months of the Civil War. He also revived an old claim to the Isles of Scilly, which had been decided in favour of the senior branch of his father-in-law's family in 1636. Presumably he claimed that the delinquent branch of Godolphins had now forfeited their right. Such actions were bound to seed offence; few friends can have remained among John's old acquaintances and the death of his father-in-law, Francis, in 1652 left him even more isolated.

During the Protectorate, John continued to serve as a JP, even working closely with the local major-general, John Disbrowe, during the 'era of petty tyranny' of 1655–6, when gambling, racing and pubs were banned with puritan conviction and the 'decimator tax' was levied on delinquents.

John used his position, as the county's most powerful men had always done, to settle unfinished personal grievances, such as in August 1656 when he sought money owed to his father by Jonathan Rashleigh. He was elected as one of the MPs for Cornwall in the elections for the second Protectorate parliament, presumably with the approval of Disbrowe. Here his focus on local issues masked a burning personal ambition.

In the afternoon of 23 October 1656, under the star-spangled ceiling of the Star Chamber room, a committee appointed by the Commons met to decide the fate of royalists who had failed to 'compound' for their 'delinquency', or who were still enjoying their estates while falling behind with their payments. John St Aubyn was among those present and he would have been fully acquainted with the fines and penalties being extracted from his many royalist relations in Cornwall. Above all, he would have been aware of the dire straights of his neighbours at Tehidy. Sir Francis Basset had expended £1620 on the royalist cause before he died[33] and his son now had to compound as a delinquent for three years' income from the family estates, before he could retrieve them from sequestration. Meanwhile, royalist sales were governed by strict regulations, which would prevent the payment of a premium, for the latent value of the vast tin deposits under Tehidy, which might otherwise resolve the Basset crisis.

Also attending in the room that day was Bulstrode Whitelocke MP, the young guest of John's father in 1627 and a fellow Middle Temple man.[34] Now in his fifties, he had risen to become one of the most influential members of Cromwell's circle. Whitelocke had once visited St Michael's Mount with a St Aubyn as his guide. Now was his chance to guide the family on how to secure the island they coveted.

Whatever enmity was flowing between Basset and St Aubyn, the proposal upon which they subsequently agreed, to transfer St Michael's Mount and its manor, was certainly a marriage of covenience. John St Aubyn would acquire the jewel of the county, a pinnacle upon which to rebuild his family's standing amongst their peers; while John Basset would receive a similar price to that his father had paid the Cecils in 1640 and save the Tehidy estate.

Plate 1. William's ship, *The Mora*, with his invasion fleet. (Detail: Bayeaux Tapestry. Alamy)

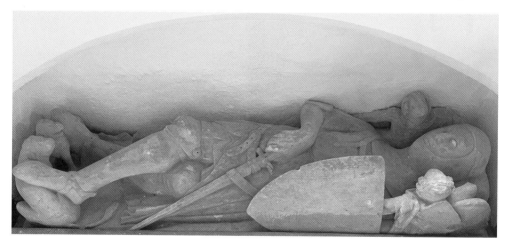

Plate 2. Sir Mauger De Sancto Albino (1291).

Plate 3. Alice, Countess of Oxford, St Stephen's Chapel, Bures. (Courtesy of Simon Knott)

Above left: **Plate 4.** Geoffrey St Aubyn (1380s–1450s) and his wife, Alice Tremere.

Above right: **Plate 5.** Thomas St Aubyn (1543–1626) and his wife, Zenobia Mallet, who was descended from Honor Basset.

Left: **Plate 6.** The Sacking of Limoges, 1370. (Alamy)

Above left: **Plate 7.** The tall, central figure is Lord Lisle. (Courtesy of the Huntington Library)

Above right: **Plate 8.** Honor Grenville, Lady Basset and Viscountess Lisle. (Courtesy of the Newberry Library, Chicago)

Right: **Plate 9.** Medieval illustration of a sea battle.

Plate 10. Clowance, West Cornwall — The seat of Geoffrey St Aubyn and Elizabeth Kemyell. (Inscribed by Dr William Borlase, for *The Natural History of Cornwall*)

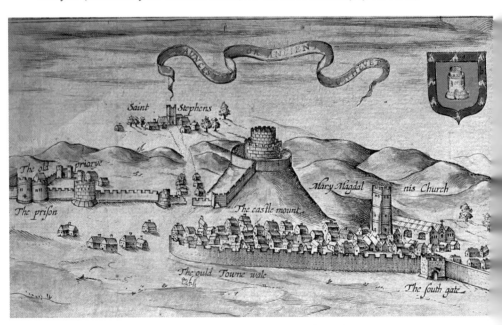

Plate 11. Launceston, from Speed's Map of Cornwall, Book 1, Chapter 11.

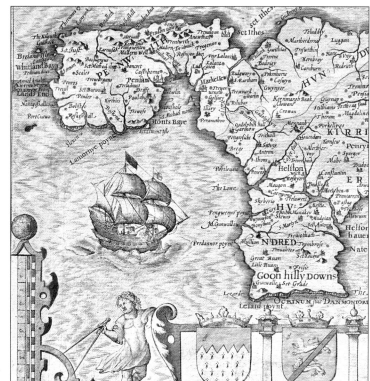

Right: **Plate 12.** Mount's Bay, from Speed's Map of Cornwall, Book 1, Chapter 11.

Below: **Plate 13.** *Tour de Calais.* Stefano Della Bella, *c.*1650. (Courtesy of Musée des Beaux-Arts, Paris)

Above: **Plate 14.** St Michael's Mount in 1582. (From Norden's *Speculi Britanniae*)

Below: **Plate 15.** The oldest sailing boat to feature in the 2012 Thames Diamond Jubilee Pageant, with James St Aubyn at the tiller and no drownings.

Above left: **Plate 16.** Colonel John St Aubyn by Edward Bower.

Above right: **Plate 17.** Thomas St Aubyn, Colonel for the King during the Civil Wars. (Courtesy of the Molesworth-St Aubyns)

Right: **Plate 18.** Sir John St Aubyn, 3rd Baronet. His deep blue coat is a Tory Jacobite emblem. (Courtesy of the Molesworth-St Aubyns)

Above left: **Plate 19.** Juliana Vinicombe, Lady St Aubyn, by John Opie.

Above right: **Plate 20.** Sir John St Aubyn, 5th Baronet, by Joshua Reynolds.

Above left: **Plate 21.** James St Aubyn.

Above right: **Plate 22.** Martha Nicholls, by John Opie.

Above left: **Plate 23.** Sir Edward St Aubyn, Baronet.

Above right: **Plate 24.** Sir John St Aubyn, Baronet, 1st Lord St Levan.

Plate 25. Campaign calling card, 1885.

Plate 26. Lime Grove, Putney.

Plate 27. Trevethoe House. (Courtesy of Tempest Photography)

Above: **Plate 28.**
Club captain, Lord
St Levan, tees off at
Pau in 1893.

Right: **Plate 29.**
John and Edith
St Levan, with their
daughters Margery
and Hilaria, on
the East Terrace
at St Michael's
Mount.

Above: **Plate 30.** James Phillippo's illustration of one of the Baptist's free villages.

Below: **Plate 31.** Gustav Hamel pays a flying visit, 1913.

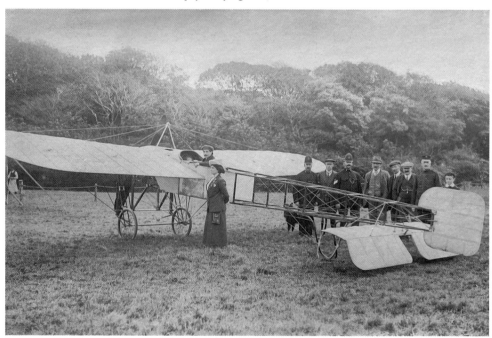

Plate 32. Detail from the Second Battle of El Teb, 29 February 1884. (Courtesy of the National Army Museum, London, Image No: 133526)

Above: **Plate 33.** Heavy German artillery at Gheluvelt, 31 October 1914.

Right: **Plate 34.** S.S. *Persia* in 1900. (Courtesy of P&O Heritage)

Plate 35. The Hon. Gwendolin Nicolson's Travelling and Wedding Gowns. (Courtesy of the British Library Board)

Plate 36. Sam and Gwen St Levan on the Mount in 1962.

Plate 37. Sub Lt. J. St Aubyn, R.N.V.R., 1940.

Plate 38. Lieutenant Piers St Aubyn in 1944. (Courtesy of Airborne Assault ParaData)

Plate 39. Gwen and Sam on their golden wedding anniversary in 1966; Jessica, Piers, John, Giles and Phillipa stand behind.

Plate 40. HRH Princess Elizabeth next to Piers at the 1951 Flower Ball. (Alamy)

Plate 41. John, 4th Lord St Levan, at the helm.

But the terms, suggesting the influence of England's leading lawyer, were fiendishly complex. Under the arrangement, Basset granted St Aubyn just a one year lease of the manor on 25 November 1657; then five days later, on receipt of £1900, he signed an indenture for £3800 to perform certain covenants, whereby Basset would disown his freehold interest in the island and its rent roll in favour of his lessee.[35] Such an obtuse arangement illustrates the extreme measures people took in these uncertain political times, when property transfers were fraught with legal difficulty.

St Aubyn's purchase was backed by his lease, so he would have a second claim to the freehold of the manor through the ancient laws of possession. His case shows how purchasers of land during the later stages of the Commonwealth had become increasingly concerned over the legality of their title. But all would have been aware of the risk in making these acquisitions and they still saw the chance worth taking. Thus a staunch Republican MP, Sir Arthur Hazlerigg, was taunted in the Commons for his large purchases of Church lands, laden with political risk, for which he was nicknamed 'the bishop of Durham'. He replied nonchalantly, 'I know not how long after I shall keep the Bishop's lands. For no King, no Bishop, no Bishop, no King. We know the rule'.[36]

But there was a special twist to John St Aubyn's dealing in this former Church and Crown land. For Robert Bennett, still Governor of the Mount, refused to allow him to take possession of 'the fort', claiming its military role was of overriding importance. If the Governor remained in residence, when the St Aubyn lease expired in November 1658, it would surely be a moot point whether John would still have the common law right, to claim possession at all.

By now, Bennett had overshadowed his West Cornwall rival in both position and influence.[37] In the early 1650s, he had already lined his pockets to acquire two former Duchy manors and the lands and castle of Launceston, where he was elected as MP in each of four parliaments of that decade. During 1653, he rose briefly to become a member of the Council of State, with his own Whitehall apartments, and his letters reveal his continued involvement in national affairs. Bennett would later refer to himself during this period as 'commander-in-chief of all the forces in field and garrison in the county of Cornwall'. In this role, he had briefly imprisoned Sir Francis Godolphin on the Mount, for writing to Sir Arthur Basset. Through gritted teeth, the delinquent head of one of Cornwall's oldest families had been forced to write abject letters, the one after his release promising, 'I am now again at home, doubly obliged to obey your commands ... your very humble servant'.[38]

But undeterred by the martinet colonel, in March 1658 John submitted the 'humble petition of John St Aubin esq.' to 'His Highness the Lord Protector of the Commonwealth', asserting that he 'hath a legal and unquestionable Estate of Inheritance in St Michael's Mount in Cornwall in which there is now a small garrison of 12 men'. He should '...be encouraged to repair and preserve the said Mount from ruin and devastation'.[39]

The matter was referred to the Lord Commissioners of the Treasury, with Bennett being asked to provide further information as to the state's own title to the island.[40] In Bennett's submission, 'in the Case of the Commonwealth and Mr St Aubyn', he reported that '... Captain Newman's judgement is that the situation of the said Mount is naturally very strong and might prove very prejudicial to the Country if an enemy should possess it'; a view endorsed by gunner Thomas Slade, who stated 'doubtless it would prove very prejudicial to the Commonwealth'. Other soldiers concurred, the implication being to maintain the status quo.[41]

But one Lord Commissioner was the recently knighted Sir Bulstrode Whitelocke. In 1627, his diary had observed the 'almost drunk' Lieutenant Newman, when he had visited the Mount with Thomas St Aubyn. Slade's father had been one of the gunners, whom Whitelocke had doubted 'whether any of them ever talked with a soldier'. Moreover under Cromwell, the English Navy had regained its former ascendancy, having recently beaten the Dutch in the war of 1652–3. This diminished the Mount's strategic importance, even more than at the time when Whitelocke was already doubting its significance in his diary. Recently reminded of his Cornish tour by fellow MP John St Aubyn, Whitelocke must surely have promoted his offer 'to repair and preserve the said Mount' and advised the Commissioners to ignore Bennett's self-serving testimony.

Meanwhile, a local enquiry was held, to consider whether the Mount had been a royal possession. Helpfully, its verdict was that St Aubyn should hold the island, on the same terms as those agreed by the Cecils with James I.[42]

In July 1658, the Treasury Commissioners' report was considered by a council committee, instructed 'to speak with St Aubyn as to how the matter may be accommodated, to maintain his right and public safety with regard to the Fort'.[43] But the issue apparently remained unresolved in August, when the committee was ordered to 'speak again with St Aubyn and report'.[44] The death of Oliver Cromwell in September put paid to any further progress, as the succession of his son Richard 'upset the delicate balance of competing interests' which his father's personality had held together.[45] In this fluid situation, Bennett and St Aubyn both had everything to play for, as the Mount lease expired.

In January 1659, John was elected as MP for St Ives,[46] where he had served as recorder since 1646. He had also secured his return for St Germans, an insurance policy which shows how keenly he wanted to be in Westminster, to press his suit against Bennett, elected again for Launceston. John's success reflected how royalist sympathisers and Presbyterians like himself had dominated the returns for this third Protectorate parliament. Yet within weeks, this fragile shift in the political mood was shattered by a Republican backlash.

Army radicals sacked Richard Cromwell, dissolved the parliament and resurrected the 'Rump' parliament banished by Cromwell's father six years before. As these new Republicans yet again set about disbarring from office those suspected of royalist sympathies, St Aubyn could feel the Mount slipping from his grasp. A summer of serious but abortive royalist uprisings across the country kept the rival factions who had fought against the king bound together by self-interest, so he continued to serve on local commissions, despite having a royalist brother. He was again appointed as a Justice of the Peace on 7 May 1659, and included in the assessment commission appointed in July. In August Richard Lobb, who belonged to Bennett's camp as the puritan MP for Mitchell, even declared St Aubyn to be 'faithful'.[47] But Bennett was unmoved. He opposed John's appointment to the militia troop of horse, for the western division of Cornwall; and on 6 August, Bennett secured his own reappointment by the 'Rump' as Governor of St Michael's Mount, with a grant of more troops and money for good measure.[48]

Then in October 1659, the rivalry between the parliamentary factions culminated in a military coup. At this point, having convinced himself that 'there was no visible authority or power for government at this time but that of the army',[49] St Aubyn's erstwhile ally, Whitelocke, accepted the army's offer, to become the president of a new 'Committee of Safety'. But in this feverish atmosphere, the normally surefooted Sir Bulstrode had for once made a disastrous miscalculation. Among those appalled by the turn of events were the gentry of Cornwall. In late December, they issued a proclamation from Truro, demanding the restoration of 'the true Parliament'.[50] John was one of the signatories, who was also named to the new assessment commission in January.

Bennett at this point shrewdly declined to join this 'Committee of Safety', and retired with haste to Cornwall to mend his fences. But his enemies in

London did not accept this damascene conversion at face value. Some saw his refusal to join the Committee as a front, saying that he had gone 'of their errand' as a negotiator. Others recalled Bennett's support for the regicide, saying mistakenly that only illness had prevented his signing the king's death warrant himself. On 24 January 1660, the Commons summoned Bennett, along with other opponents of a free parliament. Within weeks, he had been stripped of offices and military positions.[51]

In February 1660, as Whitelocke and Bennett both fell to earth, the Protectorate's overarching military commander in the field, General Monck, marched into London with his loyal regiments, on a mission to restore the Crown. In 1649, with his faction in the ascendant, Bennett had been Fairfax's favourite. Colonel John St Aubyn now looked to General Monck, both as a fellow Presbyterian and also, through John's grandmother Zenobia, as a cousin. On 12 March 1660, Monck sent this order addressed to Bennett, still preserved in the St Aubyn muniments:

> You are on sight hereof to disband those men under your command in the garrison of St Michael's Mount ... and to deliver uppe the possession of the House into Col. John Saint-Aubyn, with all the ordnance, Arms, Ammunition and provisions of warre and victual therein, to bee by him kept and preserved for the usse of the state.[52]

To manage the Restoration, reliable members of the old order were now at their most useful. John was immediately reappointed as a militia commissioner and regained his position as Vice Admiral of South Cornwall.[53] In the spring of 1660, John St Aubyn was returned once more as MP for St Ives and he must have hoped that finally, after navagating the storms and tumults of the past eighteen years, he had landed safely onto dry land. But his well honed political instincts would have warned him of a whole new sea of troubles which awaited.

CHAPTER 4

RESTORATION

*These people have so often abused their
valour in rebellions [but] have since
plentifully repaired their credit by their
exemplary... loyalty.*

Thomas Fuller, 1662[1]

Prince Charles's *Declaration of Buda,* published in April 1660 on the advice of Monck and others, set out the terms on which he would regain the throne. It promised a general amnesty, religious toleration, the equitable treatment of recent land purchases and full payment of arrears to the army. The following month he entered London as the new king, to almost universal relief and riotous celebration, as the nation threw off the yoke of puritan repression. Thirty-three regicides and other collaborators were denied amnesty by the 'Act of Oblivion', some of whom were hanged. Sir Bulstrode Whitelocke narrowly avoided the noose but never held public office again.

In Cornwall, the local gentry 'vied to outdo each other in the display of pro-royalist sentiment', as they seized the opportunity to burnish the county's royalist reputation.[2] At the heart of this 'Cornish Royalist tradition' lay three fundamental tenets, as Mark Stoyle has explained:

> The first was that Cornwall had been almost unanimously Royalist between 1642 and 1646. The second was that the Cornish Royalist leaders in general, and Sir Bevill Grenville in particular, had been personifications of the pure Cavalier spirit. The third was that the Cornish Royalist Army had been not only exceptionally courageous and successful but exceptionally pious and well-disciplined as well: that it had been a true 'Christian Army'.[3]

The truth as always was far more complicated, but it served no one's interest to labour the point. The families of former Roundheads like St Aubyn and

Bennett, preeminent during the Commonwealth, had every reason to play down their role. At one end of Chevy Chase, the Mount dining hall, John St Aubyn adorned the wall with the royal coat of arms and the date '1660'; at the other end he proudly erected the heraldic emblem of his knightly family. But it was not enough and after the spring of 1660, John's fortunes flagged. Although he was returned as MP for St Ives in the Convention Parliament, he did not secure election again.

In saving the Tehidy estate from insolvency, John had respected Basset honour by taking the tithes of Tehidy out of the Mount rent roll. So he might have expected to have earned his neighbours' gratitude. But instead, John Basset actively connived with Sir Francis Godolphin to tarnish his reputation. In April 1661, Sir Francis' loyalty to the Crown was rewarded with his knighthood. Five months later, he used his royalist credentials to undermine St Aubyn's long tenure as the recorder of St Ives, in this letter to one of the courtiers close to the king:

> ...they are about to chose Mr St Aubyn again as their recorder, of whose particular disaffection to his person [the king] had formerly taken notice, and must look upon it as an evidence of their own disaffection to him, if they should attempt to chose him again... St Aubyn is a bosom friend of Nosworthy, the present member, whom Basset hopes to eject.[4]

The following year, the authorities even instigated a formal inquiry into John St Aubyn's activities during the whole period of the 1640s and 1650s. Unless his dealings to pay for the Mount had been scrupulous, the entire transaction might be jeopardised. The stress may well have contributed to an even more bitter blow, the death of his beautiful Catherine, the mother to his four sons and six daughters, who was only in her early forties. He would live for another two decades but never remarry.

Eventually no charges were brought as a result of these enquiries and perhaps it was to amend for any feeling of ill-treatment, that in 1667 John was again appointed High Sheriff of the County. After Catherine died, he had handed over the Clowance estate to his eldest son, to whom she had given birth while enduring the siege of Plymouth, in 1645. Colonel St Aubyn retired to live on the Mount in relative seclusion.

In similar vein, John's adversary, Bennett, also retired from public life. At Hoxworthy, he devoted himself to the business of Launceston Castle and the many other properties he had acquired from distressed royalists. In

1649, he had pronounced the trial of the king as justified 'by scripture, law, history and reason'; in 1658, he had advocated the accession of Cromwell's son Richard as Lord Protector. Yet apart from a short spell in Exeter prison in 1661,[5] he was left in peace, even after attacking the new king's ministers, in a paper he delivered to the Speaker of the Commons in 1671. The old warhorse died on 7 July 1683.

Bennett had conformed to the pattern of many minor gentry in the county; St Aubyn on the other hand had broken ranks, which thereafter appears to have put him beyond the pale within his former social circle. But he had a large family and social exclusion did not extend to the St Aubyn children. In 1665, the eldest son married Anne Jenkyn, co-heiress to the Trekenning estate in mid-Cornwall. His younger brother, Francis, who followed his father into Middle Temple in 1667, wed an Arundell widow in 1690 and, after her death, Joan Crocker.[6] His St Aubyn descendants lived in Cornwall for several generations before moving to London.

After living on the Mount, a life at sea attracted one of the younger St Aubyn boys. There is a letter written by John in 1667,[7] seeking an apprenticeship with a Mr John More for his son William, enquiring 'whether he be supplied with a lad or not', adding the proviso, 'I desire that my son shall be sent beyond the sea within some reasonable time'. It appears that William's ambition to travel the world was realised, but at a cost – for he died in the busy Turkish port of Smyrna in 1685.[8]

After Catherine's death, his sister, Katherine, lived with John and appears to have assumed the maternal role in the family.[9] Her correspondence with Mrs Elizabeth Marten, whose own son had evidently become enchanted by one of the St Aubyn daughters in 1675, suggests that the number of children to be provided for was constraining their marriage portions, if not their ardour:

> Madam
> Havinge the opportunity as to kisse your faire hands with a few rude lines, which hath been my ambition this long tyme …
> I hope, distance nor tyme will not make us forgett each other's kindnesse which hath formerly beene betweene us.
> I must confesse the greatest happinesse I had since I saw you last was the enjoyment of your son in these parts. I hope you will not thinke his journey vainely spent in gettinge a faire Lady out of this family, which you had so great kindnesse for,

although she hath not that great fortune you did expect; but I hope shee will make a vertuous wife and a dutiful daughter in law unto you, hoping your part will not be wantinge.

Madam, I must confesse that I was not wantinge in this businesse, as to get him this Lady seeinge his deserts noe lesse; I must confesse he hath carried himselfe very handsomely in these parts though I heare you have hard thoughts of him, which I hope in tyme will be taken off.

Thus wishing you all happinesse, I committ you to God, and rest

Madam
Your faithfull and cordial friend
To serve you
Katherine Seyntaubyn[10]

'When you have read these rude lines', Katherine ended her letter, 'commit them to the flames.' Her niece, Gertrude, went on to marry Mrs Marten's son, William, and to live in Devon. In 1685, another niece, Jane, married William Harris, who lived at Keneggie, a manor house with splendid views over Mount's Bay, where his grandfather had once been the island captain.[11] But after continuing to care for her brother, Katherine St Aubyn died a spinster in 1687.

Life on the Mount often provided its own interest as, for example, in 1662 when the artist William Shellinks paid a visit in the company of Jaques Thierry, a wealthy Belgian ship owner, after they had first visited Penzance market, where they found 'everyone, men and women, young and old, puffing tobacco, which is here so common that the young get it in the morning instead of breakfast, and almost prefer it to bread'. That afteroon they visited St Michael's Mount, where John probably enjoyed the distraction, given his troubles:

> Mr John St Aubyn, came to us, and welcomed us with great politeness, took us back to the hall and said he was greatly obliged and indebted to Mr Jaques Theirry and a thousand more such complements, and treated us there to small beer, etc. The tide was coming in fast as they left and so we had to hurry if we wanted to go over on foot, and still had to wade through the water in boots, and Mr Veale had to have himself carried over by a fisherman.

The following morning they set out from Penzance at eight o'clock to ride to Land's End, finding 'To this uttermost westerly region mainly Quakers and such folk, also supposedly many witches and sorcerers'. The next day, John St Aubyn appeared at their lodgings in Marazion, where 'he paid for a pint or two of wine, which we drank with him for friendship's sake, and so we took our leave...'.[12]

John also continued to play an active part in naval security, monitoring ships which berthed in the Mount harbour. In 1666, England was at war with the Dutch and their French allies. Gleaning intelligence from a French merchant ship, which had docked in the Mount harbour in July, John wrote to Lord Arlington, the king's chief secretary, to warn that a 'Scilly vessel and two colliers have been taken by a French man-of-war, which still remains upon the coast, to the prejudice of the Welsh and Irish trade'.[13] On Boxing Day that December, as High Sheriff, John received a report from one Jacob Hebbelienk, who had just left France, where '40,000 horse and foot were quartered in the adjacent country [to Brest], destined for Ireland; saw the town full of soldiers; 24 men-of-war now lie in Brest, 24 at Rochelle, and 12 at Bourdeaux, with provisions'.[14]

There is, however, one incident which casts John St Aubyn and his fellow justices in a very different light. When it came to shipwrecks, it seems that old habits died hard, as a report sent in October 1671 reveals:

> The *Speedwell* was cast away at Pengersicke, near the Lizard. The rude country people plundered her of all that was between decks to a very great value, but this being noised abroad, Sir William Godolphin, Hugh Boscawen, and John St Aubyn came to the wreck, and by their care preserved all or most of the goods in the hold from the violence of the country people, and have taken care for the goods ever since to be landed with all speed, and the greatest part is now landed.[15]

All seemed well, except that in another case, the Newfoundler *Prosperous*, which apparently sank in the same storm, the report went on to say that 'Two of the men who got ashore have since died of their injuries'. Then four months later, definite foul play was implicated over the *Speedwell*. Commissioner William Noye wrote to Sir Jonathan Trelawny at St James'

Palace about 'the embezzlements of the *Speedwell*'. After those summoned failed to appear for 'rifling the cabin of the said ship':

> ... I went there myself to persuade those resolute rustic fellows to come before us, and for my Kindness as I was going home at night three or four of them fell on me, and with clubs beat and abused me, and endeavoured to throw me over a great high cliff, and had a rope with them ready fitted to hang me, and tore all my cloak in pieces. I am black at present.

Noye sent his servant to Newlyn, 'to the constable with my warrant to impress seamen', in order to bolster his authority, but:

> The town seeing my horse, fell on my man, and knocked him off, broke his head, and threw him over cliff, that he was taken up dead, so that he could not for the present go further with the other warrants, supposing it were myself (but God deliver me from them). They are about 300, resolved to stand by themselves.

Then when the embattled Noye ordered the constables of Marazion to assist him:

> ... Mr John Sayntabyn that now lives at the Mount, rebuked them, and demanded their authority, and threatened they should suffer for coming to the Mount without his leave... You may see what it is for his Majesty to loose a garrison, for were there but thirty men, ten musketeers would make those insolent rogues more submissive than all our bands of countrymen will do...

Noye also set his sights on Justice Jones, who lived in Sennen, 'a place most likely for wrecks as any within your liberty', where Jones 'has very well feathered himself by a late wreck in that place'. But his main target was St Aubyn: 'this is not the first time [he] has hindered his Majesty's interest. When we were in execution of the commission he hindered several from appearing, and received their goods, promising he would free them, being a justice of the peace, from any authority we had'.[16]

In February 1672, John St Aubyn had several motives to 'hinder' the agent Noye, sent by Trelawny. For after serving alongside John's brother, Thomas, as a colonel in the king's army, this Trelawny had proved to be one of the most active and persistent royalist conspirators in Cornwall, during the interregnum. He had been imprisoned nine times and three times even sentenced to death. In the case of the *Speedwell*, he was asserting the Crown prerogative, to usurp the Mount claim to the Right of Wreck in the Bay.[17]

But in St Aubyn's view, 'God's grace' still belonged to the Cornish, a totemic strand of separate identity and a defining limit to their much vaunted 'exemplary loyalty' to the king, even when his Majesty's representative was Cornish himself. The elevation of this old enemy to his position at the palace also made him the prime suspect, in St Aubyn's view, for the deep personal wound he had just received from the court.

For in other situations, John St Aubyn remained as energetic and loyal to the throne as ever, as we find him in 1781, committing the master of a ship from Belfast,[18] who had refused to take the Oath of Supremacy. He had also busied himself with the Stanneries, given the tin trade coming through his harbour, being elected a stannator of Tywarnwhaile in 1663 and of Penwith and Kerrier in 1673 (and elected by those tinners who would have taken a grateful interest in 'God's grace' on the *Speedwell* only a few months earlier).[19]

Charles I's order to sequester St Aubyn property in 1643 had excluded 'the barton of Clowance'. As civil war had approached, many families had taken evasive action, by setting up complex trusts and 'leases for lives' to supress the value and to protect the ownership of their land. This had helped when it came to 'compounding for delinquency', as the main tax on royalist estates was termed, or paying the 'decimator tax' levied on delinquents. Life interests were assessed at half the rate of land held 'in fee simple', for example, while there were various other rules, which almost matched modern inheritance taxes in their complexity.[20]

So John St Aubyn, at the start of the conflict, may well have sought to mitigate the risks he was taking with the family fortune, by passing on his interest in the family home, by means of some such strict arrangement. In any event, his son John now lived at Clowance with his wife, Anne Jenkyn, and it was in his son's name that the family was now reconciled with the county set. For Anne's younger sister, Mary, was married to the courtier, Sir Nicholas Slanning, and with his influence, Charles II was persuaded to grant a baronetcy to Anne's husband. Pointedly, someone had also persuaded the king not to grant the honour to her Roundhead father-in-law, who was still head of the family.

The title was confirmed in December 1671, on payment of the requisite fee, a reflection of the political hypocrisy of the age.[21] An honour which was surely earned either by the father, for risking his life and livelihood to defeat tyranny, or by the uncle, who had fought valiantly to defend his king, could only be purchased by the son, who had done neither.

Thus, on 14 March 1672 is recorded a 'Warrant of discharge to John Seyntalbyns, jun., of Clewance, Cornwall, for £1,095 due in consideration of a grant of the title of baronet conferred on him'.[22] In this era of cavalier corruption, one can only hope that proceeds from the *Speedwell*, kept out of Mr Noye's hands, covered this tariff. Perhaps they did.

Wrecking adventures may have sat easily on John St Aubyn's conscience, after this deliberate slight from the sitting monarch. But he may equally have regarded the bolt that arrived on 10 July 1676, as having been shot directly by the old one. For out of the sky, as his sister Katherine was planning her day in Chevy Chase, came a ball of fire hurtling towards St Michael's Mount. Hals tells the story:

> [It]struck against the south moorstone wall of this Mount's church [thence] by a rebound, struck the strong oak durns of the dwelling-house entry, and broke the same in two or three pieces; and so flew into the Hall, where it fell to the ground, and then brake asunder, by the side of Mrs Catherine [sic] Seynt Aubyn.[23]

Katherine survived this phenonenom unscathed, and went on to outlive her brother by three years. She could not, however, prevent one of the saddest signs of John's social exclusion, which came after his death, in the family church at Crowan. For two and a half centuries, brass memorials had honoured the lives of the squire and lady at the head of each generation of St Aubyns. From the baronetcy onwards, monuments in stone would be carved in their name. Yet for John's generation, it is his royalist brother, Thomas, whose effigy still adorns the north wall of the church, his hand on his hilt and his helmet resting by his foot, as he stares at us in full cavalier armour. In 1662, John had built a stone sarcophagus to his wife, 'Katheren … Daughter & Heiresse unto Francis Godalphen of Treveneage'. But his own grave is unmarked in Crowan Churchyard; the parish register does not even record his death in August 1684.[24]

John sat for Edward Bower, the artist who painted Charles I at his trial, and his portrait now hangs at the Mount. But it was only acquired by the family forty years ago. The 'Cornish Royalist tradition' supressed his memory for rather more than a century. But it did not alter the elevated path which his life's contribution had laid for the generations of his family that followed, St Michael's Mount epitomising their ambition.

PART FOUR

PATRICIAN HEIRS

CHAPTER 1

THE JACOBITE TENDENCY

Suspicions amongst thoughts
are like bats amongst birds,
they ever fly by twilight.

Sir Francis Bacon

Visitors to Westminster today are familiar with the green expanse of Parliament Square and the buildings that house the great offices of state running along the north side of St James' Park, before reaching Downing Street. But this is a late Victorian design. In 1690, the area was full of run-down houses, while its bars and taverns were frequented by the likes of the Tory poet, Alexander Pope, and Richard Steele, the Whig playwright who later started the *Spectator* and *Tatler* journals.[1] This whole area had come into the hands of one Peter Delahay, whose coat of arms conveyed descent from Norman nobility. But after both he and his son died in quick succession, Delahay's valuable London estate was in trust for his daughters.

Meanwhile, Sir John St Aubyn, 1st Baronet, had made little impact after securing his title, apart from representing the hotly contested borough of Mitchell, a few miles ffrom his wife's family home, in the two elections of 1679.[2] He died at the young age of 42, perhaps taken by the plague still lingering in the population. This may have spurred his son and heir, another John, to become MP for Helston for the Convention Parliament of January 1689 at the age of only 20, and only two years after his father's death.[3] He had the support of the Earl of Bath (Bevill Grenville's son) and the senior Godolphins, the county divide of thirty years before now well and truly healed. Just two months before, the 'Glorious Revolution', which replaced James II with William and Mary, had passed with no more than a Cornish spasm. Once parliament met, this new political settlement was swiftly ratified.

The new St Aubyn baronet remained an MP until 1695 and it was no doubt as a result of living more in London, that he met Mary, one of the four Delahay daughters. The young couple, bound together by the loss of their fathers as children, were married in St George's Chapel, Windsor, as was Sir John's right as a member of the Commons.[4] They had seven children, five of whom survived, spending their time both in Cornwall and at the family home in Delahay Street, next to Downing Street. Political life was becoming injected into the family veins, just as it also became a national obsession; for under the 1694 Triennial Act, the newly emerging Whig and Tory parties now had to contest elections every three years.

At this time, St Michael's Mount was in decay and it is doubtful whether either the first or second baronets spent much time there. According to Dr William Borlase, writing sixty years later, by 1700 the harbour was badly neglected and there was only one house on the island, resided in by the widow 'Orchard'.[5] The island still remained a centre of commerce for storing the tin or the fish to be traded by local producers, with the wider market abroad. But before Sir John and his wife might have realised its potential, both of them also died young and within the space of a few years, leaving five orphaned children.

The bulk of the family estate went to the 17-year-old eldest, the 3rd Baronet, under the terms of their marriage settlement,[6] with Mary dividing her Westminster house and related property between the four younger siblings, to be held by 'my trusty and well beloved Friend Luce Praed widow and unto my dear sister Martha Delahay Spinster'.[7] Perhaps she was mindful of Steele's 1701 comedy *Grief-a-la-Mode*, where the widowed Lady Brumpton says of men: 'We rule them by their affections, which blinds them into belief that they rule us... But in this nation, our power is absolute'. In June 1717, a woman could still own substantial property and designate only women as her trustees, so long as her own inheritance had allowed it.

Meanwhile William Borlase, whose uncle, William Harris, had married Jane St Aubyn,[8] was becoming a friend for life to the St Aubyn family. He had been born into his own ancient Cornish lineage in 1696, four years before Sir John and Lady Mary's eldest. Their son, grandson and even great-grandson were very fortunate that William became their mentor, as he proved to be one of the most warm hearted and thoughtful Cornishmen of his day.

Borlase had secured the living of Lugdvan at the young age of 26, after studying at Oxford during the height of the first Jacobite rebellion.[9] During the second rebellion in 1745, he would write to the younger John St Aubyn, then at Oxford himself, to warn how:

> …we, I mean pupils, tutors, barbers, shoe-cleaners and bed-makers, minded nothing but politics; the Muse stood neglected, nay, meat and drink, balls and ladies, had all reason to complain in their turns, that we minded Scotland and Preston more than the humane, softer and more delicate entertainments of Genius and Philosophy…
>
> I think if I were back again to 1715, and in my undergraduate's gown, I should let the antagonists quietly take their fate, and not go once to coffee-house to know who had the best on't. For if I can see anything in our English History, 'tis that the poor nation is always the worse for alterations'.[10]

Not everything about his Oxford days can have brought regret, as this earlier letter to Sir John St Aubyn in 1723 suggests:

> …bless my stars among all my whims and extravagances, I have not once attempted poetry, ever since I writ a couplet or two on my Oxford mistress's stays: I was (as you remember) soon after discarded by the fair one, and laughed into my senses by my companions; and this entirely cured me of what too many in this unfortunate nation are apt to call the inspiration of the Muses.[11]

Borlase would happily remain rector of Lugdvan for fifty years, for as he wrote in this letter to an uncle in 1727:

> I have had the pleasure of seeing some of the most considerable places in England, and … there is … no part … that abounds so much in the necessaries, and at the same time has so many of the elegancies of life, as that of Mount's Bay. The gentry, most of whom are our near relations, are of a free frolicking disposition.[12]

In the summer, he describes playing on the bowling green, before dining in 'a little pleasure house'. He meets his friends so frequently 'we are as it were like so many brothers of one family, so united, and so glad to see one another'.

Into this idyl, Borlase realised from the first that he needed to introduce a wife. After the Oxford mistress, the first serious object of his affections was Martha St Aubyn, one of the sisters of his friend Sir John. His predicament, in a letter to his other great friend, Philip Hawkins, sheds a light on both the man and his world. 'I could never prevail upon myself to propose that to Sir John, which you often advised me to', he reasoned:

> … I could have all the secret pleasure of being in love with Mistress St. Aubyn, without making myself so ridiculous as to discover so ambitious a passion to herself or brother.

Further on, Borlase writes: 'I had share enough of her brother's favour to excuse the folly of my pretensions if they had been discovered to him', but concludes:

> Not but I could love Mistress St. Aubyn for ever, but the little likelihood of succeeding in such an attempt, or of maintaining her suitable to her birth if I should succeed, these reasons have made me very easy in that affair. Thus you see I can please myself with chimeras for a while, but reason, kind reason, will not suffer me to be uneasy at the loss of a shadow, or the going out of a passion that has been kindled by imprudence.[13]

Yet, '… I shall be in love again, when I next see her, and please myselfe over again with a passion', and so in March 1723, Borlase wrote to console the occupants of Delahay Street in the most intimate terms, after they had lost 'Gypsy' the cat:

> As to the beloved Gypsie's elopment with her lover, if she never returns I cannot but excuse her as this case now stands; but had she not been what she is, could she have but relish'd those endearments which I have often envy'd, and been sensible of the hands that smooth'd her and the lap and bosom that fondled her, could she have had possibly any relish for those, nothing in the world should have enduc'd me to give her the least quarter for running away.[14]

Martha never married, but stayed living in the family house in Delahay Street, overlooking St James' Park, for another five decades. She was hardly a beauty and it is doubtful if any other man ever touched her heart like the equally plain faced but very lovable Borlase. Yet, his overweaning sense of propriety had protected his relationship with the men in her family; and for his friend and contemporary, the 3rd Sir John, propriety and honour were sacrosanct.

In 1714, the crowning of George I from Hanover as king of Britain, marked the start of a radical political departure, as he sought to replace the competitive parliamentary system he inherited, with one party rule under the Whigs. Places in the army, the civil service, or ecclesiastical appointments in the Crown's gift were openly denied to gentlemen of a Tory persuasion. Tory army officers lost their commissions, sometimes without compensation, against all precedent. Tory lawyers could no longer aspire to be judges or senior counsel; the lower clergy, almost all Tory, could not become bishops. Tory merchants were denied government contracts, or refused directorships in the Bank of England or other great public companies. Traditional Tory families found their sons could no longer afford to stand for parliament, deprived of the perquisites of office.

George I simply despised Tories, but by sustaining his Whig politicians in power through their rotten boroughs, not least those in Cornwall, the sovereign alienated half the nation he ruled. It was arguably the greater half, since Tories tended to represent the largest constituencies and obtained the most votes cast in every general election between 1715 and 1747.[15] So the Tory gentry in the country were drawn towards his rival, James Stuart, the exiled son of James II; 'irresistibly determined', as one of them wrote,[16] 'to lay hold of the first opportunity which shall offer, of freeing themselves from what they esteem an intolerable oppression'.

'The Pretender', as James Stuart was known, represented more than just the means to displace the one party rule of the Whigs. In the Tory view, for the Hanovarian monarch to have derived his authority by mere act of parliament was a sacrilegious offence, as well as a constitutional one; for them, kingship was a divine appointment. At the same time, the role of parliament had become entrenched since the Restoration; so Tory Jacobites regarded James Stuart's sacred belief in his divine right to rule as less of a threat to freedom, than the tyranny of the Hanovarian king's systematic corruption of parliament's elections. Lastly, resolutely Protestant Tory Jacobites could overlook James' Catholicism, because he was committed to religious toleration, of Dissenter, Jew, Protestant and Catholic alike. In the very nature of revolutionary forces, of course, other Jacobite factions – in Scotland, Ireland and abroad – held vastly conflicting views.

The upright Sir John St Aubyn, having breathed the poltical air of Westminster as a child and of Oxford as a student, had become, by the time he took his degree, a steadfast Tory Jacobite. In 1715, the Whigs had extended each parliamentry term from three to seven years, more than halving how often they had to buy their boroughs, but even so an election in 1722 was now due. Two years earlier, many people across society had speculated disastrously in the 'South Sea Bubble', and resentment still boiled at the government now led by Sir Robert Walpole, one of the few individuals to have made a vast profit from the scam.

The Jacobites now hatched the Atterbury Plot, to create a nationwide revolt against the Hanovarians, at the same time as the 1722 election. The 21-year-old Sir John was nominated as one of the Cornish leaders of the planned uprising, at the same time as he was proposed by the Tories to challenge the prestigious county seat, currently held by John Trevanion of Caerhays, who had recently defected to the Whigs in return for a post in government.

The Atterbury Plot was discovered and came to naught, but Sir John beat Trevanion at the hustings and would continue to represent the county for the next twenty-two years, alongside Sir William Carew, a fellow Tory Jacobite. They remained in secret contact with the camp of the Pretender throughout that time; meanwhile, driven by his 'deep inner fear of Jacobitism',[17] Walpole's spies sought to discover every suspicious move. But precisely because any overt expression of Jacobitism, indeed any opposition to the Hanovarian succession, was treason, punishable by death and loss of estates, Walpole was never quite sure how far its carefully disguised support extended.[18]

In 1725, John married Catherine, the sister of another Tory Jacobite, Sir William Morice, the MP for Launceston. His grandfather had been a close companion of Charles II in exile and one of his two Secretaries of State after the Restoration. He had acquired Stoke Damerel, a farm on the edge of Plymouth, before persuading the king to expand the naval base in the port onto his land, as a result of which the Morice family stood to become immensely rich. Even by 1725, her father, Sir Nicholas, could afford to endow Catherine with £10,000 as her marriage settlement to Sir John. However, it says something of the nature of Sir Nicholas that he insisted on a twenty-two-page marriage contract; and he conveyed Catherine's dowry to Clowance in two cartloads of half-crown pieces.

His other daughter, Barbara, married Sir John Molesworth, a fellow Cornishman whose family seat was Pencarrow; and the two families soon became the closest of friends, not least sharing the same Tory outlook and passion for politics.[19]

This generous dowry was invested by Sir John in restoring St Michael's Mount and in 1727 he completed a new pier, from which tin could be shipped in large quantities. But following a scarcity of corn, tinners across Cornwall had armed themselves and raided the granaries of the county. The new pier on the Mount became a focal point for malcontents and riots broke out. But in response, Sir John intervened by granting the tinners a large sum of money, to pay for their food and to save their families from starving. As a result, he won their loyal following and a latent Jacobite army at his behest. For George I had stirred the same hostility as the Tudors, by tampering with their hallowed Stannary court and the price of tin.[20]

Meanwhile, in the Commons, it was being reported that 'Sir John St Aubyn has gained a great reputation in that House' for his strong opposition to Sir Robert Walpole. As Borlase later wrote, 'he soon learnt to speak well, but spoke seldom, and never but on points of consequence. He was heard with pleasure by his friends and with respect by others'.[21] In March 1734, he seconded the repeal of the Septennial Act, describing long parliaments as 'a safe and most ingenious way of enslaving a nation', explaining eloquently:

> But this must be the Work of Time. Corruption is of so base a Nature, that at first sight it is extremely shocking. Hardly anyone has submitted to it all at once. His Disposition must be previously understood; the particular Bait must be found out with which he is to be allured; and, after all, it is not without many struggles that he surrenders his Virtue. Indeed, there are some who will at once plunge themselves over Head and Ears into any base Action; but the generality of mankind are of a more cautious Nature, and will proceed only by some leisurely Degrees.
>
> One or two perhaps have deserted their Colours the first Campaign; some have done it in a second. But a great many who have not that eager Disposition to Vice will wait till a Third. For this reason, Short Parliaments have been less Corrupt than Long Ones; they are observed, like Streams of Water, always to grow more impure the greater Distance they run from the Fountain-head.

Sir John pleaded to the House: 'Give the people their ancient Right of frequent new Elections; That will restore the decay'd Authority of Parliament and will put our Constitution into a natural condition of working out her Cure'.[22]

This speech followed on from the election that year, which had rewarded Sir Robert with another large majority. His popularity was at its height, after he had kept the country out of European wars, and could afford to halve the Land Tax. Despite the wisdom of Sir John's words, the Septennial Act would not be altered until 1911.

Walpole had now been in power for thirteen years. In the words of his biographer, J.H. Plumb[23]:

> By 1734, his life, his attitudes, his methods had been clamped into an iron mould; the years had hardened and coarsened the fibres of his personality; and as his vision narrowed into a desire to retain power for its own sake, as intolerance of criticism grew, as the fluid, sensitive feeling of the realities of men and politics were smeared by success and calloused by power, so too did Nemesis creep upon him.

Shortly after St Aubyn's speech in the House, which was triumphantly reported in the Tory press and also secretly to the Pretender,[24] the *Quarterly Review* reported '... a curious incident ... in the neighbourhood of his seat at Clowance, with which Sir John was only indirectly connected in his capacity of Justice of the Peace, but which was ultimately attended with very serious consequences to himself and his family'. The events started in June 1734 and lasted until August 1735:

> A certain Henry Rogers, by trade a pewterer, having some fancied claim to an estate called Skews, seized the manor house, and, surrounding himself with a band of cut-throats, organized a rebellion on his own account, and bade defiance to the country round. Having beaten off from his house, not without bloodshed, first the sheriff, next the constables, and finally the military themselves, the villain succeeded in making good his escape. He was subsequently arrested at Salisbury, and brought to Launceston for trial, where the grand jury found five bills of murder against him, and Lord Chief

Justice Hardwicke publicly returned thanks to Sir John 'for his
steady endeavours to bring him to justice'.[25]

The High Sheriff of Cornwall had remained supinely indifferent to
this crisis, even as (in Sir John's words) 'Skewis became an asylum for
villains'.[26] While this inaction merely mystified Borlase, as he wrote in a
letter to a cousin, to Sir John it must have appeared as profoundly sinister.[27]

For that year, the High Sheriff was James Tillie of Pentillie, in itself a
dubious choice, as he came from unsavoury stock. His wealth derived from
his great uncle, a charlatan who had married for money, and then purchased
a knighthood from James II on false pretences. On discovery, the College
of Arms 'entered his chamber in London, took down his arms, tore others
to pieces and fastened them all to horses' tails and dragged them through
the streets of London to his perpetual disgrace'.[28] The fraud built himself
a mausoleum and in his will, stipulated that his body was to be seated in
it, dressed for dinner and served with food and wine. (This macabre scene
was rediscovered in 2013.) His flawed character now haunted his great-
nephew, who shunned his responsibilities, even after his Under-Sheriff had
been attacked and two officers killed, with several more murders being
committed by Rogers and his gang during the months that followed.

Tillie's failure to act was cast in a yet more insidious light by his
appointment to the lucrative post of 'Superintendent of the Royal Foundry'.
This was announced in the *Gentleman's Magazine*, just as the drama in
West Cornwall unfolded. Tillie was the factotum of Sir John Coryton, who
controlled a Cornish seat. In 1721, Coryton had been a Jacobite, named
with Sir John in a secret government report on the Atterbury Plot.[29] But now
he had been bought. He was trading his seat to Walpole's nominee and in
return, out of the proceeds of Tillie's office, it later emerged that the toad
'paid one moiety of it to Sir John Coryton'.[30]

As High Sheriff, by ignoring what Borlase termed 'a violation of all law,
but also … a direct insult to his own personal authority', Tillie had deliberately
exposed Sir Robert's arch opponent to ten months of terror; and to the fear
that he was to be eliminated. Quite apart from his appointing Tillie as High
Sheriff, in the same month as Sir John's celebrated speech in the House, the
fact that Walpole also ran the Secret Service fund, with its remit to keep him
in power, raised the most profound suspicions in the mind of Sir John. He
immediately grasped the danger of the situation to his family.

As both the local JP and the County MP, faced with Tilley's abject failure,
Sir John resorted to every other means to secure the military assistance

necessary, to blast the Rogers gang out of Skews house with a cannon. At last, artillery was sent in March 1735, nine months after the reign of terror had started. But even once this had achieved its purpose, Sir John had to offer a £500 reward for Rogers, out of his own pocket, after the deadly rogue had somehow continued to elude capture. Thus, as Borlase later wrote, Sir John 'drew upon himself the particular odium of Rogers, and was not without just apprehensions of his house being burnt and himself assassinated'. As a result, he was 'forced to leave his own house and remove his family to Launceston, where his Lady, even there not free from fears of such an inhuman butcher, contracted so ill an habit of body as brought on a sensible decay'.

Rogers, who was finally caught in June 1735 and hanged in August, had tormented Lady St Aubyn with menacing letters, exacerbating her mental affliction.[31] She never fully recovered from this and in June 1740, Catherine died when she was only 35.[32] This left her husband equally wrought with guilt and anguish; he had been the target, but she had paid the price. With her death, 'Sir John's interest in country life came to an end'.[33] Placing his son, John, in the care of Borlase at the Lugdvan Rectory, he set out 'for a foreign land'.

———◆———

'The Landlord class', wrote the historian G.M. Trevelyan, 'in return for supporting the supremacy of the Lower House, obtained the right of nominating most of its members. That was the unwritten clause in the Settlement of 1689'.[34] One who saw the opportunities of this arrangement was Thomas Pitt, the former Governor of Madras who had made a fortune in India, including his purchase of the famous Pitt diamond for £20,000, which he then sold to the Regent of France for £135,000.[35] In 1710, he was persuaded to purchase the Boconnoc estate from the Mohuns and become a 'borough-monger' in the county.[36] One of the leading Tories predicted of Pitt that 'he will have a powerful purse and be a thorn in the side of some government men'.

By 1740, the Pitt influence in Cornwall was well grounded and for personal reasons, as well as political calculation, Pitt's grandson, Thomas, and his brother, William (the future 'Elder' Pitt statesman) now decided to throw their weight behind the 'Country' party which included the Cornish Tories. In 1734, all but seven of the forty-four Cornish MPs had been on the side of the 'Court' party of Walpole. If that balance could be shifted, in the election due in 1741, then Sir Robert's days might be numbered. Cornish revolts against the government had a sad history of failure, when decided by force of arms. But this one would be decided at the hustings.

A 'Country Party' campaign fund was started, to which Tory families such as the St Aubyns and the Morices contributed. Even larger contributions came from the Whigs who opposed Walpole, headed by the Prince of Wales, who loathed his father. As for the Pitts, Thomas was now acknowledged as the prince's political agent in the county. He systematically addressed the issue of how to win each of the twenty-two constituencies, who to pay and how much.

Thus in Tregony, by October 1740 Thomas Pitt could report that Lord Falmouth, whose younger brother had unsuccessfully contested the borough at two by-elections in 1737, 'declares he will carry the election if it costs him £5,000. The success seems to be certain, but the expense will be great'. In the event Falmouth would gain one of the two seats for the opposition, by a compromise with his opponent.

Then in Grampound, there was a dispute over the borough charter, as to who could chose the mayor, who in turn decided who qualified to have the vote. The Prince of Wales was called upon to pay £2000, of which more than a quarter went on legal expenses, 'demolishing that cursed charter and its consequences', as Pitt later put it. On top, there was £20 for each of the old freemen, and £15 for each of those newly sworn, all paid up front as they insisted was their custom.

The public mood was changing and Pitt's election agents across the county reported that 'there appears at present something like a spirit of liberty in the people'.[37] Tory demands for retaliation, in response to Spanish assaults on British shipping, had left Walpole's adminstration looking weak; especially when the press dramatised the account of Captain Robert Jenkins, who kept one of his ears pickled in a jar, cut off by a Spanish sailor when his brig, the *Rebecca*, was raided off Havana in 1731.

Pushed into 'the war of Jenkins' ear', the commander of the British fleet scored a victory at Porto Bello. But Admiral Edward Vernon was a known Walpole critic and his popularity could not transfer to Britain's ailing first 'Prime Minister'. Then Vernon's campaign went awry and the adminstration took the blame.

Returning from abroad, St Aubyn thrust himself with renewed energy into the fray, the incorruptible figurehead of the 'Country Party' opposing Walpole, of whom he said '…at my very door there are such glaring proofs, which, in less corrupt times, would deprive him of his head'.[38] But on the ground, the reality of the Cornish electorate was 'that this sort of people have been so used to corruption that little is to be done amongst them without it. Even those who would return a bribe before an election expect a gratuity when it is over'. So reported Thomas Pitt, who went on to warn: 'Men who are to be bribed into Honesty may certainly be bribed out of it'.[39]

When parliament had dissolved in April 1741, the House of Commons had consisted of 300 ministerial supporters, 115 opposition Whigs and 143 Tories. The general election that followed produced only 94 contests, less than at any other since George I's accession. Yet the results in Cornwall and Scotland cut Walpole's majority to the bone. He lost ten seats in Cornwall, seven to the prince's election manager, Thomas Pitt, and three to Lord Falmouth, whose father had once been Walpole's own election manager.[40]

Election petitions in disputed cases also went against Walpole's candidates, while the Pretender sent a letter to his supporters, including Sir John, ordering them to align with the opposition Whigs. For a while, Walpole teetered on the brink, then during a short adjournment in 1742, he resigned his office and was elevated to the Upper House, thereby escaping the judgement of the Commons, which might well have committed him to the Tower.

At the reassembly, Sir John seconded a motion brought in by Lord Limerick, for a secret committee to inquire into Walpole's administration, which was lost by two votes. But a second motion, on 23 March, for 'an enquiry into the conduct of Robert, Earl of Orford', was put by Lord Limerick for the oppositon Whigs, seconded by St Aubyn for the Tories; with a Select Committee appointed by ballot. The motion passed and now came Sir John's political triumph, as he was unanimously elected to the Enquiry Committee by all 518 members of the House; 'an honour neither then nor before (as far as the records of Parliament can reach) ever conferred on any Member, as Mr Speaker Onslow on the spot observed'.[41]

The tinners in 1497 had been stopped at Blackheath and neither Perkin Warbeck, nor Humphrey Arundell fifty years later, had reached further than Exeter. As for the royalists, in 1646 they had surrendered on home turf. But Cornish voters, suitably fed and implacably led, had finally succeeded in bringing down a government they despised.

When the committee of enquiry first met, Sir John was true to form. He declined to take the chair and so Limerick was installed. 'We are now', Sir John wrote in a letter three months later, 'winding up our bottoms as well as we can', predicting that 'we shall show the world enough to convince if not convict', despite the all too predicable limits placed on their investigation into Walpole.

They established that Walpole had expended a staggering £1.5 million on his Secret Service fund during his tenure. But this formed both 'the gravamen of the indictment of Walpole's ministry and the mystification of successive historians', as key officials refused to answer the committee's searching questions.[42] But they still discovered that huge sums had been expended on intercepting and decoding messages to the Continent. So Carte's reports on Sir John and others were almost certainly known to Walpole, giving him the motive in 1734, as well as the means and the opportunity, to intimidate the man he could not bribe. That would have pleased the bully in Walpole; just as his moral cowardice would have left any fatal consequences to chance.

Sir John was now offered a place as one of the Lords of the Admiralty, but again he declined. He was ready, he said, to serve his king and country, but would take no place unless upon the express condition that his freedom and independence in parliament should remain unquestioned and uncontrolled. Secretly, he had his own agenda, the evidence to this committee having fuelled the suspicions he had long harboured, about the strange events of 1734 and their aftermath.

Already in 1739, as his wife lay grievously ill, Sir John had discussed the possibility of an English uprising with Thomas Carte, the Jacobite historian. Carte's report to the Pretender shows that St Aubyn was being drawn into dangerous waters:

> Sir John St Aubyn gave me a commission to assure your
> Majesty and the Duke of Ormonde ... that whenever [you]
> land in England, though but with your single persons, he would
> venture himself with the power he could raise to support the
> attempt, for he did not desire a man from abroad, being satisfied
> there was strength enough in the kingdom to overpower the
> standing forces and effect your Majesty's restoration... Sir John
> has assured me he does not doubt of putting himself at the head
> of 8 or 10,000 of these [tinners] any day in the world, and they
> are the best men we have in England.[43]

After spending most of 1740 abroad, when he probably met with Fleury, Louis XV's first minister, and later playing his decisive role in the downfall and censure of Walpole, Sir John's last recorded speech was on 10 December 1742. The question before the House was on the stationing of Hanoverian troops on English soil, which Sir John feared as the king's latest step towards arbitrary power. Carte reported Sir John's increasingly fervent tone to the Pretender:

> Sir John St. Aubyn, than whom none is more universally esteemed in the House or better beloved in the country, prefaced his speech with the remarkable words, viz. that he considered that day as the last day of liberty in England, and the last day of freedom of debate in that House, and therefore it was high time to speak out, for there was no mincing matters in such an extremity ... This speech made him in a moment the darling toast of the city of London...

It is a measure of how far Sir John was now steeped in conspiracy, that the following year he was one of the MPs secretly informed by Louis XV's envoy of the plan for a French invasion, towards the end of February 1744. Parliament would be in recess, so that those in on the secret, that is Sir John St Aubyn, Sir William Carew and six others, could repair to their counties without exciting suspicion. The expedition was to be accompanied by the Pretender's son, who was to be regent, with a council including Sir John and most of the others.[44] For this role, Louis XV's envoy extolled Sir John's credentials, in this report to his master:

> The knight Jean St. Aubin, Member of Parliament for the province of Cornwall, is, in relation to his spirit, his judgment, his erudition, his probity, the beautiful role he plays in Parliament, and the virtue which appears in all his actions, universally esteemed by the whole kingdom.[45]

In the same year, similar sentiments were expressed in the following patriotic verses, which appeared in the London *Gentlemen's Magazine,* under the heading 'The Cornish Mount – A Parallel':

> Oft have I seen, from fam'd St. Michael's height,
> The ocean's rage, with wonder and delight;
> The pile majestic scorns the pond'rous shock;
> Her basis is an Adamantine rock.
> Just so (in worst of times) its owner stood,
> Serenely great and resolutely good...
> Guard him, kind Heav'n, to bless his native shore,
> When truth shall stand, and traytors be no more.[46]

At the end of February 1744, the French invasion was launched, with 10,000 men under Marshal Saxe, with arms and ammunition for their English friends, only to be driven back by a storm, which did such damage to the transports that it was cancelled. Then on 8 March, Sir William Carew – Sir John's fellow County member and co-conspirator – died at the age of 55. Meanwhile, the invasion plan had already been betrayed by a paid informer and on 31 March 1744, before it could be relaunched, Britain declared war on France.

The evident fault lines in Sir John's loyalties were now exposed. The residents of Mount's Bay became alarmed by the threat to their trade, after three of their fishermen had been seized as prisoners. They urgently needed naval cover to guard their shores and fisheries from privateers, and to defend the export and import of materials related to the mine workings. Sir John did not hesitate to act and was profusely thanked for his role in securing this protection, at a meeting of the local gentry on the bowling green at Marazion.

In 1739, he had drawn the line at using foreign troops: 'he did not desire a man from abroad ... there was strength enough in the kingdom'. Yet an irreconcilable conflict was building, between Sir John's public persona, as the most patriotic Cornish Protestant Tory, and his secret offer to raise an army against his government, on behalf of the Catholic Pretender based in Rome. The contrast between his own outlook, and that of his close Cornish friends and admirers, could not be more stark. The following year, for example, when the Jacobite Rebellion of '45 was at its height and posed the gravest threat, William Borlase's elder brother and fellow rector would write to his son:

> There is begun in Scotland a rebellion in favour of the Pretender, which should it succeed, would bring this nation to destruction. The cause is the worst against the best in the world – Popery against Protestantism, arbitrary power against liberty and law. [...] Should it come to extremity, I shall not think it inconsistent with my function to take up arms and, if it please God, to die for my country.[47]

We must leave aside the faintly comic image in military attire of the rotund middle-aged Borlase priest, who now took up fencing lessons from an old French officer.[48] It is striking that the greatest threat to 'liberty and law', as seen by the senior Borlase, was their very saviour, in the eyes of Sir John.

His powers of oratory excepted, the moment Sir John raised an army of loyal miners in open revolt for James Stuart, the gentry on the Marazion bowling green would surely disown him, along with most of Cornish society.

The bold contradiction, at the heart of Sir John's beliefs, might not have troubled a politician driven by vaulting ambition. Sir Watkin Williams-Wynn MP, resolute leader of the Welsh Jacobites, who several times promised support to the Pretender, would spend the 'forty-five' in his London townhouse. But for this inherently honest man of principle, it seems that the tragic and lingering death of his wife, caused by the terrorising of his family, had preyed on his mind; his grief, anger and frustration at the system he loathed, leading him to make irreconcilable commitments, during his lonely sojourn abroad.

But these opposing forces raging war on his conscience were suddenly resolved. For on his way home in August 1744, at the early age of 44, Sir John fell ill while visiting his sister-in-law and her husband at Pencarrow. He died there of a fever, a few days later.

CHAPTER 2

THE MORICE BEQUEST

A Wit's a feather, and a Chief a rod-
An HONEST MAN'S the noblest work of God.

Alexander Pope

Sir John's sudden death inspired political panegyrics from his friends and supporters,[1] including Alexander Pope, the Tory poet and author of *Essay on Man*. Sir John's heroic stand against power remained unsullied by triumph or disaster, either of which might have visited him, had the Jacobite uprising of the following year put him at the head of a Cornish army.

William Borlase would later write that the death of his dear friend was 'to the great loss of all who knew him; and to his country's loss of a most faithful friend... The dignity of this ancient family owes much to this gentleman'. Dr Oliver of Bath – whose invention of the eponymous biscuit left a more lasting impression than his medical expertise, which may well have failed Sir John – wrote a letter of condolence, which spoke of Sir John as:

> ... one who had bravely withstood all the temptation that honours of profit could lay in his way, and dared to stand almost single on the field of Purity, while thousands fell on his right hand and thousands on his left, the easy Prey of corruption... There is something in a character like his which renders it worthy of the admiration and the love of generations; nay, of centuries, far beyond his own.

It is hard to measure the true political impact of Sir John's extraordinary character and career; had he lived to raise his Jacobite army, it might have been tumultuous. For Walpole had sufficient self-awareness to know that his regime, built on corruption, was made of sand. He had revealed this in 1735, when he told the Commons:

> Five or six thousand men may be embarked in such a small number of ships, and so speedily, that it is impossible to guard

against it by means of our fleet … and if such a number were landed, with the Pretender at their head, there is no question that they would meet with many, especially the meaner sort, to join them … if we should draw all our regular forces away from the other parts of the Kingdom, the disaffected would rise in every county so left destitute of regular troops.[2]

But the facts are that Sir John died and the '45 narrowly failed. So we are left with Sir John's integrity, which became a legend well beyond his close circle of friends; the contrast to Walpole's venality contributing to a shift in public morality. In the next generation, both Pelham and Pitt fashioned political credit out of forgoing their own enrichment from office.[3] Sir John had provided a moral compass; above all for the seven generations of his own family, who followed him into parliament, not one of whom craved office. In 1907, his descendants erected a beautiful east window in Crowan Church dedicated to his memory.[4] But perhaps the final word should come from his arch opponent, in a saying that has echoed down the ages:

> *All these men hath their price,*
> *except the little Cornish baronet*
> Sir Robert Walpole[5]

It was Sir William Morice, the brother-in-law and Jacobite MP, who had broken the news to Borlase of the death of their 'dear and worthy friend', adding 'we are now here in the utmost distress. I have this moment sent the children to Werrington; I have all the tenderness and regard for them imaginable, and I will make it the constant study and business of my life to watch over them, and to promote their ease and happiness'.[6]

Sir William had no children of his own, his wife having left him for another man, with the unexpected result that the great Morice fortune, including that about to be realised from the expansion of Plymouth into Stoke Damerel, would now devolve onto his two sisters' families, the St Aubyns and the Molesworths.

Thus the upright 3rd baronet, simply through falling in love with Catherine Morice, had unwittingly secured for his family riches well beyond the grubby ambition of the grasping politicians he had fought so long.

Despite their grief, it was Sir John's political legacy which his friends now wasted no time in protecting. They had only recently stopped the Court Party from taking the other County seat from the Tories in their first by-election, when Sir John's fellow Jacobite, Carew, had died. So in this same letter, Sir William Morice begged leave to inform Borlase '…that Sir John Molesworth is absolutely resolved to offer himself for the County. I don't in the least doubt your readiness to serve him.' But he warned: '… our enemies are at work, and it would be a most severe mortification to us all for such dirty people to triumph over us'.

One of those 'dirty people' was the Duke of Bolton, the patron of Borlase's own living at Lugdvan, who at the Carew by-election had written to him, saying, '…I therefore desire, and in gratitude shall expect, you to give your vote and interest…' to Robert Carteret, the Court Party's candidate. The rector's reply had been a model of probity, mentioning his intimacy with 'Sir John St Aubyn … trusting his only son's education to me', before writing that 'I find myself obliged to depart from Your Grace's recommendation … impute it, not to a sense of any obligations superior to those I have to you, but to the sincere, though perhaps mistaken conviction, of what I owe to my country'.[7]

Carteret chose not to contest the seat again, much to Borlase's relief. He wrote to his cousin, Dr Oliver of '…his being put up last time on so pitiful an interest having made his journey down here the most disagreeable one he ever took, if you may believe his own words'.[8] Carteret's father was Walpole's chief spy, the Postmaster General who intercepted the Jacobite messages; his son's earlier candidacy had appeared as yet another provocation to St Aubyn. But now, Sir John Molesworth was elected unopposed; and eighteen years later, he would marry Barbara, one of Sir John's orphaned daughters, thus bringing the two families even closer together.

As for Sir John's only son, Borlase bid farewell to 'the young baronet', who 'goes to Werrington this week, on his way to Oriel College in Oxford'.[9] With the help of his uncle, Sir William Morice, the young Sir John was elected MP for Launceston in 1747.[10] On this news of his former pupil, Borlase wrote to Oliver that 'the House of Commons … would be the best of schools for the young gentlemen of this nation, if there was less of party there… Party, I think, makes children of us all, nay infants, for it takes away the use of our legs, as well as of our choice'.[11]

On securing the County seat in 1761, this 4th Sir John began to display that sense of independence, so popular with Borlase and the like-minded Cornish freeholders who had chosen him. Thus the record shows[12] that 'every known vote by him in the Parliament of 1768 was with the Opposition… He even attended the Opposition dinner on 9 May 1769'. That year marked the founding of The Cornish Club, which in 2018 would celebrate its

250th anniversary with its president, the Duke of Cornwall (the future King Charles III) and the descendants of many of the founding members, including Sir John's. The 'Object of the Club was to induce such gentlemen connected with Cornwall as might be temporarily or permanently residing in London to dine together several times a year'. Eligible candidates had to be born in the county or own property there, which included many of the forty-four Cornish MPs.[13]

The election year 1768 was also significant for the Wilkes affair, when the Commons voted to prevent the member returned for Middlesex from taking his seat, on the grounds he was an outlaw. This was after Wilkes' newspapers had campaigned against political corruption and for press freedom. He had been sued for libel and forced to leave the country, then imprisoned on his return. Wilkes was elected by Middlesex and rejected by the MPs three times in quick succession, his campaign sparking riots in London, which culminated in the Georges Field Massacre, when troops killed eleven rioters.

Wilkes' campaign captured the spirit of the 4th Sir John's father and so hardly surprisingly, he voted with the opposition on Wilkes, and on every other occasion.

With the Morice inheritance, on Sir William's death in 1750, Sir John had furthered his father's restoration of the Mount, writing to his old tutor for advice, as 'I am certain I can't consult with a more proper Person than your self about Its inside'. The results played on the idea of the Mount as a castle and anticipated the more decorative aspects of the Gothic revival.[14] Later, Borlase described them in a paper on the Mount, written in 1762:

> The whole house has lately undergone thorough repair from the present and late worthy proprietors; the courts are enlarged and neatly laid with well squared Bristol slate, the parlours and bedchambers very elegantly furnished, particularly in the niches of a handsome parlour lately erected where the Antechapel of the Nunnery formerly stood; there are two large vases of oriental jasper with an alto-relieve of statuary marble in each, relating to hymeneal happiness, fit to adorn the largest and most magnificent saloon. The Church has an handsome organ erected.[15]

In 1756, when the 4th baronet married Elizabeth Wingfield, he ordered delicate Gothic chairs for their 'Blue Drawing Room' (as this 'handsome parlour' became known), and the chairs bearing the couple's combined coats of arms still furnish the room today. It was also about this time that the family developed the 'Mount Livery', still worn by their boatmen, when described here by their great-grandson:

> A long red watermans coat with yellow facings with a large brass badge on the left sleeve stamped with the St Aubyn arms – a frilled shirt – white canvas sea petticoat, a sort of hunting cap made with leather with the family crest in brass on the front.[16]

In August 1754, the family enthusiasm for boats had nearly ended the St Aubyn line. Borlase wrote to Dr Oliver, as '…you desires a particular account of the danger Sir John St Aubyn was lately in of being drowned, and his narrow escape'. It was thus:

> Being very fond of the sea, and having got a fine new boat made on purpose to attend his yacht, he had a mind one day, the weather being fair, to try how she would sail, and accordingly set out in this bark from the Mount towards Penzance. But the boat being made very crank, the ballast they had taken in was not sufficient, and the Bart: as they were coming near the town, being fond of showing his boat to the greatest advantage, ordered more sail, which presently overset her.
>
> The steersman immediately leapt off, Sir J. after him so close as to get hold of him: the man with such a clog, though a good swimmer, was soon spent, and just as they were both sinking, another taking hold of Sir John then under water, supported him by the help of an oar till a boat from the shore took 'em both up, just as they were ready to sink. The steersman was gone to the bottom.
>
> Sir J had no appearance of life for some times but by rolling being brought to vomit, he at length revived…[17]

We learn something of the 4th Sir John's character from an anonymous pamphlet from 1771, which has survived in the family archives. 'A Curious Letter' was aimed at the Reverend Blackett, the rector of Stoke Damerel. It followed the consecration of St Aubyn's Chapel in Dock-Town, which Blackett had tried to prevent. But 'Sir John had no objection to his tenants and neighbours being accommodated with a place of worship suiting their convenience'. The pamphleteer went on:

> Sir John St Aubyne, is a protestant gentleman, as such he takes the liberty of thinking for himself; and as a worthy member of the British legislature, allows those who differ from him, to worship God in a manner they deem most consonant with scripture, without oppression or abuse. His tenants, of every persuasion, are in this respect happy in their honourable landlord, and sincerely pray for his felicity... It will be well for you, sir, to learn candour and generosity from the example of the *baronet*.

Sir John and Elizabeth had one son and four talented daughters, who formed a musical quartet and planted a walled garden on the Mount. But like their parents and grandparents, these five also lost their father far too early, when he was only 46; so that the full benefit to come from the Morice property, now developing into 'Dock-Town', would fall into the young hands of the 5th baronet. As this Sir John soon realised, he was about to become one of the richest young men in England.

———◆———

The 5th baronet was 14 years old when his father died in October 1772. He was swiftly sent to board at Westminster School. Here, as reported in the London papers[18]:

> In order the more readily to obtain the money he wanted to supply his extravagances, he procured a schoolfellow just come of age to join with him in the bonds, to whom he pledged his honour or the repayment of every sum borrowed, so soon as he should come of age.

On one occasion, when these bond holders arrived to demand money, he hid himself in a big open chimney, but left one leg exposed. He was saved by a maid, who marched up and down in front of the fireplace singing a poular song of the time '*T'other leg up Sir John, Sir John*'.[19]

In court, his barrister having pleaded that the under-age Sir John was 'incapable of judging the nature of the securities he was induced to grant', the Lord Chancellor ordered settlement in full, with interest at 4 per cent. By the time this case was heard, the 5th Sir John had reached the age of

21 and had escaped from his creditors to France, where he formed a liason with an Italian woman, by whom he had a daughter, while spending three years on an extended Grand Tour. Sadly, both the mistress and the daughter died.[20]

Returning home, he was appointed High Sheriff in 1781 and quickly assumed the responsiblities of head of the family. In March, just after granting his mother 'an additional Annuity of £900 a year', he was alarmed to discover she was going to marry again and wrote:

> I have thought it necesasary to give Mr Baker Notice of my Designs by a letter of which I enclose you a copy:
>
> Sir,
> Being informed that a Treaty of Marriage is on foot between my mother and you I think it proper to inform you that … I am injured to the amount of upwards of [£]10,000 and am come to a Resolution to … file a Bill against her in the Court of Chancery forthwith.
>
> I am Your hble Servt[21]

But it seems that Sir John's concerns were soon assuaged, for Lady St Aubyn married John Baker the following year and they lived happily on his estate in Essex until her death in 1796.[22]

The St Aubyns' Godolphin neighbours had long since soared onto a far higher plane. In 1740, the last heiress had married the Duke of Leeds, for whom her Cornish estate was no more than a detail. The east wing of Godolphin House now served a tenant farmer, the rest given over to servants, farm staff and even a pigsty. The great hall, library and chapel were demolished in 1805, while the gardens and deer park returned to nature. The ancient ties between the Basset and St Aubyn families, on the other hand, had been rekindled by the marriage of Sir John's aunt, Margaret, to Sir Francis Basset of Tehidy in 1756. In 1784, their son, Sir Francis, persuaded his cousin, Sir John St Aubyn, to stand for parliament. Sir Francis was a year older than Sir John and would prove a lifelong friend, one who burned with dynastic ambitions which his cousin was only too happy to assist. St Aubyn was elected alongside Basset as MP for his pocket borough of Penryn and for the next six years joined him in opposition with Charles James Fox, against William Pitt's ministry, but without once making a speech in the House.[23]

The following year, he became Provincial Grand Master of Cornwall's Masonic Lodge, while his friend was proposed by Fox to join Brooks's Club in London, a temple of gambling for its 300 members. 'The gaming', wrote Horace Walpole a few years earlier, 'is worthy the decline of our Empire. The young men lose five, ten, fifteen thousand pounds of an evening'.[24] Brooks's had recently moved to St James' Street and while John remained Grand Master until he died, he was more in his element at this centre of Whig intrigue and excitement, which he joined two years later.

The extent to which St Aubyn risked his fortune is not clear, as his name is absent from the original betting book, but its flavour comes from a typical entry for March 1774: 'Lord Clermont has given Mr Crauford 10 Guiness upon condition of receiving 500 £ from him whenever Mr C. Fox shall be worth £100,000 Clear of Debts'. Gambling at dice or cards was unlimited, with counters for credit. A set are still displayed in the Castle on the Mount, as a caution to later generations, although the extent to which Sir John lost money at the tables has probably been exaggerated.

Meanwhile, at 24 he had fallen in love again, this time with Martha Nicholls, whose large blue eyes, fine features and delicate frame shine out from her portrait by John Opie. She was the 17-year-old daughter of the respected landscape gardener, John Nicholls, who at this time was laying out the grounds at Clowance. Hebe, the first child to come out of their affair, appeared in 1780, followed by James in 1783, who was said to be his father's favourite.[25] Martha was ensconced as chatelaine of St Michael's Mount, where she bore Sir John four more children.[26]

At this point, John found himself enmeshed in the bitter personal rivalry between his cousin Sir Francis and Sir Christopher Hawkins of Trewithen. The Basset estate of Tehidy had earlier been managed by Hawkins' grandfather, during a sixteen-year minority, when as their lawyer he was accused of having misappropriated £60,000. There were long-winded suits in Chancery and the case still rankled with the younger generation. Now Basset and Hawkins, having competed over the control of Cornish boroughs, extended their feud in an attempt to control the County seat returns.

But County politics had always provided a contrast to the borough-mongering: 'For most of the eighteenth century, representation had been monopolised by four familes – the Carews, Bullers, Molesworths and St Aubyns, all families of moderate wealth and great antiquity'.[27] Thus until the 1770s, contested elections had been a rarity, as the gentry agreed the candidates behind closed doors. While many of the borough seats were chosen by the town corporation members and mayor, who could be bribed by the local landowner, the County MPs were elected by all the freeholders. If they were to be swayed in a contested election, it would call for new methods of communication and campaigning.

In 1790, the mood in the country at large was very favourable to Pitt, the young reforming Prime Minister, to whom Hawkins had given unfailing support. Francis Gregor, Hawkins' chosen candidate, declared he was in the running, and Sir William Molesworth, the sitting Whig member, chose to retire. Basset responded by pressing St Aubyn to take up the challenge against this presumptuous newcomer. A leaflet organised by Basset gives a flavour of the mean spirit in which the campaign that followed was orchestrated: Gregor's vanity had, it claimed '…induced him to aspire to a station for which his connections and situation in life evidently never intended him'.[28]

This was not at all the sort of fight to which the free-spirited Sir John was suited and it presented him in entirely the wrong light. Most obviously, in the eyes of the Cornish gentry, his own 'situation in life' was quite at odds with the 'great antiquity' upon which rested the credibility of his claim to the seat. Gregor scored a convincing victory and Sir John retired wounded, and disillusioned with politics. He had other interests to pursue and even seventeen years later, when he returned to the fray and won Helston, he gave up the seat in 1812, two years before the end of the parliament.[29]

Politics had proved a rough trade and the strain it put on John's relationship with Martha Nicholls is only to be imagined. But we do know that around this time, he realised that he no longer loved her. According to the painter J.B. Lane, as he later explained to fellow artist Joseph Farington, John had embraced an unorthodox lifestyle, due to the influence of a profligate clergyman at an early age, who had led him 'into scenes of vice with women and familiarised him to this kind of intercourse'.[30]

This was certainly not William Borlase, who had died in 1772, the same year as the 4th baronet. Evidently, the wisdom of the Lugdvan rector, who had guided the father through adolescence, was sorely missed by the son. This budding baronet had matured surrounded by his four sisters and his doting mother.

But at last Sir John had found his soul mate. Her name was Juliana Vinicombe, an enthralling 21-year-old with deep set eyes,[31] who came from a respectable but modest local family. Like Martha, she was quite outside the social circle from which he was expected to choose a bride. Her father, Martin, was a farmer near Marazion, who had persuaded Sir John to help pay for her education in Cheltenham[32]; her cousin John Vinicombe had recently been ordained as a deacon, at Pembroke College, Oxford, where he remained.[33] Juliana's mother, Margaret, was a Polgrene, from the same yeoman stock as Peter St Aubyn's wrecking and rebel accomplice, Thomas Polgrene, three centuries earlier.[34]

John and Juliana would stay together until death, nearly fifty years later. But in their own act of rebellion, they would only marry in church, after she had borne him eight more children.

CHAPTER 3

REGENCY STYLE

*A large income is the best recipe
for happiness I ever heard of.*

Jane Austen[1]

Sir John and Juliana's relationship was a radical departure from the norms of Cornish society, acknowledged by Winston Graham as an inspiration for his well-known fictional characters, Ross and Demelza Poldark,[2] but hardly so remarkable in a London awash with rakes – a role which John disavowed (but one which his eldest son would eagerly embrace). For the generous baronet remained devoted both to Juliana and indeed to all of his twelve surviving children. The artist, Joseph Farington, noted in his diary: '[a]ll the Children He educates as He wd. have done legitimate Sons and daughters: the latter are placed under the care of His Sister... The eldest Son ... has been at one of the Universities, & His Father now allows Him a separate establishment'.[3]

This conduct fitted with the times, at least among the wealthiest members of society.[4] In 1787, Sir John's sister, Dorothy, had married Thomas Barrett Lennard, the illegitimate son and designated heir of Lord Dacre. After raising a regiment against the French, Thomas would be awarded a baronetcy in his own right in 1801, as wealth once again trumped decorum.[5] Sir Thomas inherited the Dacre estate of Belhouse in Essex, near to Lady St Aubyn and Mr Barker, which suggests how he and Dorothy met.

A more extreme case was George Wyndham, 3rd Earl of Egremont, who fathered more than forty children from his many mistresses, all of whom lived with him at Petworth. But he married his favourite, Elizabeth Ilive, after their five sons had been born. The eldest of these was George Wyndham, a distinguished soldier who was made Lord Leconfield before he died. He inherited his father's Petworth estate, while the entailed Egremont lands went with the title to a legitimate cousin.[6]

The most public example was Mrs Jordan and William, the Duke of Clarence, later George IV. They had nine children together and at first were pilloried for immorality. But after William's 'domestic habits' and desire to live in 'the unpretending quietude of a private country gentleman' endeared him to the public, ballads and pamphlets began to praise 'Dora' Jordan for her maternal 'tender affection' and William for his paternal 'liberality and generosity'. Even Farington, who took a prurient interest in the private lives of the rich, conceded: 'The Duke is equally kind to the Children [Mrs Jordan] had before she lived with him as to those which He acknowledges'.[7]

Among Sir John St Aubyn's four sisters, next to him in age was Catherine. She had married her cousin, John Molesworth, a younger son who had entered the Church. In 1829, their second son, Hender, listed 'a few of the almost innumerable proofs that might be urged of my dear uncle's disinterested generosity, & affectionate disposition of heart'.[8] As well as making generous provision for his sisters and his children, his uncle had paid for Hender's education and holidays too. Hender wrote of how Sir John's...:

> ... old servants are always most nobly pensioned. As a landlord there can not be a kinder. Kind to his own species, he is kind also to the other creatures of God's hand. This merciful man is merciful to his beast, and whenever a faithful horse for instance arrives at a certain age, he is not neglected, but permitted to roam at large on good pastures for the remnant of his days. As a public character his parliamentary conduct was uncorrupt, &, I fully believe, incorruptible.

In 1811, Sir John would lobby the Chancellor as the local MP and even spend thousands of pounds 'out of his own pocket' to save the Packet Station at Falmouth, whose ships were a conduit for information from around the globe, as well as serving the needs of travellers. Sailing from Falmouth in 1809, in his *Poems* Lord Byron wrote: 'I shall not survive the racket, Of this brutal Lisbon Packet'.[9]

Yet following the 1790 election, John evidently became increasingly detached from Cornwall, spending less time there, while still taking care of his responsibilities. From an interlude when he was at Clowance, these notes transcribed from his *Short Abstract of Letters received in 1795* give us some insight into what this entailed.[10]

In January, Mr Smith writes that 'he will come down to Clowance with James and Robert [two of his sons by Martha Nicholls], as soon as Lord Clemons and Lady Jersey has left his House'. A few days later comes 'a very friendly note from [12-year-old] James'; meanwhile 'his mother would not let him go with Mr Smith into Cornwall, until she received an answer to her letter of the 13th'. Then another note from James – 'Been with Mr Baker and Lady St Aubyn visiting'. Then a letter arrives 'from Mrs Nicholls, objecting to the children coming into Cornwall, the holidays being so near'. A few days later, Mrs Nicholls worries that 'her mother very ill'.

Despite his mother's objections, young James left town. But after a few days:

> The Rev. Mr Williamson confesses to 'his uncomfortable situation … Mr James and 2 others had made their escape'. While regarding their youngest ones, Mrs Nicholls 'sends me the Children's Bill with the addition of Jane's wages'.

Hebe, their eldest child, was now aged 15. She informed her father that 'Bedford has desired Mrs Lennard [her aunt Dorothy] to recommend him to [you] as Butler'. Sir John also received news that:

> Mrs Molesworth is staying at home 'on account of the illness of her daughter Barbara'. She expresses 'thanks for the lend of my Horses. Mr and Mrs Prideaux [another married sister] called on them on their way to London and left Hebe with them until their return'. Then Hebe writes again, complaining that Mrs Molesworth 'makes her read to her every morning … will not suffer her to put out her washing'. From Mrs Molesworth, on the other hand, while 'her daughter Barbara has been very ill, Hebe [has been] very attentive to her etc'.

Two years later, Hebe would escape this domestic drudgery, by marrying the younger brother of her Prideaux uncle. Meanwhile, a stream of enquiries flowed from suppliers, such as Captain Wolfe who offered 'to bring …from the Barbados and Jamaica Pine Plants etc'. These would be for the walled garden on the Mount. Among other taxing demands:

> Sir John starts the year being chased by a creditor 'to pay her bond of £1000'. For Irish lottery tickets, Sir John learns that he owes 'a sum of £10/0/0'. Then 'from Mr J. Hunt – arrears of £9/9/0 due to the Devonshire Club'. 'From Mr Wallis, desiring my attendance at a meeting of the Cornwall Agricultural Society.' 'From Sir Francis Basset: Desiring me

to be a subscriber to Mr Collins. Desires to know if I am quite determined not to come into Parliament at the next General Election.' 'From Brooks's Club. I owe £20/0/0, two years subscription to the Club.'

By March, still not a line from Juliana: she was there at Clowance, by his side.

Sir John evidently enjoyed swimming in this world of domestic concerns, temporary crises and unending burdens on his time and money. When he returned to the sophisitication of the metropolis, his town house was for some time at Portland Place, with a country seat variously at Woburn Farm, Chertsey, or Woolmers, in Hertfordshire.[11] In London, he kept in touch with the Cornish MPs, not least through the Cornish Club founded by his father's generation. One of these was Sir William Lemon, from Carclew near Truro. The sitting member in 1790, he went on to become the father of the Commons. His passion for playing his organ at night disturbed his London neigbours in Bryanston Square. In 1791, Sir John bought it from him for £800 and had it installed in the church on the Mount, where this organ, designed by John Avery of Bristol, is still being played today.[12]

The development of 'Dock-Town' next to Plymouth was now proceeding exponentially. At the time of the new chapel built there in 1771, 5000 houses had existed; a century later, there would be more like 20,000,[13] together with all the infrastucture of the Dockyard itself. The area became known as Devonport and it proved even more rewarding than Sir Francis Basset's mines at Tehidy. Tin could only be extracted and sold once, but under the widespread leasehold system at this time, houses reverted to the landlord at the end of a building lease, and the sale was repeated next time, not of just the land, but of the bricks and mortar as well.

The system had advantages. Before planning controls were introduced in the 1940s, landlords were the main protection against overdevelopment, with a vested interest in the long term quality of their freehold estate. Young aspiring couples and the elderly alike, benefitted from the low cost of short leases, giving greater security than a rack-rented home. But leaseholders were always on a moving staircase going in the wrong direction and there were many traps for the unwary, who failed to trade up or move on before the value of their holding was dissipated, especially if their landlords were ruthless.

Hender wrote of John's 'delicacy and honour with respect to the leases on the Clowance estate [which] can not be too highly praised', while in

Devenport such dealings were in the hands of his steward John Coles, of whom John wrote in his will as follows: 'my sense of his attachment to me and of his care and fidelity and of the interest he has taken in my concerns'. The fact was that the revenues pouring in from the development meant that John could afford to be as fair to his tenants, as to others, and it gave him pleasure to be so.

For tradesmen, feelings were rather different. Apart from the ferry, there were two turnpike bridges connecting to Plymouth and Stoke, where the lucrative toll income was jointly shared by the St Aubyn and Edgecumbe families.

Sir John needed an outlet for these riches beyond family, clubs and betting, and he found this in the arts and sciences. In 1780, he had come across the 'Cornish Wonder', the mostly self-taught painter John Opie. On St Michael's Mount, there is his first full length portrait of his patron, at the age of 22, in brown coat, knee breeches, powdered hair, hat and cane in hand, with a greyhound. The island castle looms in the background.[14] He had just met Martha, whom Opie also painted.

He was to paint Sir John several more times, including making copies of a portrait by Joshua Reynolds, which John had given to his cousin Basset, in return for one of Sir Francis by Gainsborough. The two young MPs smiled at each other across the walls of the Blue Drawing Room on the Mount; then in 2012, the copy which Opie had made for this purpose was replaced by the Reynolds original, which had been bought back from Basset's descendants at auction. The Opie currently hangs in the main dining room of Brooks's, lent to Sir John's old club.

Opie's second wife spoke of Sir John as 'that early and just appreciator of the merits of Mr Opie, who, through the whole of his professional career, united the kindness of a friend to the services of a patron'.[15] His first marriage had been a disaster, something to which his patron could perhaps relate, as well as enjoying his Cornish sense of humour. Asked what he mixed his colours with, Opie replied 'With brains, Sir'. Walking past St Martin's Church with his friend Godwin, an aetheist, 'Ha!' said Opie, 'I was married in that Church'. 'Indeed', said Godwin, 'and I was christened in it.' ''Tis not a good shop', replied Opie, 'for their work does not last.'[16]

Sir John commissioned Opie to paint Juliana and also her cousin, the Oxford don John Vinicombe, who left his image to Pembroke College.[17] Juliana's portrait was mislaid for a while and then found at auction in 1900. It has since hung close to that of her husband on the Mount castle drawing room wall. He also introduced Opie to his sister Catherine, who became a fine artist in her own right.[18]

The respect in which both the Royal Academy and the public held Opie, lost to art at the age of only 46, is reflected in the solemnity of his funeral. A hearse and six horses, three mourning coaches, with six horses each, and twenty-seven other mourning coaches and pair, with thirty private carriages, formed the procession to his grave in St Paul's Cathedral, next to Reynolds, his friend and mentor. Sir John St Aubyn and his Basset cousin, Sir Francis – whose political manoevres had by now elevated him as Lord de Dunstanville to the Upper House – were two of the six pall bearers, who also bore the cost.[19]

Sir John was also a voracious collector of engravings and etchings, and when auctioned by Phillips after his death,[20] their sale attracted 'the principal connoisseurs in the kingdom; and ... lasted for seventeen days'. The collection retained by Juliana, when sold on her death in 1856, amounted to a further one thousand lots auctioned over six days, at their Lime Grove residence in Putney.[21] Sir John had taken this house on lease in his final years and to provide for Juliana in widowhood.[22]

But Sir John's lasting contribution as a collector were his fossils. Dr Borlase's moral teachings fell on deaf ears, but the scholar's lifelong study of Cornwall's mineralogical riches inspired his boy pupil, some of his own rocks forming the basis of Sir John's assiduous collecting.

In 1794, he commissioned Count de Bournon, a refugee from the French revolution, to arrange his portfolio. The count was the foremost minerologist of his time, behind the founding of the Geological Society of London. Sir John's work in the field earned him election as a fellow of the Royal Society, the Society of Antiquaries and of the Linaean Society.

In 2009, the Geological Society mounted a nationwide exhibition of the St Aubyn Collection, which he had donated to the Devonport Library, later presented to the Plymouth Museum. The exhibition noted that 'Sir John St Aubyn's ability to network and communicate ideas is well respresented by the diversity of labels in his mineral collection. He obviously had many connections with dealers during his lifetime'.[23] He never contacted the Cornish collector, Philip Rashleigh, who was perhaps his rival, but his acquisition of Lord Bute's collection in 1799, which he had catalogued by Dr Babington, secured its future for science.

Not everything in Sir John's life was so successful. Martha Nicholls, as the mother of six of Sir John's children, remained an extended but disconsolate part of his family for forty years, as her worrisome correspondence suggests. When Martha died in 1829, she was buried in the cemetery at St Michael's

Mount, a desolate epitaph carved on her gravestone: *This stone is erected to the memory of an affectionate Mother by a dutiful son.* This was James, her eldest son, who had rushed to be by Martha's side at the last and was the chief mourner at her funeral.[24]

Sir John was not present. A glimpse into their relationship comes from this record by Martha's descendant, Diana Hartley, writing in 1977:

> Miss Eileen Mudge, an old inhabitant of Marazion, can remember talking to one of the old hereditary Mount boatmen when a bright light appeared in one of the upper windows of the castle, and he said 'That do be the window where the old Sir John used to put a light to be seen over to Ludgvan by Mrs Nicholls, who he used to call his other wife'.[25]

Living in Sir John's shadow, on an allowance of £300 a year,[26] must have been hard to bear for Martha, even if out of consideration, he left Juliana at Clowance during those times when we imagine he received her and their children on the island. Nor did the children find it easy to come to terms with their situation, faced with society's vexed attitudes, accepting the child as innocent while viewing the parents as steeped in turpitude.[27] In her highly perceptive work *Illegitimacy,* historian Kate Gibson has recently portrayed these tensions with incisive detail, not least in her study of James St Aubyn.

James – Martha and Sir John's eldest son – was only 7 when he witnessed the trauma of his parents' separation. He grew into a charming libertine, imbued with good looks and a lustful insouciance. In his twenties, he had three daughters by his first mistress, Sara White. He felt he had to keep them secret from most of his family until the youngest was at least 5, and no St Aubyns attended when they were baptised under a false name in 1811. Seven years later, when one of them died, only two St Aubyn relatives whom James had 'acquainted with this secret part of my family concerns' attended her funeral. Even in 1822, his mother Martha refused to meet the other two girls, which he found 'indelicate, unpolite, and unfeeling'.[28] Yet once better known, the surviving girls were warmly embraced into the whole family.

We know this from James' diaries, where he bared his soul from 1810 into old age. They begin with 26-year-old James falling for Henrietta Caldwell, whose father had just inherited her family's Irish estate in County Meath. They met at a New Year's house party at Belhouse, the seat of James' uncle, Sir Thomas Barrett Lennard. After a six month courtship, Henrietta eluded her chaperone and absconded with James '…to Henley where we slept.

A night never to be forgotten!!!.' James now became engaged to Henrietta, but for another five months hoped to leave his mistress, Sara, and their children, without causing a scene:

> I had been obliged to use means for breaking with Sara, with whom I had lived upon terms of the most uninterrupted affection ever since June 20 1806. To accomplish this, my letters became colder, and my presence less frequent... I could never find courage to break to her the cause of my actions, but was in hope that a continuance of such a conduct would [lead] her in time to the knowledge of the truth.

Almost inevitably, this attempt to skirt disaster invited it:

> '... in this however, I was deceived, for she fancied that I had ingaged in another Connexion equally injurious to my honour [i.e. another mistress] and hurtful to her feelings. At length ... she discovered the evidence of her, who had stolen my affections from her; upon her she called while I was out of town... As I had never divulged the secret of this connexion to Henrietta, so she was confounded....

But Henrietta, either deeply in love, or fearful now that she was compromised by James, chose to act 'as mediator between my injured Sara and myself'. In his diary, James describes the ensuing break with Sara as 'the saddest story which befell man', relating 'the agony which struggled in my bosom' at leaving 'my little children... After this sad interview', he went to stay in his lodgings in Knightsbridge, 'there to dine & spend the evening with Henrietta'.[29]

Yet three weeeks later, after seeing his father for Christmas and exactly one year after first meeting his betrothed Henrietta, James visited Sara again on 1 January 1811. This was in fact her birthday:

> ... the day of course was passed in alternate pleasure and tears, for the memory of the exceeding happiness which we had enjoyed so much together was clouded by the consciousness that it was vanished for ever ... who can describe my feelings in leaving the arms in which I used to repose, and permitting her to go to that now solitary bed, which I used to share with her?

Over the next two and a half weeks of mid-winter, James dined with Henrietta nine times and with Sara once, as each vied for his affections. By late February, these conflicts had brewed into another crisis:

> I went to town for the purpose of seeing Henrietta, who had written a letter to me, absolving me from my engagement towards her, a step she took in consequence of some misrepresentation of me from Sara: upon seeing her she was fully satisfied that my poor friend had been actuated to mislead her from the wish of bringing me back to herself...

Then three weeks later, at St Andrew's Church, Holborn, on 20 March 1811, James' and Sara's second and third daughters were christened, in a bizarre attempt at reconciliation between the rivals:

> Anne Henrietta was my second child christened, Mrs Fr Halliday, her mother's sister being Godmother & whose name is Anne and for whom Sara stood proxy, and Miss Caldwell, whose name is Henrietta being the other Godmother. The third child was christened Elizabeth Sara, Lady Elizabeth Halliday [Sara's sister-in-law] and the child's mother being Godmothers, Miss Caldwell standing for the former, and the mother for herself: I was godfather to both children.

The little girls' parents, as recorded in the parish register, were 'James and Sara West'.[30] His true family name he reserved for his betrothed.

All this time, his diary indicates that James moved easily among both his siblings and his legitimate cousins, as well as between Sir John, Martha and Juliana. Like the Egremont boys, he had been educated at Westminster, and then at Oriel College, Oxford, giving him the 'ready-made stamp of belonging'. When he was in London, he attended the Westminster School annual dinner, with its enduring friendships.[31]

James would eventually inherit his father's free estate at the age of 56. Before this, he qualified as a barrister, living in lodgings and dependent on his paternal allowance. His diaries reveal his love of theatre, both as a critic and as an actor, who performed on stage in the innovative farces of his friend, the playwright John Poole.[32] His diary sometimes reads like the script for one of them. James often decried his father's 'cruel and deliberate treatment', by controlling his income, for example when he was at first 'exceedingly averse to the match' with Henrietta. Two years later Sir John relented, but for James it was too late – Sara was now carrying yet another daughter by him. A son born of his affair with Henrietta died in childhood, and thereafter she chose her own path.[33] Meanwhile, James sped around England in his horse-drawn tandem, hunting and horse racing his diversions, as new romantic liaisons filled his diary. Appearing as the protagonist in *The Mountineers,* he declared on stage: 'I will go prowl – but look I meet no fathers'.[34]

Sir John's alleged harshness may simply have been owing to his strained finances from time to time; in 1816, for example, he suddenly left England to spend three years in Geneva, where he had sheltered in his youth from his creditors. But by 1819, after disposing of the extravagant Wolmers estate – which he had only purchased seven years earlier – Sir John could return home and indulge James with a Grand Tour of France, Switzerland and Italy.[35] James eventually wed Sara in 1829, his two girls acquiring their father's name at last. He had embraced his friend Poole's advice, to find happiness 'settled quietly down in the country…[where] every creature about you loves you, purely, wholly, distractedly'.[36]

The eldest son of the 5th Sir John and Juliana Vinicombe was William. He was born eleven years after his half-brother, James, and chose to conform. He married his cousin, a daughter of Sir Thomas Barrett Lennard and his father's sister, Dorothy. The 'natural' born Sir Thomas doted on animals. He instructed his servants to leave out water bowls for the thirsty rats in his houses, and balanced his love of hunting by laying false trails across his land, so the hounds never caught a fox. He wore shabby clothes and was once tipped when he opened the gates to his house, and his visitors mistook him for a servant.[37]

William St Aubyn's eccentricities were less charming. His father held the advowson of Stoke Damerel and in 1828 he nominated William for the rectory. But to the people of Devonport over the next fifty years, William became known as 'the bad St Aubyn'. He began his ministry by immediately dismissing the Reverend Hawker, a popular curate who had long had the running of the church, under William's absentee predecessor. This was in flagrant breach of the undertakings William had given parishioners just before his induction. Hawker remained a thorn in his side, building with public subscription his own church, where he held episcopal services of common prayer for many years, in defiance of William and his bishop.[38]

This set the tone for a series of disputes between William and his parish, many concerning the graveyard – imposing ruinous charges for burials, cramming too many bodies under its turf, levelling the ground of burial mounds. Every attempt to resolve disputes met with a legalistic response. It was as if William had consciously abjured the memory of his grandfather and embraced the mean spirit from 1771 of his erstwhile predecessor, the Reverend Blackett.

William was no kinder to his parents Sir John and Juliana, constantly upbrading them for living in sin; they finally married in 1822, the same year as he did. The Anglican hierarchy to which William now aspired disdained illegitimacy; none so labelled was ever appointed a bishop.[39] So unlike James, as a churchman William evidently agonised over his birth status. He seems to have been driven to desperation by the sanctimony exuded by the Anglican prelates of his day. This is evident because four years after his society wedding, he committed a family solecism of the worst order.

The 'King's Most Excellent Majesty' received a petition purporting to come from Sir John, expressing 'a great affection for his aforesaid natural Children who have always borne and used the Surname of St Aubyn'.[40] As he intended to settle his free estate on his children, the letter expressed the wish 'that the said Surname of St Aubyn should be confirmed to them by your Majesty's Royal Authority and that they should bear the Arms of the ancient family of St Aubyn with due distinctions ... according to the Laws of Arms'. Such a request was not unusual at this time. Between 1811 and 1823 alone, 'Garter King of Arms' at the College of Arms had had to deal with no less than five petitions from the illegitimate sons of peers, for a confirmation of their surname.[41] So matters proceeded under the auspices of General Nayler, Garter, who wrote accordingly on 14 June 1826:

> Not being fortunate enough to see you before you left town, I beg to inform you that the several Patents of the Armorial Ensigns for your Children are now nearly completed – and being called upon to defray the usual fees which amount ... to the sum of £629/2s/6d, I shall feel much obliged by your favouring me with a draft for that sum.

But it was not only the demand for this enormous sum which drew an immediate and startling response, as we can surmise from this second letter from Garter to 'Dear Sir John', just eight days later:

I am favoured with your letter of the 19th instant and beg to assure you that it contains the first inclination I have ever received that you were not fully aware not only of the object of the petition signed by you but also of the probable expense... Upon which the warrant signed by His Majesty was founded. Not having the smallest doubt on the subject, the *nine Patents* of the Amorial Ensigns have actually long since been emblazoned on vellum...

I cannot but feel as extremely unpleasant, namely to request that the Royal Licence be cancelled – but nevertheless should such be your wish, I shall endeavour to get this done. *All this might have been avoided had Mr William John St Aubyn even hinted to me that you had the least objection to the Arms being assigned to your Children...*

William had apparently enveigled the grant of this licence. Meanwhile, his half-brother James had been gaily flaunting the family insignia, without a care for the consents or protocols required by law, in cases of so-called 'natural' children.[42] For even when 'natural' children were formally granted armorial bearings, they still had to observe the 'due distinctions ... according to the Laws of Arms'. Specifically, the Arms derived by an illegitimate offspring require a truncated strip that runs from the upper right to the lower left of the armorial shield – a cruel heraldic slur, for it is known as the '*baton sinister*'.

Whatever supercilious Anglicans might think, by marrying Sir John four years earlier, Juliana had at last legitimised her children before God, under the canon law of the Church. Yet ever since the barons had held the Convocation of Merton in 1341, the civil courts had refused to recognise the heraldic lineage – or any other right of inheritance – of children born before a marriage.[43] So it surely appalled Juliana, having at last achieved something of the legitimacy she had so long craved, to think that this mark of bastardy would still attach to her children and to all her descendants, under the terms of this Royal Licence. It must have seemed that yet again, William was tormenting his parents with the circumstances of his birth; and indeed had perhaps obtained his father's signature to this petition by a subterfuge.

Garter fortunately proved most sympathetic to the distress this caused the St Aubyns, accustomed as he now was to dealing with Royal Licences for 'natural' children. Thus an early letter ended 'PS. All my family desire their kindest remembrances to Lady St Aubyn and the Ladies', while in another he wrote 'I feel much obliged for your kind enquiries as to my family – They are all at Hayes and quite well – May I beg my respectful Comp[limen]ts to Lady St Aubyn and the young Ladies...' But it was three whole years later, before this letter from Garter signalled a resolution of the delicate issues involved:

> My dear Sir John,
> I regret not being at home yesterday when you did me the honour of a call as I should have mentioned to you that after a great deal of pro and con Mr Peel agreed to *a new warrant to bear the name only* and this morning on my calling at the Secretary of State's Office I had the pleasing intelligence that the Royal Warrant was just returned from Windsor signed by the King ... permit me to add that I assure you no delay in the least has occurred as it is no small favour to get a Royal Warrant cancelled. I beg my best regards to Lady St Aubyn...'

It would take reform of the House of Lords and the social upheaval of the Great War, before the civil laws of inheritance were changed by the Legitimacy Act of 1926. But even after futher legislation in 1976, the inheritance of arms and titles still accords with the Convocation of Merton.

A decade after this episode, there can have been little surprise that in his will, Sir John left William and his wife a mere £100 each.[44] For taking account of their marriage settlement, '...[and] otherwise by Cash advances made by me to him and on his account and by presenting him to the Rectory of Stoke Damarel in the County of Devon, I have made sure such provision for him as I think expedient sufficient and proper'. William remained as rector in Stoke until his death in 1877, when his nephew William succeeded him until his own death in 1894. This younger St Aubyn did much to restore harmony, recalled in 1901 as 'the late beloved rector', in the parish magazine which he had started.[45]

To his other surviving children, meanwhile (Juliana's second and third boys had died in infancy) Sir John left £10,000 each, as a debt on the estate, to be paid out of the Devonport rent roll.

Devonport and St Michael's Mount, with its historic endowments in West Cornwall, were left to James. Clowance and the old Cornish estate, which in value were now only a modest part of the whole, were entailed to the elder son of John's now deceased sister, Catherine Molesworth, on condition that he took the St Aubyn name. As the legitimate heir, John also left him 'a silver embossed tankard partly gilt formerly presented to Sir William Morice by the States of Lubeck at the Restoration'.

John's legacy was a generous and liberal expression of his beliefs, but also accorded with the custom of his time. While Clowance was entailed, lawyers in the Middle Ages had devised the means to break an entail and since 1540, the process had been enshrined in law. Indeed, it is probable that the Mount and Devonport were also entailed. So where John drew the line may simply have reflected his desire to spread his huge wealth around the family, in particular among those of whom he was most fond. But at the same time, to have denied his legitimate Molesworth heirs the original St Aubyn birthright would have offended social convention and even spawned a legal dispute[46]; while the fact that the 'barton of Clowance' had escaped the royalist sequestor in the Civil War suggests a form of inheritance which was ironclad.

John Molesworth was already 58 and without an heir when his uncle died, and so it must have pleased Sir John St Aubyn to know that the eventual beneficiary of Clowance would be Hender Molesworth, to whom he was obviously so close, and whose own son would also inherit the Molesworth estates and baronetcy in 1912. Likewise, Juliana could be confident in the prospects of her fourth son Edward, to whom his half-brother James' inheritance was entailed.

—◆—

Sir John's long life thus produced the greatest disruption in the St Aubyn family story since the Devon line's extinction during the Hundred Years' War. The period then begun, when the family's focus had become almost entirely centred on Cornwall, was now closing. At a time when the British Empire was about to enlarge to a third of the globe, so would the spread of the St Aubyn family.

This change was dramatically marked by the complete destruction of Clowance, the St Aubyn seat since the 1350s, in two fires which struck the house in quick succession, the first only shortly after John had made his will. It was reported on 17 November 1836:

> It appears to have ... been occasioned by a beam in the kitchen chimney taking fire, owing to a defect in its construction. It was first discovered about five o'clock, by a servant, who with much difficulty, escaped with her life, but the fire by that time

gained such strength as to baffle every attempt to subdue it. At half-past nine the whole of the roofs of the back wings had fallen in.[47]

Then fire engines arrived from Helston, 'with a body of constables and yeomanry from the neighbourhood', who saved the rest of the house.

It is curious that only a month before, a local man had sent a letter to Sir John at 63 Portland Place, his London home, concerning 'George Beckett your keeper', warning that 'many Gentlemen is thought feared of by the Public owing to the wickedness of their Servants'. This writer's dog had run loose in a field near Clowance and '… Beckett saw it and as it is the delight of his heart to kill such animals, soon it was shot. I would rather he had gone into my field and shot one of my horses'. He went on to disclose:

> The same day thousands of people was at Clowance seeing the Masons going to church and some little dogs followed their owners their [sic]. Beckett saw them, and as soon as the main body of the people had left he shot two, I think one more by the hind legs, beat out its brains against the pale.
>
> I should hope there is not such another monster of cruelty to be found in the Kingdom. He is a disgrace to any Gentleman to have him in his service… You would have heard of some of his tricks long ago, but the general opinion is that he would not dare to do as he has where he not sanctioned by you.[48]

The writer referred John to his own son or to the rector at Crowan, for 'my character and the character of my family'. Whatever was coming to the keeper, he would 'as Beckett of Canterbury didn't, thickly deserve it'.

This letter reveals so much about the nature of society at this time, especially that a keeper could hold the neighbourhood in thrall, because the inhabitants thought their landlord intended it. This is perhaps why it was preserved in the St Aubyn family papers, as an insight, even though Sir John had ordered all his personal correspondence to be destroyed when he died. He must have been horrified by this account and no doubt Beckett was dismissed on the spot. Whether this would have left him with such a grudge that in revenge he caused the fire a month later, is of course the stuff of novels.

There can be no connection with the second fire, which took place four years after John had died and completely destroyed the old house. But it was insured and a new Victorian Clowance emerged, where the Molesworth St Aubyns continued to live happily until the Great War. The paintings and furniture had mercifully been saved and now grace the rooms at Pencarrow, the Molesworth seat near Bodmin.

Three years after the first fire, the 5th Sir John St Aubyn died at Lime Grove, Putney. The majestic procession that transported his body to Crowan left London on 17 August 1839, and drew 20,000 followers along the way. There was the hearse, drawn by six horses dressed with feathers and velvet; seven mourning coaches dressed likewise; and twelve gentlemen's carriages attended by the coachmen, and twenty-six porters and footmen, all in black silk hat bands and gloves. They did not arrive in Devonport until the 23rd, as the West Briton reported[49]:

> Here the remains were attended by the Mayor and Council, and other dignitaries of the town; the Board of Commissioners, the Borough Police, the boys of St. John's School (of which the baronet had been a patron); the girls of St. John's School; the Town Sergeant (with the mace of the Corporation covered with crepe); four clergymen; two beadles, and numerous attendants on horseback, not to mention the private carriages of mourners from the locality.

All along the route the shops were closed, and the tolling bells of the neighbouring churches and chapels proclaimed that a great man was passing to his grave. On 28 August, after mourners had paid their respects in St Austell and Truro, Sir John's coffin finally reached Clowance:

> ... the body lay all day in state under a canopy of black cloth, with plumes and feathers. Here it was attended by twelve boys from the Free School, in crepe scarfs; eight poor men in cloaks, standing bareheaded; eight male servants in crepe bands; twelve girls from the Free School, in crepe sashes and bows; seven female servants in hoods and scarfs; twelve poor widows in hoods and scarfs; and two mutes.

Early the next morning, the gates of the park at Clowance were thrown open, as people from the neighbouring towns began to assemble. All who could gain admission to the house were treated with refreshments. By the start of the funeral, two rows of spectators, 20,000 or 30,000 in number, had lined the road from the house to Crowan church. The crowd parted as the procession now made its solemn way, led by the master and mistress of the Free School and 150 of their pupils:

> Following these walked a hundred members of the Order of Freemasons, bearing their banner, Sword of State, a Bible on a black cushion, with the vacant jewel, etc. Then came a hundred tenants wearing silk hat-bands and gloves, an undertaker, two mutes, and thirty poor widows, the latter in black gowns, hoods, and scarfs. Before the body, which rested on a car, 'impelled by tenantry' walked the officiating clergyman and two leading mourners, whilst behind it in their respective order came thirty relatives, a hundred clergy and gentlemen, twenty-five servants, and, finally a hundred and fifty more tenants in hat-bands and gloves.

Following John's burial in the family vault, where Juliana would join him seventeen years later, the Masons held their own ceremony, on 3 September 1839 at Bodmin parish church. In his address, the Reverend Henry Grylls spoke these words[50]:

> His charity and generosity were unbounded, his honour of the brightest lustre; and his later years were devoted to the best objects; to the support of useful and scientific institutions; to the encouragement of youthful talent.

Sir John's love of his family was ' blended with a fidelity of attachment not to be surpassed to one from whom he had never swerved, and to whom he had for many years been united by the most sacred ties'.

CHAPTER 4

VICTORIAN VALUES

*The history of England is emphatically
the history of progress.*

Thomas B. Macaulay

James St Aubyn's inheritance of the Mount proved something of a millstone, deprived of the fabulous income which his father had enjoyed. For many years, no member of the family lived there and when Queen Victoria paid a visit, as the royal yacht sailed past Mount's Bay in 1846, she was met by the housekeeper, Thomasine Simms.[1] There was the sinking fund to raise £130,000 in bequests to John's children, while Juliana's Lime Grove residence cost £5000 a year. This left James with an allowance of only £1200. Yet after both Martha and Sir John had died, he often visited Juliana or even stayed with her in Putney.

James was now nearing 60 and apparently settled with Sara White and their daughters. But with independent means returned the restlessness of his youth. Eleven years on, well into the queen's reign which exalted traditional family values, he defiantly fathered yet another child. Sara brought proceedings in Doctor's Commons – the civil law court for matrimonial disputes – and James agreed to 'settle the unfortunate Law-Business [with] Mrs St A'. Six weeks later, his boy was christened 'James St Aubyn the son of James and Mary St Aubyn Luke'. No family members attended and it was five years before Sara could forgive this ultimate betrayal. After she returned to him, they chose life in London and lodgings in Great Portland Street. Here his diary ends.[2]

Devonport, the main source of James' income apart from the Mount endowment, was left in the capable hands of his half-brother Edward, the heir to whom he had drawn close. Edward was born sixteen years after James and by then, Sir John's extended family had settled into a comfortable pattern. This stability no doubt helped him to emerge as the one to inherit the family mantle, after proving himself as a diligent London lawyer. Like George Wyndham in Sussex, given the direction of a flourishing estate, he acquired a natural authority, rendering the incidence of his 'natural' birth irrelevant.

By now, most of the 1810 acres of Stoke Damerel belonged to 'the devisees of the late Sir John St Aubyn, and let on liberal building leases'. Nearly 24,000 inhabitants by 1800 had, by 1840, grown to nearly 34,000. Apart from Devonport itself, as 'Dock-Town' had been renamed in the 1820s, there were the 'handsome and populous suburbs' of Stoke and Morice town within the municipality, which since 1832 had also enjoyed its own MP. But as the first Mayor of Devonport, Edward wielded a great deal more power than a backbencher.[3] He planned the town's development, as it grew to 50,000 inhabitants by the 1870s and more beyond, from 1859 spurred by the railway connected to Saltash, on Brunel's wrought-iron masterpiece of engineering across the Tamar. The revenue from the toll bridges, reconstructed after securing an act of parliament, provided a growing income, until sold in 1890 for nearly £250,000, shared between the St Aubyn and Edgecumbe estates.

As estate manager, Edward drew a generous salary. His father had left him an extra £5000, plus an allowance to send his eldest son, John, to Eton and Cambridge. In 1828, Edward had married Emma Knollys at the British Embassy in Paris, where her father was posted. He and Emma were well placed to provide for three more sons and three daughters.

As a fifth-former, John St Aubyn took part in the last Eton 'Ad Montem'. This 'most picturesque of all school customs', as scholar Wasey Sterry later recorded, was being abolished 'after lasting certainly three, probably four, hundred years'.[4] John ranked as a corporal, which meant wearing 'a red tail-coat with gilt buttons and white trousers, with a crimson sash, sword-belt with gilt buckles and sword, and cocked hat and plume like a field-marshal's'. The 'Captain of Montem' led 500 Etonians – some as sergeants, others as musicians, corporals, polemen or servants, according to place – three times round the schoolyard, with the queen and Prince Albert among the guests looking on, from the windows above the cloister gate. Once the ensign waved his flag, 'the corporals drew their swords and slashed in half, if they could, the polemen's staffs, and the procession started off through the playing fields to Salt Hill'.

On arriving 'ad montem', the procession and their onlookers stood around the base of the mound. The ensign again waved the flag: 'backwards and forwards, round the neck, round the waist, round the knees and then the ankles, aloft, below, with a final flourish supposed to mean "God save the King!"' So ended the ceremony.

Travellers on the Bath Road to London were now forced to stop 'ad montem' and pay 'salt money', which by 1844 could raise a thousand pounds during the rest of the day. But after the expenses of the riotous feasting that followed, the Captain of Montem would be lucky to clear £200 as his perquisite. The railway had arrived in 1841, and the unweildy crowd of spectators combined with the wily evasion of the route by others, heralded a long-sought end to this wild tradition, by the sober new headmaster. But its memory lives on, not least in John's splendid uniform, still displayed in the Mount castle.

Dr Hawtrey was a modernising head, who encouraged the teaching of mathematics for the first time at Eton, although only as an optional extra while John was there.[5] But it was one where he excelled, even preserving exam questions and his answers for his scrapbook. Later, at Trinity College, Cambridge, he would obtain a double first class ordinary degree in maths and religious studies. But Cambridge would come after spending more than a year on the Continent, where revolution was formenting.

Three decades before, the Congress of Vienna had brought peace to Europe, at the end of the Napoleonic Wars. But it had looked backwards, restoring ancient kingships, when their citizens were already alive to the lure of freedom. In 1848, the political and social strains of this faultline erupted.

Meanwhile, John St Aubyn had started his travels as soon as he left school, writing in July 1847 to a German friend Moritz Wiessner, from a hotel in Dieppe, after his recent stay with him[6]:

> … finally we came to Amiens, where we spent a whole day around the cathedral, the most beautiful Gothic building in existence, with the possible exception of Cologne. And so to Rouen, this capital of the Gothic architectural style, where we stayed for eight days. On the fourth day I had the pleasure of seeing my father and the rest of my numerous family, which made me very happy since I hadn't seen my brothers for a year and a half.

He had written in German, ending with 'We are generally satisfied with France, although I would very much like to be in Dresden at this moment', where the Wiessners lived.

By December, we find John in Rome, reading *The Roman Advertiser*, a weekly journal for English tourists, where he stayed until March, by which time the first rumblings of discontent were being reported. Then on reaching Naples, on 15 May he was caught in the bloody repression of the Neapolitan liberals by Ferdinand II's Swiss guard. His letter home, written two days later, describes how the Swiss troops let him past their barrier to the Toledo, after he 'gave them a 5 franc piece to drink the health of the Inglesi'. His friends held back, so John 'advanced with a fat Italian from Milan whom I got very intimate with in the course of the day'. There was 'no one near us but an officer, when on a sudden a window in house No.3, opened and a shot through the head laid the officer dead, close to us':

> At that moment as if by magic every window in No.4, not 30 yds. from where I was standing ... opened upon our battery and the infantry close to it. Three cannons were immediately wheeled forward and at a distance of 20 yds, pointed at this unfortunate house. The moment the firing began all the lazzaroni etc., in the square ran away like smoke and my Italian friend and I were the only people besides the troops in the whole piazza.

The engagement then nearly cost John his life:

> The soldiers in the piazza ... and the 3 cannons all fired at the windows at once, and the people inside fired from every window. At last they blew the door open and soldiers rushed in... The whole thing from the time the first shot was fired, when I bolted behind the battery, was over in five minutes. I saw three carts of killed brought out of that house alone... I saw a soldier shot where I had been standing half a minute before, the ball went in at his temple and came out, at his ear. I saw him carried away... he was in a horrible state. Altogether I had rather a providential escape. Austin and the rest of our party who saw the firing but could not get near us were in a dreadful fright on my account, they say Austin looked as white as a sheet and it certainly took away his appetite for dinner.

In the evening, John's party 'went on board a French three decker and passed the night there, as it was not considered safe on shore'. But the next day, they were back at their hotel, where:

> We were awoke this morning by a sergeant and four soldiers with muskets, who begged our pardons, but said their 'devoir' obliged them to search our beds etc, for arms, which was accordingly done. They found some pistols in Tell's room next to mine which they gave him back, after complimenting him upon the make.

John's parents may not have been too relieved to know that 'To-morrow we take the steamer for Sicily, she stops a day each at Messina, Syracuse and Catania, and then goes on to Malta where we stay a few days and then come back here'. He ended his letter affectionately, letting his little sister know he had 'expended £4. in a coral necklace and bracelet for her which I hope she will like ... also bought a quantity of Neapolitan music, Tarantelles etc., for her'.

After Cambridge, John set off on his travels again, with his school friend Wyndham, carrying letters of introduction to Portugal and Spain. After that he came up to London, where his grandmother's house at the base of Putney Hill was handy, now served by a railway station, opposite the front gates:

> The mansion derived its name from a grove of limes which formed an avenue to the house. The structure was one of those thoroughly English mansions, erected for convenience and comfort rather than for display. The apartments were spacious and lofty, and contained a rich store of pictures and articles of vertu; among the former were several by Opie.[7]

John joined the Amateur Musical Society, whose patron was Prince Albert, playing in the violin section. Before the last concert of the season, the young bachelor had won the heart of Lady Elizabeth, the second daughter of the Marquis of Townshend. The *Illustrated London News* announced their engagement on 3 May 1856 and this knowledge must have filled his grandmother with pride. Juliana died only a month later, reflecting on how far life had changed in the nine decades since her primitive childhood in Marazion. Her beauty and intelligence had played their own part; and not least ambition, as when she steered Sir John to entrust the entail of his free estate not to the eldest, but to the most promising of their sons.

One of the greatest changes in Juliana's lifetime had been the extension of the franchise. Her son Edward was the first, after nine successive generations of St Aubyns since 1551, not to be elected as an MP. The rules of the game had shifted across the nation, while in Cornwall potential candidates had to contend with the 'Lemon connection'. Sir William Lemon, the MP whose organ had been bought for the Mount church in 1790, continued as the Tory member for the county until 1826, when he retired as Father of the House. Then in 1831, his son Sir Charles confounded his opponents by drawing on his father's Tory support, while standing as a Liberal. He held his seat until 1857.

The borough seats were still controlled by a few local magnates, such as the Tory Lord Falmouth. But the more electors they registered, the harder it became to maintain influence. So Falmouth and other leading Tories neglected to build new supporters, with the result that the Liberals gained a preeminence in organisation and registrations at the county level. Meanwhile, the historic sense of Cornish difference had now transmuted into nonconformism. Wesley's sweep through West Cornwall – to the anguish of the Borlase rectors in the eighteenth century[8] – now meant that ' by the time of the 1851 Religious Census, Methodists of various types far outnumbered followers of the Church of England'. Thus Liberal activists could take advantage of 'the obvious nexus between Methodism and Liberalism'.[9]

The retirement of Sir Charles Lemon nevertheless offered the Tories an opening in 1857, as he had occupied the seat held by tradition for the agricultural interest, the other one being for mining. The most likely candidates to step into this role were all Conservative. Enter Sir Richard Vivyan, 'nemesis of the Western Conservatives', whose ancestor Sir Richard had been an early Jacobite MP and the sponsor of the 3rd Sir John in 1722. His descendant now sought out the recently married John St Aubyn to step forward, as another liberal minded candidate with resonant Tory antecedents. But John demurred, and so Vivyan's choice fell to the elderly Michael Williams, who went on to win in 1857, but died a year later. John St Aubyn was now ready to take his chance.

Vivyan swiftly secured the support of the Tory gentry, for this new scion of the St Aubyn line, assuring them that he would support the then Conservative government of Lord Derby, even though fully aware that John was in fact an opponent. Meanwhile, Conservatives put forward Williams' son, who as a prominent miner struggled to convince the farmers that he would attend to their grievances. Tory factions all began to fall into line behind St Aubyn, and Williams gave up without a fight. Come the General Election of the following year, Gladstone's support for disestablishment confirmed the nonconformist vote in John's favour, while the Tory gentry were content with one of their own. So West Cornwall gained another MP who would stay the course unopposed, until the county seats were abolished amid the crisis for Liberal Unionists in 1885.

The following letter, addressed to J. St Aubyn Esq, arrived from the Prime Minister, resident at 94 Piccadilly, on 16 January 1860[10]:

> I hope you will not think that I am taking too great a liberty, if I say that I and my Colleagues would be much gratified if you would kindly undertake to move the address in answer to the Queens Speech at the opening of the approaching session. I am sure you would inform the Parl[iament] with satisfaction to yourself & with advantage to the Government.
>
> I should be happy to give you any information you might wish to have on any of the topics to be dealt with
>
> My dear Sir
Yours faithfully
Palmerston

To make the 'Loyal Address' is a distinctive honour, usually given to a promising backbench member of the government. John was being invited onto the first step of the ministerial ladder and it was vital that he perfom to the utmost, in front of the most discerning debating chamber in the English-speaking world. There followed various exchanges with 94 Piccadilly, leading up to a dinner at the house in June, the night before the opening of parliament. John was warned the Address would '... be read at my dinner tomorrow but must not get into the newspapers before it is delivered by the Queen'.

The Address once delivered by Her Majesty, John's moment had come. In 1853, he had joined the Cornish militia and he now stood up in the chamber in the uniform of a major in the rifle regiment. It was also his maiden speech and he spoke boldly, being as well received by those with Tory sentiments, according to *The Times*, as by his own party[11]:

> England is now in a position to enforce, with the greatest possible effect, the policy which in my humble opinion should ever be the policy of this country – viz. to allow every other country to be the best judge of the form of government under which they would live (*Hear*).

After surveying the successes of Lord Palmerston's foreign policy and expressing his firm support for the promised bill to expand the franchise, John ended with this expression of hope:

> That our Queen might long continue to rule over a nation which presented the spectacle of a loyal and contented people, attached to peace but not afraid of war, must be the sincere desire, not only of every member of the House, but of every man who owns the name of Englishman (*Loud cheers*).

A resounding success in the Commons gives little room for a seconder, in this case Lord Henley, to make an impression. Benjamin Disraeli, as Leader of the Opposition, rose in response and began by making something of this contrast:

> As I listened to the noble lord it appeared to me an address suited rather to the atmosphere of a French Senate than to that of an English House of Commons (*hear, hear*); and the noble lord will allow me to say that I do not think it favourably contrasted with that graceful and ingenuous speech with which the mover of the address (*loud cheers*) introduced his sentiments and observations to the consideration of the House.

After such a promising start, it might be expected that John would soon be invited into the government. But apart from valuing his independence, he knew that his West Cornwall constituents, sharing his frame of mind, would not be impressed by a ministerial portfolio. Instead, he earned their respect by piloting the reform of the Stannaries, making mining property liable for rates and mine investments subject to company law. He served two years on the commission which reported into the health and safety of those mine workers not in the coal pits.

There was one further matter, his father having succeeded as head of the family, when James St Aubyn died in 1862. As Edward's parents had legitimised their marriage in church, one option might have been to seek the grant of a royal licence of succession, to the baronetcy of 1672. But as the eldest, that would have gone to his uncle William, the unpopular rector of Devonport, whose own attempt at a royal licence in 1826 had provoked such embarrasment. So instead, John sought a new royal grant – with no appendage of the '*baton sinister*'. When this honour was mooted for himself, he asked that instead it be granted to his father, not least for his distinguished role as Mayor of Devonport, one of the most successful town expansions in the country.

But time was starting to run out for the Liberals, as their reform of the franchise encountered opposition from their own side and tactical manoeuvres by Disraeli. In June 1866, their majority collapsed, while the baronetcy was still in abeyance. The Home Secretary, on whose influence John was depending for the honour, resigned as part of the outgoing government. Yet on July 4 1866, his former office wrote to John's father, Edward:

> Having received directions from herelong Sir George Grey for Letters Patent to be prepared and passed under the Great Seal granting you the dignity of a baronet, I will thank you in order for me to be able to defray the stamp duties and fees on the Letters Patent, which will amount to about £280, to cause that sum to be placed in my account at Messrs. Drummond's, Bankers.[12]

This scrupulous transaction stands in stark contrast with that in 1672, when a fee of over £1000 was extracted by the Crown for the privilege of a baronetcy. That the grant of title still proceeded under the auspices of the new Conservative Home Secretary on 31 July, may have owed something to the fact that he was Spencer Walpole, a cousin of John's wife, Lady Elizabeth. John's luck had held once again, and a Walpole had advanced a title to a St Aubyn, with not even the whiff of a bribe taken.

John's father, Sir Edward, lived on until 1872, a year which marked the final break in the family link with Clowance. Ten members of the family, from the second baronet in 1714, were buried in the family vault at Crowan. These were now moved to a new one in the graveyard on St Michael's Mount. Here Sir Edward was also laid to rest.

At the same time, the family commenced the most ambitious building progamme at the castle, since the church was erected in 1135. Piers St Aubyn, Martha Nicholls' grandson and by now a successful architect based in Kensington,[13] designed an entirely new Victorian wing, to be built out of blocks of granite against the precipitous rock face running below the south-eastern face of the castle. He also designed kitchens and servants' quarters under the north terrace, connected by tunnels blasted through the rockface by Cornish miners. This was a massive project, which would take five years to complete and cost £100,000. As Sir John and Elizabeth's eldest son John later recalled[14]:

> The architect Mr Piers St Aubyn had by no means an easy task to carry out these additions in such an exposed situation without detracting from the appearance of the old building. Some of the granite was found on the spot – notably the chimney piece in the drawing room which was quarried in the place where it now stands.

The result was to create the comfortable country seat, in one of the most august settings in the world, that this side of the family had long sought to replace its entailed Kemyell inheritance. But the exposed island situation had its disadvantages, as this John went on to explain:

> ... life at St Michael's Mount must be very different in many respects from ordinary life in a country house – Carriages cannot get nearer than the opposite shore – And it is always necessary to walk up the hill to get to the castle – unless you wish to be carried in a chair kept for that purpose.
>
> Altogether it is a residence adapted for fine weather – and it is in summer that it should be visited unless indeed the visitor should be curious about the force of the wind and sea – a subject which he would have ample opportunities for learning about were he to pass a day here during a winter's gale.

The family needed to find a complementary base on the mainland and for a time took Trevethoe, a large, late Georgian house sitting above Lelant and Carbis Bay near St Ives.[15] The local MP also needed a home in Truro, the centre of activity in West Cornwall through which the main London train now passed; as well as in London, to attend to his parliamentary duties and the pleasures of town. This generation of the family had reached the summit of English society, at the time when it enjoyed the most power and prestige in the world, under the detached gaze of their widowed sovereign, from 1878 also an Empress.

Sir John frequently returned in style to the Continent, his passport in 1872 including Elizabeth and their son, accompanied by a maid and valet; in 1878, 'with two daughters and two maid servants'. He loved golf and one of his favourite courses was at Pau, near Biarritz, the oldest course on the Continent and a winter enclave of British society before the First World War. Victorian Baedeker Guides, with their superb maps of continental Europe, still line the bookshelves of one of the Mount bedrooms, along with Murray's *Handbooks to Travellers* covering the length of the United Kingdom. From passenger steamboats on the Rhine to luxury railway journeys through Switzerland, this was life lived with a grandeur and style more than a match for Sir John's grandfather.

Eleven of Sir John and Elizabeth's fourteen children survived birth. Five of the eight who married found titled spouses, four of them the heir or the daughters of an earl. One son, on the other hand, went out to Jamaica where he was a police commissioner and married Katharine Phillippo, the alluring granddaughter of a Baptist minister.

Many of Martha Nicholls' descendants had also spread their wings, to Australia, Africa and America; through the Navy, colonial opportunities, or prospecting. Lyon St Aubyn became an Irish priest, where he narrowly escaped being shot by the Fennians. After staging a shooting contest at his vicarage, where he scored a bullseye with an old revolver, there were no more threats. His offspring emigrated to Fiji.[16] Other St Aubyns gravitated back to West Cornwall, where they were welcomed warmly to the Mount. One became a dentist on the Lizard peninsula, several had houses in Marazion. A descendant of Martha's, Diana Hartley, wrote *The St Aubyns of Cornwall 1200-1977*, which tells their stories in loving detail.

———————

By the 1880s electoral reform had established the secret ballot and limited campaign spending. The Liberals and Conservatives now brokered a compromise which extended the franchise, abolished the old county seats, and reduced most other two member consituencies to one. Boundaries were redrawn across the country and nowhere more so than in Cornwall, where the number of seats sunk from thirteen to seven. Sir John withdrew to where his home was, the far west and the newly drawn seat of St Ives. His Liberal Party was sharply divided over the issue of home rule for Ireland, the singular mission of Gladstone as the Prime Minister. Sir John was a Unionist, reflecting not least the Cornish fear that an Irish parliament might exclude them from their favoured fishing grounds. In the new politics, standing under the Unionist banner did not prevent the Tory Charles Ross, MP for the old borough seat of St Ives and former Mayor of Penzance, from mounting a formidable challenge. Come the winter election, 'the fight was severe', according to *The Times* and victory over Ross was secured only by a few hundred votes. Nationally, Gladstone had lost his majority and only hung on with the support of the Irish MPs led by Parnell. When his Home Rule bill fell six months later, another election was called.

This time, Liberal Unionists like Sir John openly aligned with the Conservatives and he comfortably held the seat, establishing a Liberal Unionist stronghold for the future. He had been an MP for thirty years, whose long service had now twice been mandated by the new broad based electorate. In 1887, Queen Victoria's Golden Jubilee prompted a showering of knighthoods, and also six peerages. Lord Salisbury, the Prime Minister, wrote to the ducal heir Lord Hartington, 'some have been made because they are Liberal Unionists … the mention of your name as Sir John St Aubyn's proposer will in his case sufficiently indicate that fact'.[17] Sir John became Baron St Levan, after the small parish running down to Land's End, where the St Aubyns had owned land since the time of Sir Mauger in the thirteenth century.

Three years later, the Duke of Edinburgh was appointed Port Admiral at Plymouth and the Devonport town council thought it fitting to invite Lord St Levan to become their mayor. In 1891, a delegation came to St Michael's Mount to ask him to stay on for a second year, to which 'His Lordship expressed himself as rather surprised that after a year's experience of his shortcomings they should make the request … because he was so often absent from the borough'.[18] This seems to have made them only more determined and he stayed. The same year, the St Levans warmly welcomed the visit to the Mount of the Speaker of the Commons. Arthur Peel had been a contemporary of John at Eton, a fellow Liberal MP from 1865 and had left the party as a Unionist at the same time.

In 1883, J. Bateman's fourth report on wealth in Britain had placed the St Aubyns among the forty 'wealthiest landowners in Britain', with a revenue of £95,000 a year from 6500 acres.[19] This overstated their standing, but nevertheless a news report of the marriage of their eldest son in 1892, at the Guards' Chapel in St James, gives the sense of the social world where the St Aubyns were now at home:

> The Lady Edith Hilaria Edgcumbe, who was married on Thursday at the Royal Military Chapel, Wellington Barracks, to the Hon. John T. St Aubyn, is the youngest and fairest daughter of the earl of Mount-Edgcumbe. The bridegroom is the military secretary to the Governor-General of Canada, and is very popular in the social circles of Ottawa. He belongs

to the Grenadier Guards, whose officers presented him with a service of massy silver. The queen sent the bride an Indian shawl. The Duke of Edinburgh's gift was a bracelet of diamonds and sapphires. Major and Lady Elizabeth St Aubyn are now the guests of the Duke of Northumberland at Albury Park.[20]

The St Levans were evidently enjoying life after politics; John playing more golf, including a season as captain at Pau.[21] Until the fourteen club rule was introduced at St Andrews in 1939, it was common for a golfer to carry twenty to thirty clubs in his bag. Either Pau already set higher standards, or John St Levan prided himself on his play by burdening his caddy with only a handful. His clubs, with names like 'driver', 'spoon' or 'masher', had shafts made of hickory wood, leather bound to club heads forged in iron. The balls were moulded out of the dried sap from the Malaysian Sapodilla tree, with a bramble pattern on the surface. A world away from its origins, but also from the game we know today.

The following piece in the *Daily Express* confirms the picture of a very contented retirement a decade later:

> Lord St Levan, who celebrates his seventy-second birthday today, is one of the youngest looking men for his age, and is most extraordinarily active. He swims like a fish, and is an expert 'trick' swimmer, while his walking feats would be equalled by few men half his age.
>
> He is a man of most kindly disposition, and is a notable host, having entertained almost everyone of note at his beautiful place, St Michael's Mount, from their Majesties downward. His hospitality is always most lavish, and altogether he is quite one of the old school of English gentlemen... He is extremely popular in the county of Cornwall, where he spends most of his time, though he is also fond of travelling.[22]

The next year, 1904, the royal yacht HMY *Victoria and Albert* sailed into Mounts' Bay, her 'tall masts and shapely funnel' instantly recognised by an excited crowd on the shoreline, as she anchored off St Michael's Mount. The St Aubyn barge, with six oarsmen bedecked in the ancient family livery, rowed King Edward VII to a landing in the Mount harbour, where his first step on the keyside is still marked by a brass footprint.

This time, forty years after his mother's visit, the family were at home to welcome their sovereign and show him around the castle. One eye-witness recounted later how, on the return of the party to the mainland, 'the full-skirted Victorian figure of Lady St Aubyn' curtseyed on the wet sand as the king left the boat; His Majesty 'very gracefully helping her to her feet, taking both her hands'.[23]

Four years after the portrait of Juliana by John Opie had been rescued from obscurity, visitors to the Mount castle also found its walls hung proudly with ancestral portraits from Raynham, the Townshend's Norfolk seat.[24] In 1904, John St Levan bought these from his cash-strapped brother-in-law. They included Lettice Knollys, the mischievous granddaughter of Mary Boleyn, whose affair with Henry VIII is now believed to have produced Lettice's mother, Katherine Knollys, the queen's favourite. There was also a full length portrait by Knellner of Charles Townshend, 2nd Viscount, the early patrton of Walpole, who married his sister.

In 1906, the St Levans celebrated fifty years of marriage, and the next year they acquired the ideal winter home to complement the Mount – a large regency house called 'The Rookery'. Set in five acres of grounds in Marazion, it enjoyed a view of the castle and bay from the top floor window in the 'smoking lounge'. In another three years, leaving the Edwardian party while the music was still playing, they had both died.

But their son, John, had already experienced the military limits of Empire, in the Sudan and South Africa, while at home the peerage he now inherited was under seige from the Liberal Party, so altered from the body his father had joined fifty years before. Meanwhile, Britain's period of 'brilliant isolation' was about to come crashing apart, in a forty-year-long maelstrom of division, death and destruction, for Europe, for Britain and inevitably, for the St Aubyns as well.

PART FIVE

SCIONS OF EMPIRE

CHAPTER 1

MEN AT ARMS

No man, however strong, who kept a house could,
if he were not armed, keep his house in peace.
Sir Redvers Buller, VC

Seen from across one of the rivers that run through the city, the three spires of Truro Cathedral rise sublimely above the wooded hills beyond. Pearson's design combines the influence of Early English and French Gothic, its vaulted ceiling and magnificent arch uplifting the spirit as the building is entered. The foundation stone was laid in 1879, three years after Cornwall attained its own diocese, beyond the ambit of Exeter. Its first bishop, Edward Benson, was consecrated at St Paul's. He had been the founding headmaster at Wellington College before becoming chancellor at Lincoln Cathedral, the inspiration for Truro's design and where Pearson was working at the time. On Christmas Eve 1880, Benson introduced his Festival of Nine Lessons and Carols to Truro, a service since adopted by Anglicans around the world.

Piers St Aubyn, the architect, narrowly missed out to Pearson in the competition to design the new cathedral. The chairman of the building committee was Lord Edgecumbe, Lady Edith St Aubyn's father. His task was constantly challenged by lack of funds and only completed in 1910. At one point, when Benson was giving a sermon in St Mary's, the Truro parish church becoming absorbed into Pearson's design, the story goes that he pleaded with all the ladies present to give up the jewels they were wearing that Sunday, in order to pay the bills. It is said a surplus of precious stones gathered that day has ever since been embedded in the cathedral communion chalice.

John St Aubyn supported his father-in-law in this role, while he pursued an active army career; he and his two brothers would be the first St Aubyns to see battle since the Civil War. He had joined the Grenadier Guards in 1878, after Eton and Cambridge, at the age of 21. Five years later, he was sent out to Egypt as ADC to Major-General Earle, at a turbulent time, with unrest stirred first by the politics of Ahmed Arabi Pasha, a charismatic Egyptian Army officer, then by the religious zeal of Mohammed Ahmed ibn Abdullah, who in 1881 had claimed to be the 'Mahdi', from the Arabic for 'divinely guided one'. He had all the characteristics of the Mahdi, including a mole on his right cheek and a V-shaped gap between his two front teeth. But to British officers, he was 'the mad mullah'.[1]

In the background to this developing crisis was the Christian lobby inspired by Dr Livingstone, a missionary with the single aim of eliminating the East African slave trade. This trade was a linchpin of the economy and society, from the Sudan to Zanzibar and the Mahdi approved of slavery, as a method of dealing with non-believers. Anglican and nonconformist voters were putting pressure on Gladstone's administration to stop this appalling human suffering, at the same time as commercial interests sought to displace the Arab and Swahili traders, whose slave labour gave them an unbeatable advantage in businesses along the coast.

Before John had arrived in Egypt, General Wolseley had outwitted Arabi, secured the Suez Canal and overwhelmed the Egyptian's heavily fortified camp at Tel El-Tebir. Under his command had been the King's Royals, which included Edward St Aubyn, a year younger than his brother John, who had already distinguished himself. But now a poorly equiped Egyptian force led by Major General Hicks in November 1883, sent to defeat the Mahdi, was annihilated at Kashgil, south of Khartoum. The Mahdi's followers then began to attack Sinkat and Tokar and beseige Suakin, a key port on the Red Sea. A first Egyptian relief force in the new year, led by the previously disgraced General Baker, fell into a trap at El Teb and were also massacred.

The Egyptian army having failed twice, the British responded by sending a force of two infantry brigades, a cavalry regiment and other units. Sir Redvers Buller, who had recently married John's aunt, Audrey, was sent in command of one of these brigade to rescue Suakin from this menace. He took John St Aubyn as his ADC.

A second and ferocious battle was fought at El Teb, at the end of February 1884. The British lost only 35 men, with 155 wounded. Two thousand of the dervishes, as the Mahdi's followers were known, were killed in this second battle. The British followed this up with a second engagement two weeks later at Tamai. The two battalions, comprised of 4500 men with guns and machine guns, fought against 10,000 dervishes in a bloody confrontation. When they were temporarily overrun by tribesmen in hand-to-hand combat, the day was only saved by the discipline of the British troops. The Mahdi army lost at least another 2000 men, but on the British side 214 were wounded or killed, 10 of them officers.

John was mentioned in dispatches and awarded the Egypt medal and clasp and bronze star, as was his brother Edward. Major General Graham's report also praised Buller's 'coolness of action, his knowledge of soldiers and experience in the field, combined with his great personal ascendancy over officers and men'. He was promoted to major general. Later, Churchill dismissed this campaign as punitive: 'they fought without reason, they conquered without profit', as it failed to force the Mahdi's surrender. But it did avert a strategic threat to control of the Suez Canal.

Meanwhile General Gordon, defying orders to evacuate Sudan immediately, had sought to inflict one final defeat on the Mahdi before he left, to deter an advance on Egypt. Denied reinforcements, his base at Khartoum was soon surrounded by dervishes. Buller, with John as his ADC, then joined the Gordon Relief Expedition, where disagreements between the commanding officers fed into fatal delay. Gordon and his men were butchered, two days before the relief force arrived.

Buller was now put in command of the Desert Column, while John St Aubyn was reassigned back to General Earle as ADC. The General led the 1000-strong Nile Column, which included the newly formed 'Camel Corps', directed to disperse a dervish force holding out in the heights of Kirbekan. In the battle that followed, in February 1885, the Mahdi forces were totally routed, with heavy loss. The British dead came to only sixty men, but included among them General Earle. His ADC was again mentioned in dispatches and awarded two clasps.

John's military career now led him to Hong Kong and then to Canada as the Military Secretary, before his marriage to Lady Edith. A tour of duty in South Africa then beckoned, where his younger brothers, Edward and Piers, were already fighting in the Boer War under General Buller. 29-year-old Piers had joined Thorneycroft's Mounted Infantry from the Rifle Corps and had already been mentioned in dispatches as 'conspicuous both at Colenso and Spion Kop for great galantry ... an excellent second in command'. He was again commended when he had 'shown great tact in dealing with colonial troops', before he was invalided out in July 1900.[2] Edward, now in his forties, had served as a staff officer and returned home unscathed.

By the time their brother John arrived, however, the war was over and his battalion was turned back home. John's troops were soon assigned to duty at the Tower of London. At the end of this posting, Major St Aubyn informed the Lord Mayor that his battalion would accord with ancient custom and their special connection with the City, by marching through the streets 'with colours flying, drums beating and bayonets fixed'.

Then in 1906, John St Aubyn accompanied Arthur, Duke of Connaught, on the Garter Mission to Japan. They arrived on February 19 to wild enthusiasm. In a break with protocol, the Emperor greeted them himself at Shisabi station before they rode in a court carriage to Kasumigaseki Palace, accompanied by the Crown prince, the Imperial Lancers and a military band playing the British national anthem. After the duke had invested the Emperor with the Garter, to mark a new treaty with Japan, John returned home with the gift of a 100-year-old Samurai suit of armour, which today stands resplendent in the castle armoury.

As for Edward and Piers, they remained the epitome of the London bachelor of their time, enjoying a private income and an army salary. Edward 'Bean' St Aubyn had in 1891 also been a founding partner of the Discount House, Smith St Aubyn, which for ninety years played an intergral part in the London money market. But it was said he was only encouraged to go to the office when business was quiet.

———◆———

By the time of John St Levan's death in 1908, the Liberal government was losing patience with the blocking majority of Conservatives and Unionists in the House of Lords. Then the Lords rejected Lloyd George's radical budget of 1909, whose higher rates of income tax and death duties would hit them hard. This offended an iron constitutional principle, established in the Middle Ages: that the knights of the shires and the burgesses of the towns having agreed to collect the taxes demanded by the Crown, the Lords would not impede their task. So by committing one constitutional outrage, the Lords had invited another – the threat of an overwhelming number of new peers, if necessary, in order to curtail their powers. The king was not unsympathetic, but insisted that the Liberals would have to win an election on the specific issue of Lords reform, before he would cooperate with this threat.

In the General Election which followed, self-serving speeches from obscure peers failed to impress the voters, who again returned a Liberal government. Members of the Upper House now divided into 'hedgers' and 'ditchers' over the bill to reform them. Then King Edward VII died, and the Liberal government sought assurances from the new King George V, that he would create up to 250 new peers to force through its reform programme, if the majority in the Lords resisted. A second election was then called, with almost exactly the same result as the first.

By May 1911, the Parliament Bill had passed the Commons and came to the Lords for its second reading. The 2nd Baron St Levan rose to speak, 'as a backbencher, not a backwoodsman'. He supported reform because 'rightly or wrongly, I believe that the people of this country are not prepared to support a Second Chamber based entirely on the hereditary principle'. But he rejected the solution put forward in the bill, because the Second Chamber would be emasculated and '...it is absolutely necessary to defend not only the interests but also the liberties of the nation (*Opposition cheers*)'. This view was echoed by Lord Rosebery, who said 'I can see no use in prolonging the existence of this House as a useless cham to delude the people ... that they still have a Second Chamber with control over the First'.

But by August, the bill had returned to the Lords for its final reading, without any of the safeguards that the 'ditchers' were seeking. Lord Morley, for the government, twice simply repeated the threat to create new peers. To which one of the 'ditchers' retorted: 'We ourselves, as effective legislators, are doomed to destruction. The question is – shall we perish in the dark by our own hand, or in the light, killed by our enemies?'

The House divided and by 131 to 114, the bill was passed. The 'ditchers', like John St Levan, had overlooked two points. First, that the power of delay remains a political weapon, which is why the Second Chamber even today has not yet been 'doomed to destruction'; secondly, that it was precisely because 'the people' had rejected the Second Chamber's claim to 'control over the First', that reform was inevitable.

While St Levan did not speak in the House again, John and Edith could console themselves with the London season, in 1913 throwing a ball at the Ritz for their two daughters, Marjorie and Hilaria. The girls were presented at court to the king and queen, who also included the St Levans among the 2500 guests at the State Ball in honour of the President of France. At Westminster Abbey, they attended the reinauguration of 'The Most Honourable Order of Bath'. Young flying ace, Gustav Hamel, soared above the Mount in his 'flying-machine', performing 'brilliant flying feats', before being invited to lunch in the castle. (Months later, his flying feats would prove fatal.) At the end of 1913, at the Plymouth Drill Hall,

Sir Edward Carson spoke, 'Supported by all the Ulster Unionist Members of Parliament', including St Levan.

The beginning of 1914 saw Lord St Levan elected as a member of the Royal Society for the Protection of Birds. Then, as one of his valets later recounted,[3] 'We always went abroad as soon as Christmas was over. We'd leave about the second week in January and stay away until April'.

So in February 1914, John and Edith found themselves in the Sudan. The Governor General was now Lord Wingate, whose letter to John following their visit expressed a forlorn hope:

> What a real pleasure it was to see you again – especially in Khartoum, which we had struggled together and failed to reach nearly thirty years ago ... if we are allowed a fairly free hand and immunity from internal or external troubles, we shall make of the Sudan a very valuable possession for the Mother country, especially if our cotton cultivation projects develop as we anticipate.

But an impromtu visit to Kirbekan, where John had fought in 1885, had to be cancelled. As this telegram explained:

> Owing to fact no rains fell last year at least five to seven days notice necessary to enable Arabs to bring in camels as grazing grounds far away. Unless longer time can be given regret not possible to arrange tour.

Back in England in April, John was involved in a trading standards dispute, over what constituted a 'sardine'. His extensive knowledge of fish was put to good use in a sworn witness statement to the county council officers in Bodmin, which concluded: 'I rely on the label of this class of goods. If I order sardines in my household I want the particular fish I know as a sardine and am not satisfied with any fish that is canned in oil of suitable size'. Quite so.

But come August 1914, the gravity of the crisis in Europe brutally exposed the complacency at the heart of British policy. A chain of treaty guarantees, combined with a misplaced faith in British deterrence, now ensnared the country in a fatal and bloody conflict. Tinned sardines of any description would soon be sought as a luxury, for the millions of soldiers embedded in opposing trench lines stretched across Belgium, France and Germany.

John St Levan and his younger brothers, Edward and Piers, had all joined their father's London club Brooks's, no longer the iniquitous gambling den where the 5th Sir John had allegedly lost a fortune, but a bastion of Victorian privilege, dubbed by the editor of *Punch* as 'probably the most aristocratic club in London'.[4] In 1783, William Pitt the Younger had been dragged from his coach by Brooks's members; it had taken resolute supporters from Whites, on the other side of St James' Street, to rescue the young Prime Minister. The only political scandal Brooks's members in the 1890s could manage, on the other hand, was an internal row over Liberals and Tories blackballing each other's candidates.

Today, as one enters the hallowed portals of this old club, it is impossible not to be struck by the extravagance of the enormous glass dome which hangs over the hall, framed by the cantilevered staircase rising to the first floor gallery. But also not to be missed is the stone memorial, adorning the left side wall, listing all those members of the club who gave their lives in the two world wars of the last century. There are more St Aubyns on that plaque than any other family.

The first to fall was Piers. Fourteen years after he had been wounded in South Africa as a captain, at the age of 42 he signed up as a second lieutenant in his old regiment, the King's Royals, along with his much younger brother, Lionel. By October 1914, they found themselves in those same fields of Flanders as their ancestor Sir John St Aubyn, more than five centuries before. Only Piers and Lionel were part of the most highly trained army in the world,[5] fighting alongside the French and Belgians. Every British soldier was required to pass the 'mad minute' exercise, firing 15 rounds in 60 seconds, at a target 300 yards away. A veteran like Piers might manage 20 rounds a minute or more, the record being held at 38 shots in 60 seconds, all of which had hit the inner bullseye.

But the British Expeditionary Force had little with which to answer the heavy artillery fire possessed by the Germans; by the end of the month, the iron law of attrition threatened to crush the defenders, the loss of whose skill was irreplaceable. A critical moment was reached at Gheluvelt, just four miles ahead of Ypres, where a German breakthrough would threaten the Channel ports and Britain's critical supply lines. A perilously thin line faced an overwhelming German assault, which was launched at 6.00 am on 31 October:

> The fighting was close ranged and desperate; many British units fought to the last man…With the line broken, the Germans surged forward and soon reached the village.[6]

But at 2.00 pm the British counter-attacked, with such ferocity that the Germans fled, thinking they faced far greater numbers. Lionel survived Gheluvelt, but not his elder brother. The recapture of Gheluvelt was 'the tipping point in the First Battle of Ypres' and the Germans never came so close to a decisive breakthrough again.[7] So at least Piers' sacrifice had not been in vain, although his body was among those never found, his name one of the 35,000 commemorated on the Menin Gate. Come the end of November 1914, the British had suffered some 89,000 casualties from an original force of about 120,000 men. In the words of one survivor, 'the old army was finished'.[8]

Whereas Piers had died in the heat of battle, the death of his brother Edward was a German war crime. A decorated lieutenant-colonel in the 12th Battalion, King's Royals, by the outbreak of war and at the age of 56, Edward had risen to chief of staff within the General Staff Branch, responsible for training, intelligence, planning operations and directing battles. In December 1915, he was serving as a King's Messenger on board the SS *Persia*, a luxury ocean liner sailing to India. Without warning, on the orders of Max Valentiner, one of the most notorious U-boat captains of the First World War, a single torpedo struck her amidships. SS *Persia* keeled over so quickly she was still moving forward as its funnels touched the waves, drowning 343 of the 519 mostly civilian passengers on board. The Palace's letter of condolence remarked of 'Bean' that 'Their Majesties knew him for so many years and had followed his career with interest'.[9] It was said that Bean never married because he was in a complicated relationship with one of Edward VII's mistresses. The souls lost also included the mistress of Lord Montagu of Beaulieu, Eleanor Thornton, whose image went on to adorn every Rolls Royce in the world as the Spirit of Ecstasy. Her lover survived.[10]

———◆———

These St Aubyn brothers had died without issue. John St Aubyn only had two daughters and the youngest brother, Lionel, was another bachelor who remained fighting in the trenches with the King's Royals.

The St Levans would have appeared at this point in as much danger of extinction as their Devon forebears, were it not for one other descendant in the male line. Francis St Aubyn had been born in Jamaica in 1895, where he had lost his father when he was only 2 years old. He came to England, with a bronzed complexion and a soft lilt in his voice, and had instantly been nicknamed 'Sambo'. He would be known as Sam for the rest of his life.

Sam's father, Arthur, had been John and Elizabeth St Levan's fourth son, sent out as a captain of the Mounted Police to join the Royal Jamaica Constabulary. Here he fell in love with Katharine Phillippo, the captivating daughter of a local doctor. Her grandfather, James Phillippo, had emigrated to the West Indies as a Baptist minister. With two other ministers, he had led the campaign to abolish slavery. They raised the funds to buy up land, defying the wrath of the sugar plantation owners, in order to establish free villages, where former slaves could start a new life for themselves, without fear of eviction. Their mission to instill an idealised Victorian ethos would in time clash with Jamaica's own cultural norms, but these villages with their chapel, small houses and neat gardens left a core legacy of home ownership.[11]

Phillippo raised self-consciousness, by flouting the law against preaching the gospel to slaves, before he returned to England for medical treatment in 1831, just before the slave insurrection known as the Christmas Rebellion. Its harsh repression by government troops, with 200 slaves killed outright and a black Baptist deacon executed, spurred Phillippo to campaign in England.

The Slavery Abolition Act came into effect in 1834, but it was only with the end of apprenticeships in 1838 that emancipation was celebrated in Spanish Town. Phillippo was invited by the Governor to lead a procession into a crowd of 8000 in front of Government House, where the Proclamation of Freedom was declared.[12] He lived in Spanish Town for another forty years, where he would have known his grandaughter, Katharine, as a small child.

Arthur St Aubyn had been married to her for merely three years when he died from pneumonia and exposure, after strenuous duty during a storm and earthquake, in October 1897.[13] At a packed service in his memory, held in the church on the Mount, a twenty-nine-gun salute was fired from the terrace, one gun for each year of his brief life.[14] Then some time after his burial in Kingston, his widow sailed for England with her little boy, where they were taken in hand by the family. Introduced into their circle, it was not long before Katharine found herself surrounded by admirers.

In 1904, she married Patrick Crichton-Stuart, by which time Sam had been dispatched to the harsh disciplines of an English boarding school where, as he told his grandson, he was once beaten four times in the same night. His path to Eton and thereafter to Sandhurst followed a now established family pattern. By 1914, Sam was widely seen as the eventual heir to the Mount.[15] But first he would have to survive the call to arms.

As soon as war was declared, a Reserve Battalion of the Grenadier Guards sprang into existence in Kensington and within five days,

1700 reservists from across the country had come to join. Sir Frederick Ponsonby, in his account of the regiment, lists Sam as one of the young officers commissioned to convert this mass of men into a disciplined force. As he also wrote:

> The whole conditions of service were now different. Instead of the usual apathy on the part of the men to learn anything new, they now eagerly seized every opportunity to acquire knowledge. The Army was no longer a profession, where a man could reduce to a science the practice of doing the least possible amount of work without getting into trouble. It was now a matter of life and death.[16]

On 20 April 1915, just after it had been decimated in the battle of Neuve Chapelle, Sam joined the 1st Battalion, Grenadier Guards at the front. Only a month later, he had his own taste of death during the battle of Festubert. A shell burst into the middle of his platoon, killing four men and wounding many others. Sam was struck in the face by a piece of shrapnel and he was invalided behind the lines to recover.[17]

Yvo Charteris, who had been an Eton scholar and contemporary of Sam, joined the battalion in September 1915, while his elder brother Hugo was dispatched to Egypt. He came just in time for the start of the Loos offensive.[18] By the time Sam rejoined him as another second lieutenant, two weeks into the attack, it had successfully breached the German line with massive artillery support, which now included heavy cannon as well as field guns. Gas had also been used for the first time against its German inventors.[19]

But the inherent problem with trench warfare was that the skill of the 'mad minute' marksman had been superseded. In 1915, in the account of Yvo Charteris' great-nephew, James Wemyss, 'the machine-gun emerged ... as the queen of the battlefield, seconded by thickets of flesh-tearing barbed wire'.[20]

On 14 October, the 1st Battalion took over Quarry Trench, the captured German front-line trench east of Big Willie. Just beyond its northern end, the Germans had built a substantial block. Between this block and the part of Quarry Trench occupied by the Grenadiers, a distance of about 140 yards, German shelling had much reduced the depth of the trench – now a sap – which was enfiladed by German machine-guns.

The next day, the men went out over the top at the crack of dawn, with their expert bombers, to eliminate this threat, but on arrival they found two

German machine-guns opening fire. The men wavered, and Yvo Charteris was sent up the sap to rally them and to lead a fresh attack around the enemy guns.

But according to Ponsonby's account:

> Second Lieutenant the Hon. I. Charteris and Second Lieutenant H. Alexander, two very promising officers, were killed at once, and a large number of men were killed and wounded. ... Lieut. Lord Lascelles, on coming up, quickly grasped the whole situation. He saw that while the two German machine-guns were in position, it was a practical impossibility to take the trench, and he very wisely withdrew what remained of that Company to our trenches.
>
> It was well that he did so, for soon afterwards the Germans commenced a heavy bombardment, which lasted till noon. The casualties were 2 officers killed and 3 wounded, with 125 of other ranks killed and wounded... Lieutenant St. Aubyn was also wounded during this bombing attack, but not seriously. In the evening the body of Lieutenant Charteris was recovered, and buried at Sailly-la-Bourse, Lord Stanley superintending the funeral.[21]

The British had broken through the German line, as they had at Neuve Chapelle a few months before, but 'faulty staff work, confusion of command and the sheer friction of war meant that there were no reserves on hand to exploit the breach'. By the end of the offensive, 'the British had lost 60,000 men and the Germans 51,000'.[22]

One can well imagine the guilty feelings of the bandaged Lieutenant St Aubyn, at his younger schoolmate's funeral. Yvo had celebrated his nineteenth birthday only a few days before. He was the bright scholar and classicist, and had been offered a place at Balliol College, Oxford, of whom his headmaster had written that he 'expected him to make his mark in the world'. Yet Sam would survive to inherit his family's Cornish estate and peerage, while one of the heirs to the Scottish castles and earldom in Yvo's family had now been lost, his brother soon to follow. Thus could the random pattern of the pitiless German killing machine dispose of talent, titles and fortune at opposite ends of the United Kingdom.

After Loos, Sam secured some leave back home and was present for the memorial service for his uncles, Piers and Edward, held in St George's, Hanover Square, in February 1916.[23] On leave, the twice wounded Guards officer and heir apparent presented quite a catch, in a marriage field reduced by war. In the few months before he would have to return to the front, Sam cast his eye among the young girls whose debutante season had been so cruelly blighted by the fighting.

The 19-year-old daughter of Sir Arthur Nicolson, head of the Foreign Office and former ambassador to Russia,[24] was one of those whose horizons had been curtailed. Gwen was petite, shy and vulnerable, but also pretty, bright and full of spirit, with a veneer of worldly erudition after growing up in the splendour of Edwardian diplomatic postings. Her elder brother Harold, who described Gwen as 'a passionately affectionate personality',[25] had been close when they were the ambassador's children, and remained so throughout the inter-war years as his star shone.

In Russia, Harold Nicolson had played a game on his 12-year-old sister, at the time when the British embassy installed electricity. Persuading her to lie like a corpse on the embassy drawing room floor, he attached wires to her feet and hands and then instructed her not to move an inch, on pain of electrocution. When their mother entered the room with a grand lunch party, half an hour later, she discovered her daughter still transfixed to the floor.[26]

Now Harold was married to Vita Sackville-West, an only child reared in the great house at Knole Park in Kent. He had been exempted from military service because of his high-flying career at the Foreign Office, where his and Gwen's father had just reached retirement as Permanent Under-Secretary, becoming ennobled as Lord Carnock. On the face of it, this gifted intellectual circle had little in common with that of the gangly Cornish lieutenant, in whose company she was soon to be found.

Yet in August, this extract from *Tatler* conveys the frenzy of matrimonial proposals in the summer of 1916:

> Another big wedding this week – the Cadogan-Mills one – and I hear plenty of nice presents even if there *is* a war. Next week Lady Helen Brassey marries her publisher-soldier-man, Major John Murray, 'quite quietly', and there are several more fixed for the next week or two… (Ah, well as everyone knows, man wasn't made to live alone!) and Mr Astor's to Lady Charles Mercer-Nairne… And Miss Gwendoline Nicolson's to Captain

St Aubyn, Lord St Levan's heir-presumptive... But that's about enough to go on with, isn't it? Looks as if the parsons and people'll be kept busy anyway this August.[27]

The following month, 'Lieut. Francis Cecil St Aubyn was summoned for not having a rear light on his motor car at Swanley Junction – P.C. Nash stated the defendant said the lamp was an electric one, which had gone wrong, and as he did not understand it he could not put the lamp right. – He was fined £1'. Fortunately, this scrape did not stand in the way of Sam and Gwen's marriage, which was solemnised on 6 October at Holy Trinity, Sloane Street, as *The Queen* magazine reported:

> Lord Carnock gave his daughter away, and very pretty she looked in her simple bridal gown of ivory crepe de Chine, the bodice gracefully draped and completed with a vest of chiffon and lace, a cluster of white heather holding the folds of the drapery at the waist.[28]

They left their wedding to enjoy a short honeymoon on the Mount. There the butler, the housekeeper and the cook were waiting to greet Gwen and Sam as they stepped off the family barge rowed to the island by the liveried Mount boatmen. Over nine in ten men from Marazion had volunteered at the outset of war,[29] so the pre-war retinue of servants – footmen, valets, hallboys, lady's maids, housemaids, stillroom maids, and kitchen maids – must have been somewhat reduced in the line-up, to offer their congratulations to the happy couple. Nevertheless it no doubt dawned on Gwen that governing this domain would one day prove her daunting task to master.

Only a week later, Sam was ordered to rejoin his battalion in France, spending three days out of ten in the trenches, until finally relieved of front line duty in April 1917.[30] Gwen had joined the Red Cross, so that if he was wounded again, she might be allowed to go to France to nurse him. These two were still too deep in the first bloom of love, to realise quite how complicated their union had just made their lives.

Meanwhile, 'poor little Gwen, so white and quiet' had been the observation at her wedding of Gwen's sister-in-law, Vita. On Sam's return from the front, she and Harold rented their London base in Ebury Street to the newlyweds.[31]

CHAPTER 2

THE LOTUS EATERS

*Civilisation is ... the enhancement of pleasure, the love
of loveliness, the refinement of relationships, and the
embellishment of life.*

Harold Nicolson[1]

Our perceptions of the inter-war years are unavoidably coloured by
the horror of what followed. But for those entering the 1920s, after the
slaughter of the Great War and the devastation wrought by the Spanish 'flu'
epidemic, there was a reckless urge to rediscover life's pleasures. War also
presses the human spirit into great feats of imagination and invention, in the
battle for survival. As the motor car, the telephone, motion pictures, radio
and television burst onto a mass market, the sense of a new world vision
seized the popular consciousness. In the 'coupon' election of December
1918, Lloyd George promised to build 'a land fit for heroes'; while in
America, President Harding was elected in 1920 on the pledge of a return
to 'normalcy'.

But many wealthy families found the new reality as starkly altered as
their tenants and servants. One in ten titled families lost heirs in the war,
leaving widows and children bereft or a family line facing extinction.
The tragic loss of a son in the trenches was often compounded by death
duties, while rent controls designed to alleviate the burden on the returning
heroes, left little money to improve the quality of housing. Class divisions
and strife, which the wartime spirit had muted, erupted with new energy
under a labour movement led by its own party, demanding improvements
in workers' conditions, which Britain's weakened economy struggled to
afford. Before the war, Britain had been the world's largest creditor and
America its debtor. Now the position was entirely reversed.[2]

The reaction of the St Aubyns, like so many landed families, was to
withdraw to their parochial rural idyll – and few familes could have found
it simpler to do so.[3] Life in the island castle and on the Cornish farms was
sheltered from the harsh conditions which confronted the residents of their
Devonport manor across the Tamar. The toll bridge income had been sold

and the urban estate was fully developed. But as the building leases granted a century before expired, the resale or letting of Devonport houses provided a vital source of support for the lifestyle of the family, without burdening its tenants in Cornwall. Soon the castle hummed with forty servants to cater for their every need and that of their weekend friends. Clean bedsheets were laid every day and for every house guest from the island laundry. So many bottles of champagne was opened, that the butler, Henry Lee, used the corks to craft a splendid model of the island and its castle. Today it stands proud in the Map Room as visitors pass by. As for house parties, Stanely Ager, who was for three years Lord St Levan's valet, describes the typical invitation:

> When I accompanied the second lord on a weekend away, we rarely stayed in any house for longer than three nights. Even so, he traveled with at least three cases as well as his dressing case, all of which were my responsibility. We generally left home Friday morning and arrived in time for tea that afternoon. The weekend finished on Monday and we left immediately after breakfast, unless it was a weekend's shooting. Then he would shoot on Monday and we would leave on Tuesday.[4]

Sam and Gwen St Aubyn were invited during the holidays, with their five children, to stay in the 'Rookery' on the mainland opposite, at other times joining Sam's uncle, Lionel St Aubyn, and his three young sons at their home in Devon. They imbued a love of sailing, swimming and fishing in summer, shooting and riding in winter. After one hunt had set off after a fox, as the field mounted the Cornish hedges (as they do in Ireland), there was a moment when four St Aubyns had lost their seat in the saddle at the same time.

But like the residents of Devonport, once out of sight the St Levan heir apparent was out of mind, left to live on a shoestring budget. He was the first St Aubyn heir in 900 years to inherit from an uncle, with nothing from his own father; and the first heir to feel really short of money, since Geoffrey in the fifteenth century. Sam had returned from the war at the age of 23, without time to gain a professional qualification, but with a young family to feed. They led a peripatetic existence, in a series of rented houses in the more bohemian parts of London, as Sam scratched a living as a 'half-commission man' in the City, while Gwen launched herself on a modest writing career, in the slipstream of her more prominent brother Harold and his wife Vita.

When Harold Nicolson had entered the diplomatic service in 1909, it was 'still preponderantly a small, close-knit, aristocratic and hereditary profession, much favoured by patricians of limited resources but good connections'.[5] Nomination by a senior Foreign Office figure was a preresquisite of entry and Harold was the protégé of Lord Curzon. By 1917, with Arthur Balfour as Foreign Secretary, Harold was assigned to work on the thorny issue of Jewish settlement in Palestine. Over thirty years later, when her nephew Piers had just served in the Holy Land, Vita sent Sam a volume of essays as a Christmas present. This included Harold's recollection of Balfour's momentous handling of the Zionist quest for the ancestral Jewish homeland[6]:

> We were accorded two small rooms in the basement of the Foreign Office...[which] had been fitted up as an air-raid shelter for the Prime Minister, who would nip across from Downing Street when the Zepplins approached. They had been repainted in vivid suffragette colours and furnished with armchairs, tables, a sofa, and a harmonium on which, it was said, Mr Lloyd George would when the bombs fell, play Welsh hymns....

Sir Mark Sykes, to whom Harold reported, had just signed an agreement with France and Britain's other wartime allies to divide up the Ottoman Empire after the war, with Palestine to become Britain's responsibility. Sykes wrote everything in his green ink pen, which often strayed into caricatures and comic drawings on the side of his official papers. On one occasion, when Balfour's lift became caught between the floors, Sykes illustrated the scene with himself up a ladder, holding the Declaration towards Balfour to sign, the Zionist Dr Sokolov waiting anxiously below. Despite the genial atmosphere, Harold later wrote:

> 'Dr Sokolov would visit us daily, slow, solemn, patriarchal, intense ... the Balfour Declaration was not some sudden opportunistic statement made at a time of difficulty; it took weeks to draft, and every word was scrutinized with the greatest thought and forethought.

Nicolson joined the British delegation to the Versailles peace conference in 1919 and played his part in the establishment of the League of Nations.

After a few years back in London, he was posted abroad to Tehran and then to Berlin. As a diplomat's wife, this world was never going to attract Vita; although Harold's enforced absences abroad were most useful in facilitating her open pursuit of her own interests, both romantic and literary. But without her support, Harold's career was limited and so he developed his own talent as a writer. Although never meeting quite the same success as Vita with her history of Knole (1922) or her novel *The Edwardians* (1930), by late 1929 Harold had become sufficiently established as an author, to resign from the Foreign Service. He became a journalist on the *Evening Standard*, while seeking a seat in parliament as a second string to his bow.

Then in 1933, by which time the Nicolsons had acquired Sissinghurst in Kent, they were brought back into Sam and Gwen's lives after Gwen had been in a bad car accident, which had damaged her skull and shaken her nerves to the core. Gwen would be in need of rest and medical care for months to come and Vita began seeing far more of her. Sissinghurst was suggested as the ideal setting for her recovery, apart from her five children.

Gwen's vulnerable condition had evoked Vita's tender concern. A visiting friend at this time described Gwen as looking like 'a battered, a dissolute child'. But quite apart from Vita's ministrations, she was sustained by her faith. For despite opposition from her family, Gwen was receiving instruction from the Jesuits at Farm Street and her growing Catholicism betokened a profound influence on Vita's writing.[7]

Gwen had already written two books on raising children, *Nursery Life* and *Parents' Problems*. Now she was commissioned to edit *The Family Book*, a modern guide for parents with expert advice on every subject from marriage, sex and religion to child psychology and education. Harold would write the introduction. But it was with Vita that Gwen delved into discussions on the intricacies of family relationships and the inner lives of women.

Meanwhile, Gwen's condition gave constant cause for anxiety and her doctor said she would need a year of treatment.[8] A 'red-hot rabbit-hutch' was placed over her head twice a day, as Vita explained to Virginia Woolf, which made her faint. 'They seem to think', Vita wrote, 'that this will dispel the injury to her brain'.[9] Gwen's doctor put it to Sam that the tranquillity of Sissinghurst was aiding the healing process and, according to Harold, Sam 'quite sees that Gwen must be left to make her own arrangements, and not bothered by obligations, domestic or otherwise'. A room for Gwen was provided at the top of Vita's tower.

Vita's consuming interest in the romantic objects of her desire had until now been satisfied by bodily possession. But in the case of Gwen, as with

Harold, it was her powerful intellect, combined with her current physical vulnerability, which made her sister-in-law so attractive; together with the covetous sense, that while Vita's stately home had cruelly passed to her cousin after her father's death, the death of Sam's uncle would elevate Gwen to chatelaine of an even more inspiring and romantic seat.

In January 1934, Gwen had an operation on her head, the first of several. So Vita took her to convalesce on the Italian riviera, in a castello she had rented for a fortnight. The medieval villa, replete with staff, stood on a craggy outcrop at Portofino. As well as a garden in bloom and olive groves descending to the sea, it was the setting of *The Enchanted April*, a wildly successful novel by Elizabeth Russell.[10]

Published eight years before, this portrayed two wives cowed and neglected by their husbands, who escape from their household chores to this romantic castle and a carefree way of life; when at last joined by their husbands, their lives and their marriages are renewed.

Harold wrote to his wife, 'It all comes from Gwen reading Tauchnitz editions of the works of Lady Russell. I hope you are both very uncomfortable and happy. Bless you both'.[11] Gwen responded that she was happier than she had ever been before: 'You see for once I have no responsibilities, Vita having taken them all'.[12]

Harold briefly joined the Portofino couple, before going on to Cap Ferrat where he had tea with Somerset Maugham.[13] Thence to Marseilles together and a boat to Tangier, where Gwen had been born during her father's posting to Morrocco in the 1890s. In Casablanca, one evening after Gwen had retired, Harold mused with Vita that Gwen 'thirty years ago would have felt herself fortunate at having a faithful husband and five adoring children. But now she feels that these obligations limit herself, that there is a more important function for her somewhere beyond the function of a mother'.[14]

The Family Book was published in 1935 to general acclaim and in the same year, Gwen completed her journey into the Catholic faith (as she later described in *Towards a Pattern*). The truth was that she really did have 'a more important function' awaiting her in Cornwall. But it was one whose image Vita portrayed in crudely distorted colours in her next novel, *The Dark Island*. In the book, Venn is the sadistic heir to a Norman castle atop Storn, an island where he lives with his manipulative grandmother. The heroine is Shirin – which just happened to be Vita's nickname for Gwen, meaning 'sweet' in Persian – whom Venn chains up and whips in a cave, after they marry.

For the easy-going Sam and his many friends, a literal interpretation of this storyline provoked bemused incredulity. But Venn either represented

Vita herself,[15] who was struggling to accept the fact that Gwen's strong-willed call of duty to Cornwall would soon end their intimacy; or personified the Catholic Church, whose doctrine inhibited its physical expression.

In April 1935, Gwen joined Harold, Vita and their son Nigel on another trip across France, before boarding a cruise ship to Greece. All this time, Harold had been anxiously seeking a footing in parliament, 'as a sort of alibi from literary failure', because he feared his books were 'not good enough to justify myself having cut adrift from public service'.[16] He had flirted with Oswald Mosely's New Party, but found his plan to wear 'brown shirts' offensive: 'if you must choose a uniform', he had asked Mosely, concerned not to lose the middle class vote, 'could it not be grey flannel trousers?'[17]

Harold having come bottom of the poll in Cambridge under Mosely's banner in 1931, Vita's cousin Lord Sackville was unable to swing the nomination for Maidstone his way four years later. Then Leicester West came up, if Harold would stand as a National Labour candidate. Ben and Nigel came to help on election day, along with Sam taking voters to the polling station in his car.[18] But Vita had refused all requests to appear alongside her husband during the campaign, instead spending October touring Provence with Gwen. This left Harold 'puzzled and disappointed and rather cross'.[19] Nevertheless, he squeezed in by eighty-seven votes and his ten years as an MP would ensure that his diaries retained their fascination, even if his political career never found its mark.

By the mid-thirties, divorce was becoming as common among the upper reaches of English society as elsewhere. The trauma of war and the lack of opportunity during the slump had both contributed to an accelerating change in social attitudes. The total number of divorces in England and Wales each year rose from 1654 in 1919 to 5000 by 1936. By 1939, four of the twenty-seven dukes of the English peerage were divorced, whereas in 1918 none had been.[20]

So when Harold described Sam as 'a faithful husband' to Gwen, he really meant one who would stand fast by the institution of marriage and never desert her. But at least since their children had gone to boarding school, this couple had led lives as separate as Harold and Vita's, yet without the constant flow of letters and sharing of minds. They shared a love of their five children and a focus on the prize that Sam's Cornish inheritance dangled over them; but tasted individual freedom while it lasted.

For Gwen's children, such freedom was harder to come by. Years later, her eldest son John explained why he enjoyed watching old films on television, which was to discover the endings. He related how he and his brother Piers could only sneak away to the local cinema in Chelsea, if they made it home in time for their mother's tea. The editor of *The Family Book* had espoused that adolescents should 'learn to think twice before they rush off for the first amusement or visit that offers'; the matriarch in charge of five children kept a stern eye on pocket money, as well as punctuality. Gwen's older children were made to keep a pocket-book, itemising their weekly expenditure. At the cinema, to maintain their subterfuge, Piers would beg John for the ticket money, before he paid it in at the booth.

Later, pocket book in hand, his brother would be asked:

'So John, how did you spend that last sixpence?'

'Mother', he could reply with a straight face, 'I gave it to a beggar'.

Sam's Aunt Edith had died in 1931 and for a while the St Aubyns feared the prospect that Uncle Jack – as the second Lord St Levan was known to the family – would marry again, to a wife of childbearing age. But fortunately, the romantic in the old soldier had long pined for a girl who had turned him down in his youth. Julia Wombwell had instead married the older and grander Earl of Dartrey. Now she was a widow and two years after Edith had passed away, the countess gave up her superior title to marry her Cornish admirer.[21]

In April 1937, the German ambassador to England, Joachim von Ribbentrop, paid a visit to West Cornwall. From Exeter, he was conveyed on a private train to St Ives, where he was greeted by the mayor and stayed at the recently refurbished Tregenna Castle Hotel. Historian, Charles Spicer relates how in a moment of acute embarassment, it was discovered that the ambassador from Japan was a fellow guest. 'Appalled in case their meeting was construed as a secret conspiracy against the host nation, the Japanese diplomat made his excuses and returned to London the next morning'.[22]

The St Aubyn family friend and Penzance neighbour, Colonel Bolitho, as the Lord Lieutenant and local master of hounds, was prevailed upon to lend well shod hunters to the Ribbentrop entourage. One of his diplomats, Reinhard Spitzy, later wrote of how deeply he fell for the colonel's daughter. He started dating her and through this romance:

> Ribbentrop's empty prattle about a degenerate Establishment, which was run by plutocrats, a jaded aristocracy and Jews, was clearly revealed to me in all its primitive superficiality.[23]

When the Nazi ambassador demanded a tour of St Michael's Mount, Uncle Jack resolutely refused to allow his group to set foot on the island. This spun Ribbentrop into one of his petulant outbursts. To a Bolitho guest, owner of the local newspaper, he boasted that the Mount would become his country seat, once the conquest of Britain was complete.[24] With this in mind, he used tourist postcards to prepare a secret dossier of the coast. Meanwhile, the innocent staff at the Tregenna hotel 'went to great lengths to make him feel at home, even arranging a cake decorated with a swastika at a tea party to meet the local press'.[25]

The looming international conflict had not prevented the St Levans from enjoying four happy years together. On the wall of the Mount Church, there is a memorial to Jack's first wife, Edith, with a line from St Matthew: *Blessed are the pure in heart.* Below is the one to Julia, where the text is taken from Zechariah: *In the evening there shall be light.*

Jack lived on until November 1940, marshalling his home guard at the outbreak of war in September 1939 and ordering the building of concrete pillboxes around the island to defend them from the invader. The pillboxes are the last defensive battlements ever erected on the island; they are the only ones that were never used. Ribbentrop was hanged for war crimes in 1946. He had it coming, said his Nazi rival Göring, 'just for being so stupid'.[26]

CHAPTER 3

TOTAL WAR

*We shall fight on the seas and oceans, we shall fight with
growing confidence and growing strength in the air,
we shall defend our island.*

Winston Churchill, June 1940

When war was declared, Sam and Gwen's elder two sons, born a year apart,
were both of fighting age. But at first it was 'the phoney war' and so the
eldest, John, claimed the place he had won at Cambridge, to study law. His
brother Piers, having recently returned from a year at school in Maryland,
had begun a six-year London course to become an architect. Jessica, the
eldest of the five children, had already 'come out' as a debutante and
married the week war was declared; while their younger sister, Phillipa,
was homebound with Gwen at Sissinghurst, as was a third son, Giles, now
boarding at Wellington College.

Their Uncle Harold was a governor at Wellington, his old school, which
since its foundation in 1859 had built a reputation for educating the sons
of soldiers and diplomats, in recognition of the school's founding spirit,
the Iron Duke. So while John had continued the family tradition at Eton,
Piers as the son of a former Guards officer had been admitted to Wellington
on favourable terms. The two schoolboys, who had fought against this
separation, arranged to meet covertly and every week they each began to
cycle seven miles from their schools into Windsor Great Park; a ruse only
foiled when a housemaster inspected one of their letters.

Six years later, living in their London flat, Piers had joined the Territorial
Army, while at Cambridge, John's love of sailing had translated into
membership of the University Naval Cadets. But by May 1940, the war
with Germany was being fought in earnest as the Nazis stormed through
France and Belgium, trapping the British Expeditionary Force at Dunkirk.
On 25 May, just two weeks after Winston Churchil had become Prime
Minister, his War Office gave the order to evacuate. In the next eleven days,
nearly 340,000 men would escape, including 140,000 French, Polish and
Belgian troops.

On reading the news of the evacuation, John spoke with a fellow member of the Cambridge cadets and the two of them decided to leave their college on the spot and catch the train to Chatham.[1] This was the control centre for the 'small boats' being urgently commandeered to ferry the troops home across the Channel.

On the train to Kent, learning that they were officer cadets at Cambridge, a fellow passenger cast doubts on their being accepted as such by the Royal Navy. He asked pointedly whether they even knew their sexton from their compass. So on arrival at the docks, the two cadets marched into a shipwright's and inspected both items, politely requesting a lengthy tutorial, before making a hasty purchase. With this briefing under their belts, they sailed into their interviews with confidence.

'Do you know how to handle a sexton?', John was asked.

'Of course', came the reply.

'And can you read a compass?'

'Nothing simpler'.

John was promptly dispatched to Ramsgate, where he found that the Dunkirk evacuation was creating chaos. As he entered the command centre, the cry went up for an officer to captain a Belgian merchant ship which had just been seized. Looking around the room, when no one else put their hand up, John held his high. At the age of 21, he had his first command.

Inspecting the ship's quarters as they sailed, John found an enormous double bed in the captain's cabin and could not help but ruminate on what a wasted opportunity this voyage was proving. But on reaching Dunkirk, his ship took on board about 150 men under a hail of shells from the German artillery and Messerschmitt fire from above. They made it home, where it was by now realised that a more senior officer should be found, to join John for a return trip. Many years later, John related how the rescued troops disembarked at Ramsgate:

> They marched off so smartly as if they were on the parade ground – it was then that I knew we were going to win the war.[2]

Later, flushed with success, John made his way from Ramsgate to Sissinghurst, where his mother Gwen and Aunt Vita were taking refuge. He longed to recount his adventure, only to find them far too engrossed in discussing garden plants to listen to his Dunkirk exploits. They would have been equally uninterested to know that the family yacht, the *St Michael*, had also been dispatched to rescue troops across the Channel, while one of the Mount family barges would soon see action as a commando landing craft.

After completing a training course on mine-sweeping, John was gazetted as a sub-lieutenant in August 1940 and posted to the minesweeper HMS *Salamander*.[3] He would be awarded a DSC for his service on the Arctic Convoys, providing Britain's Soviet allies with vital supplies of both munitions and food. Finding that he had a particular facility for this work, he volunteered to serve on nine missions, including the fateful PQ17.

By the spring of 1942, thirteen convoys had made the successful passage to Russia, with the loss of only one out of more than a hundred merchant ships. But the enemy had now directed some of its heavy battleships to Norway, preparing to stop the flow of supplies to the Soviets by every means at its disposal.

Meanwhile, PQ17 was the first large Anglo-American naval operation to be put under British command; HMS *Salamander* was one of three minesweepers assigned to the close escort.[4] The full escort was led by six destroyers and four corvettes, along with anti-aircraft ships and submarines, sufficient to protect the convoy's thirty-four merchant ships. They set off on 27 June 1942, with 200,000 short tonnes of supplies for Archangel, from the allied naval base at Hvalford in Iceland.

Not least through the summer midnight sun, the convoy was soon being shadowed by a German U-boat and Luftwaffe flying boats. Five days into its mission came the first aerial bombardment, followed by more attacks, which were beaten off by the convoy escort. Then on 4 July, British naval command received information that the most feared enemy battleship, *Tirpitz* and its battlegroup were advancing on PQ17.

While USS *Wainwright* had broken up one air attack that day, in the evening SS *William Hooper* was sunk by twenty-five torpedo bombers. At 21:36 hours, the Admiralty lost its nerve and ordered the convoy to scatter. The high command might be willing to risk British ships, but not to lose American units on the first joint mission they had orchestrated.

But in fact, *Tirpitz* was heading nowhere near PQ17. Meanwhile, the vanishing cruisers and destroyers had left the convoy and its remaining close escort fatally exposed to the ever present enemy threat. The next day, the 8400-ton British oil tanker RFA *Aldersdale* was one of the merchant ships bombed and heavily damaged by German aircraft; John's HMS *Salamander* managed to pick up all fifty-four crew members, before the tanker was sunk by a German U-boat.

In all, twenty-three of the thirty-four merchant ships which had left Iceland were sunk; only nine reached Archangel, while two made it to Murmansk. Barely a third of the tonnage to have left Hvalford was delivered. PQ17 had suffered the worst losses, of both men and cargo, of any convoy in the Second World War.

Reaching the naval port of Archangel on John's other missions was therefore a source of relief. There was the occasion when John enjoyed a vodka-induced camaraderie with Soviet naval officers in the forest, before a mad dash on Cossack horses to join his ship leaving port. Another time, an endearing Russian girl gave him a scarf which years later, he revealed he still kept in his sock draw. But on his next visit to Archangel, he was told she had been transferred to Siberia, for fraternising with a British officer.

Later on, John served on a naval mission to New York, hoping to meet up with a girlfriend he had known in London before the war. But when his ship docked in port, he learnt that she was getting married the next day. He consoled himself at her society wedding on Fifth Avenue.

On D-Day, John's minesweeper was supporting HMS *Warspite*. Then towards the end of hostilities, he was awarded command of the minesweeper HMS *Prospect*. His orders were to take ten German barges loaded with poisonous gas through the heavily mined Norwegian fjords, to be sunk without trace. It was a perilous journey. An accident occurred when the men failed to disarm some ordinance, which exploded on one of the barges. A mushroom cloud appeared over the barge and began to drift towards Copenhagen. John signalled that the city was at risk from a wave of poisonous gas, causing a crisis meeting of the Cabinet in London, to decide whether to inform the Danes. Deciding against, it was argued that the danger of causing undue alarm outweighed the risk from the gas, which fortunately wafted away from the populace.

Of his five years of service in the Royal Navy, John would later only say how relieved he was never to have been put in the position where he had to kill another man. Unlike his brother Piers, who would be one of only three officers of the 156 Parachute Battalion to emerge in one piece from the battle of Arnhem in September 1944.

Piers' call-up papers came two days after the outset of war and after being sent to Sandhurst, he obtained a commission in the King's Royal Rifles as a second lieutenant, like so many St Aubyn men before him. He was stationed at Hove, then in 1942 his battalion was sent out to North Africa.[5] Here he spent a week as a platoon commander on night patrol duty at El Alamein, before being posted to the Turkish-Syrian border. At this point, he applied to transfer to the new Parachute Regiment and in April 1943, Piers was assigned to 156 Battalion.

After making trainee drops near the Sea of Galilee, 156 Battalion was assigned to 'Operation Slapstick', a diversionary plan to seize the Italian port of Taranto, while the main offensive was being made on Salerno. Piers and the others arrived on the Italian coast at Taranto by cruiser, because there were no aircraft available. He immediately commandeered a bus and earned a mention in dispatches for the way he fought through olive trees and farm buildings.[6] Later he demonstrated his marksmanship on night patrol by bringing down a German officer with two pistol shots before leading a charge on a machine-gun post. Before moving on, the platoon paused to eat grapes they had discovered in an upturned German helmet.

Eventually, by the end of September, the British 1st Airborne Division had advanced 125 miles to Foggia. Reinforcements from two infantry divisions had by then landed behind them, which allowed the airborne troops to be withdrawn to Taranto. Soon after, the division, minus the 2nd Parachute Brigade, sailed for England in preparation for 'Operation Overlord', the invasion of Normandy.

By February 1944, Piers' 156 Battalion had eventually been gathered at one base in Melton Mowbray.[7] This was superb hunting country, where the enthusiastic young officer was freely offered horses for the rest of the season.

Training continued through the summer of 1944, as fifteen airbourne operations were planned and then cancelled in quick succession, between the Normandy landing on 6 June and early September. Finally, on 10 September, Field Marshal Montgomery outlined the plan for 'Operation Market Garden' to the airborne commanders in Brussels, Generals Dempsey and Browning. The British airborne troops, together with the Polish Brigade, were to capture the bridge over the Rhine at Arnhem, securing a bridgehead in advance of ground forces, as they had done in Italy. If the plan worked, it could foreshorten the war by six months and the western allies would reach Berlin before Stalin. But the entire operation had been betrayed to the Nazis by a worm, caught on the hook by the Soviets. His name was Anthony Blunt, a senior MI5 officer whose treachery would cost hundreds of thousands of lives, so that his Russian paymasters could reach Berlin first.[8]

Piers had acquired a reputation for leading from the front, by the time he and 33 other officers, with around 600 men, dropped near the Dutch town of Arnhem on 18 September 1944, as part of 4th Parachute Brigade. They were to reinforce the party already fighting to take the bridge. But the operation was 60 miles behind enemy lines, and owing to Blunt's betrayal the Germans were found in far greater strength than expected.

Although he had been appointed battalion intelligence officer, Piers was leading thirty tired and hungry men two days later when they came across the enemy firing down into the brigade headquarters, established in a hollow by Brigadier 'Shan' Hackett. Being low on ammunition, Piers told the Germans, with a mixture of hand signals and choice Anglo-Saxon words, to put down their arms and 'f*** off'; which, to his relief, they did. After clearing a neighbouring wood, he brought the Germans' weapons to Hackett, half of whose men were killed or wounded in the next four hours. Hackett then called together all those who could walk and led them in a wild dash through the astonished Germans to his division's defensive position several hundred yards away. It was 'a beautiful little charge and chase' by the men of 156 Battalion, Hackett commented in his battlefield diary.

By now the battalion consisted of little more than two platoons, one under Lieutenant St Aubyn and the other under Captain Stevens – the battalion's forward observation officer – who each took possession of an empty house. Major Powell was in overall command. St Aubyn's building had strong walls, but it was clear that the platoon could not survive there long. When Powell went to ask General Urquhart for permission to withdraw, the shock in the general's face indicated that he had forgotten all about them.

After resisting two fierce attacks, in which he lost eight more men, Piers decided not to await Powell's return, and joined the rest of the battalion holed up in three nearby houses. By now the bridge had been lost, and his men had only boiled sweets to eat. On visiting brigade HQ to obtain rations he found no food, but happily fell into conversation with a Nicolson cousin, Lord Buckhurst, until Hackett told them sharply to get into a trench before they were killed.

Back in his house, St Aubyn dispatched a foraging party, then settled down to read *Barchester Towers*, reasoning that if he seemed relaxed it would have the same effect on his men. When a private started to run from window to window, shouting 'I'll get you, you bastard' at a German sniper, St Aubyn told him to be quiet, and returned to the reassuring story of Victorian clerical squabbles.

At dawn, enemy infantry were beaten off with grenades, and two paras ran across the street to drop bombs from the first floor of a building opposite onto a self-propelled gun. Piers withdrew his men from their house only just before a tank reduced it to rubble. The following day, as his men were digging trenches, the enemy tried a new tack, using a loudspeaker to play the Teddy Bears' Picnic and to relay a female voice telling them to surrender if they wanted to see their wives and sweethearts again. Some Typhoons swept low to make a rocket attack, but they did not stop the enemy drawing closer. As a private was about to fire his bren through a hedge, Piers placed a hand over the barrel, coolly saying that they did not want to give away their position.

When the withdrawal was ordered on the eighth day the platoon retreated into some remaining houses, where the men wrapped their boots in carpet and curtain material to deaden the noise. At nightfall, Lieutenant St Aubyn led them through the woods, each man holding the unfastened smock of the soldier in front, as if they were children playing a game. After they had reached the riverbank, a Canadian engineer beckoned from a boat: 'Room for one more'. As St Aubyn held back to offer another man the place, a fresh machine-gun burst decided the issue, and the passengers pulled him aboard.

On his way back to England, Piers went through Brussels, where he met up again with his friend 'Billy' Buckhurst. They took themselves out to dinner in the city's finest restaurant. In all, out of 603 members of 156 Battalion, only 27 had escaped,[9] among them the quartermaster, Lieutenant Bush, as well as St Aubyn and Powell, both of whom would be awarded the Military Cross. The summary of Piers' citation would read: *This officer displayed conspicuous gallantry and great powers of leadership.*

At a civic dinner held in their honour, after the Paras returned to their base at Melton Mowbray, Lieutenant St Aubyn was told that there was 'a young lady' at the door. Thinking that it was his girlfriend, he strolled out with a glass of wine and a cigar and was shocked to find his batman's widow, who had come up from London to ask how her husband had been killed. Piers was then given a few days leave on St Michael's Mount, where he wrote letters of condolence to the next of kin of all those men under his command who had fallen. He always said it was the hardest thing he ever had to do.

While the fighting continued in Europe, bombs were falling all over England and one of them came quite close to killing John and Piers' younger brother, Giles. On 8 October 1940, a stray bomb dropped on Wellington College and by a freak chance killed the headmaster; other bombs on the school that night hit the old hall, chapel and library. Although the boys had been sent to their shelters – and would be sent there every night for a year after the event – Giles later remembered the shock of being told what had happened the following morning; but also the calming influence when the king and queen paid a visit, attending a memorial service in the college chapel. Apart from Eton, and from a slimmer cohort, Wellington would go on to mourn more war dead, than any other school in the country.

At the same time, bombs falling on Wellington were nothing to the fifty-nine bombing raids which hammered Plymouth during the war, which killed 1174 civilians and injured a further 4448.[10] The raids destroyed 4000 properties and 18,000 were damaged. St Aubyn tenants and their houses skirting the dockyard, a strategic military target, suffered their fair share of this misery.

On leaving Wellington in 1943, Giles was swept along by the school spirit into joining the Royal Navy, but he was entirely unsuited to be an ordinary seaman and was invalided out within a year. A lifelong academic, he went up to Oxford, where he read history for the next three years. Someone else who had come up that year was Mary Southwell, a beautiful young student of philosophy, who had won a place from her home in South Africa. Her father had trained as an engineer in the Cornish mines, before emigrating to work for his uncle, one of Cecil Rhodes' business partners. His expertise brought rich rewards, but also the poor health synonimous with mineshaft duty. Giles and his daughter, Mary, now became good friends.

In 1942, Sam and Gwen had finally come to live on the Mount, where they feared failure stared them in the face. Although Uncle Jack had excluded Sam from any role in the management of the estate, he had at least taken care to make the sort of family provision treated as usual by this time, to mitigate death duties. But just before he had died in 1940, the government had passed a hastily drafted Finance Act, which appeared to circumvent his arrangements and impose crippling taxes on Jack's estate.

The war call-up had at least reduced the staff levels on the island, making the urgent need for economy that much easier to impose. The newly installed St Levans had the support of their daughter, Jessica, who came to live in the steward's house in the island village. She now had a baby daughter and was expecting another, while her husband, Pat Koppel, had joined the Welsh Guards as a second lieutenant.

Gwen found the castle in poor decorative order, but discovered an ingenious way to circumvent the wartime rationing of paint. An exemption had been made for religious buildings and Gwen determined that one of the rooms in the castle should be blessed as her Catholic chapel. Powder blue paint was administered to the walls and the RC Bishop of Plymouth was invited to bless the room. Only Gwen kept on changing her mind about which room, resulting in a succession of episcopal visits and a surfeit of castle rooms decorated in fresh light blue paint. Throughout the thirty years that she remained there, Gwen never altered those room colours.

Virginia Woolf, Vita's earlier love, had only recently committed suicide, leaving Vita still distraught. She did not hold back on her feelings about Gwen – her leaving Sissinghurst to assume this new role was 'a betrayal and a dereliction'.[11] Vita even called Harold a 'quisling' for visiting his sister's new home and admiring it.[12] Arriving by train in September 1942, Harold described how, with Sam and Gwen he had '...walked across the causeway. Then up the steep grass path between hydrangeas, fuchsias and pink lilies like hemerocallis. Great granite rocks above us among the pines and ilexes, and the blue sea below'.[13] He tried to mollify Vita, by emphasising the frustration of living on an island so often cut off by the sea: 'If you had been born to it you would have become a sea-gull, perching on rocks and screaming sea-gull cries'.[14]

But the brutal truth was that Gwen had chosen this island jewel over Vita's consumate garden. With Sam, she had put aside the years of drift and waiting, to embrace their uncertain destiny.

CHAPTER 4

GIFT TO THE NATION

*At the Mount, everything went
through Her Ladyship first.*

Stanley Ager, Butler[1]

By the spring of 1945, it was evident that the tide of war in the Allies' favour was unstoppable. John and Piers were home at the Mount on leave, Giles was there on vacation from Oxford and Jessica now had three small children living with her on the island. Two distant St Aubyn cousins had been killed in action, but for once war had treated the senior family line with mercy. Sam St Levan now wrote to his uncle's old valet, Stanley Ager, inviting him back to the island as his butler. Ager, who had returned from the war to find that his most recent employer had died, agreed to come on a three-month trial. He stayed for thirty years, although as he later explained, he had to adjust to radical new circumstances, for a butler:

> After the war most people were unable to afford the same amount of staff. I saw great changes in service as our people's life-styles became less grand. In my youth the butler was always available if the family needed him; otherwise, he merely supervised the staff. He had worked hard all his life, and he wasn't going to continue if he could help it!
>
> A butler in the old days would never have dreamed of doing as much day-to-day work as I did. He wouldn't have cleaned the silver, laid the table or seen to it that the reception rooms were orderly: those jobs belonged to the first footman. Nor did any of my staff wait on me as they would have done on a butler in the past.[2]

Ager found that footmen, who used to work their way up through service, now had to be trained from scratch; but he did it so well that his protégés became butlers to royalty and embassies around the world. In 1980, in collaboration with Fiona St Aubyn, he published *Ager's Way to Easy*

Elegance – The Butler's Guide, a bible for all aspiring domestic staff (and their employers); to which the screenwriters of *Downton Abbey* acknowledged 'a deep sense of gratitude'.[3]

While Sam indulged his sailing, attended to his pigs, or met the tenants on the farms with his agent, Gwen and Ager formed an unshakeable alliance to ensure the smooth running of the island. It was as if Gwen had imbibed every detail of Blandings Castle, as created by P.G. Wodehouse, except for one difference. Apart from royalty, dignitaries and close family, she refused to countenance guests. Her years of solitude in Vita's company had done nothing to conquer her innate shyness, or to ease those feelings of anxiety which her head injury in 1933 had accentuated. Gwen could be the most delightful company in a private conversation, warm, generous and amusing; but in a crowded room, she either vanished, or wore a cold, intimidating carapace.

One occasion was in 1951, when Sam and Gwen's nephew, Nigel Nicolson, aspired to follow his father into parliament, by standing as the Conservative candidate in Falmouth. Nigel later wrote:

> Always in those days my refuge was St Michael's Mount...
> Once I begged my uncle to entertain Rab Butler there for
> a night when he was visiting Cornwall, and such was his
> astonishment and delight, that I could wheedle anything out
> of him, including the promise of Government subsidy for the
> Cornish tin-mining industry.[4]

Gwen had agreed to this alien intrusion only reluctantly. The next morning, determined to make the esteemed Tory statesman leave her island bastion with all due speed, she informed Butler that she feared a storm was brewing. So the harbour master had advised that if he did not leave before the causeway closed, he might be trapped on the island for days. This had the desired effect. As for Butler's effusive promises to Falmouth, they were never put to the test, as a few weeks later, Nigel lost to Labour by a thousand votes.

Another time, Piers and Mary St Aubyn were staying on the Mount with their children, when their closest friends from Sussex were on holiday nearby. Mary asked if the Shands, whose daughter the future Queen Camilla had just met Prince Charles, could come to tea. After careful consultation with Mr Ager, her Ladyship announced that it was impossible to receive all six members of their party, 'because the footmen would not be able to serve everyone with matching teacups'.

Meanwhile, after a series of decisions in lower tribunals, the threat of death duties hanging over the St Aubyns had finally wound its way into the Royal Courts of Justice, nine years after Uncle Jack had died. The family were represented by Sir Andrew Clarke KC, a decorated war hero who, according to *The Times*, had established his position as 'the leading advocate at the Chancery bar'. Against them was the Solicitor General, appearing in person for the Crown. If tax was to be levied on the family estate, it would be at seventy-five per cent. The family contemplated having to move out of the castle and live in the laundry building on the side of the island, while Lord Beaverbrook let it be known that he would be prepared to purchase the Mount for four million pounds. It felt as if the tax demand was striking at the very heart of the St Aubyn family identity.

Sir Andrew had qualified at the Bar by correspondence from Monte Carlo and his gambling instinct evidently infused his strategy, to defend the family fortune. With subtle tactics as well as an intricate grasp of the obscure details of the case, after winning judgement at the Royal Courts, he informed Sam and Gwen that he fully intended to lose on appeal; so that his confidently predicted victory in the House of Lords would be final. Stripped of its complexity was an important question of principle: where a law on taxation was ambiguous or vague, should the courts interpret it in favour of the king, or his subject?

After the war ended, John resumed his legal training as a solicitor. His father held that many Cornish families had been ruined by London lawyers, so he urged his son to become one instead. But taking a room at first in Chelsea, invited to innumerable parties, legal detail was not John's metier. His career at a Knightsbridge firm was not improved when he met Baroness Orczy (celebrated author of *The Scarlet Pimpernel*), to sign her will. On the way back to the office, he left it on the No. 9 bus.

John was also an investor. His eye for an opportunity would warm to any scheme with a social purpose, to create new jobs or improve the housing stock. His chain of launderettes in South London relieved housewives of the drudgery of the mangle. A joinery in Plymouth trained skilled carpenters. Housing schemes helped to rebuild the bombed-out city.

Meanwhile, there was a succession of romances. He became engaged to one girl, but all foundered when they ran out of conversation on holiday. With a view to a proposal, he invited another into the garden for a game of croquet. But so cunning were her tactics with a mallet, that John abandoned all thought of a union.

His brother, Piers, had more success in that field. He had been discharged after a year in Palestine as a captain, part of the British mandate force holding the line between Palestinian and Jew. Here he had earned the nickname 'Port St Aubyn', after a six-bottle case fell out of the back of his truck, as he drove across the desert to his battalion HQ. On his return home, Piers reluctantly abandoned his architectural ambitions, to become a gilt-edged broker in the City with the firm of Grieveson Grant, where his father was remembered as the half-commission man and port was a staple of the lunchtime menu. He moved to Greenwells, where his 'gilt' team established an enviable reputation for expertise and research.[5]

Piers went to a dance in Cornwall also attended by Giles, down from Oxford. He had brought his friend, Mary Southwell, along and the war hero insisted that his younger brother introduce them to each other. Mary's philosophy tutor that year was Professor 'Freddie' Ayer, whose masterly *Language, Truth and Logic* had made him the star of Oxford. But when he attempted ardent advances on Mary, she put him firmly in his place. Her cousin, Jim Bailey, the decorated Spitfire pilot, who was up at Oxford at the same time, later told how Mary's friends dubbed her 'Freddie's Frigidaire'.[6]

Mary felt no such coldness towards Piers and they became a couple. A little later, Piers arranged a sailing trip around the Lizard point to the Mount, which proved to be a stormy experience. Soon afterwards, Piers proposed and Mary accepted, but on the understanding that she need never go sailing again. They were married in the Anglican cathedral in Johannesburg, by a bishop who on his way up the aisle, pinched the bottom of a good-looking usher.

Giles St Aubyn never married but became an acclaimed historian and one of the most flamboyant housemasters in modern times. At Eton, where he taught for nearly forty years, he owned a succession of fast cars. One was a D-Type Jaguar – even then so valuable he had to keep it in a lock-up garage in Windsor. He bought another car, in order to visit the Jag. He adorned his study with paintings of St Michael's Mount, while inviting interesting friends to lunch – Sir Martin Gilliat, the *Sunday Telegraph* diarist Kenneth Rose, the artist Derek Hill. The Queen Mother graced his house plays. As a young master, he would turn up at school still wearing white tie and tails, having come directly from debutante balls in London. Rumours that he had dated Princess Margaret were avidly circulated by his charges at the time.

Sir Nicholas Coleridge, the future Provost of Eton, was in Giles' house. He gave the eulogy at his memorial service:

> Giles' signature was like a coil of barbed wire above a First World War trench, and boys routinely attempted the perfect imitation. At a reunion dinner many years' later, middle aged men revived their efforts and Giles judged them all. I was taught Theology A- Level by Giles, who as a teacher was exceptional, even brilliant. Chinese missionaries, who made up half the course, were covered in one swift lesson. The remainder were devoted to the Victorian Tractarian Movement, the subject of his final book, *Souls in Torment*.[7]

Giles wrote twelve books, all of which were reviewed with distinction in the national press. He was elected a Fellow of the Royal Literary Society, to whom he later made a generous bequest, to fund a prize for budding historians; he was also made an LVO. His long life – he lived well into his nineties – combined many aspects: from the years living at Sissinghurst, to his friendship with the poet John Betjeman; from his love of remote islands, which led him to buy one off the coast of Wales, to his love of film, which prompted him to start the Eton Film Unit, by purchasing all the equipment himself; from his Worcestershire finishing school for recalcitrant students, which won renown as 'the Hilton of crammers', to his discreet friendship with the Royal Family – whether tutoring the Duke of Kent or cruising with the Queen Mother on HMY *Britannia*.

But it seems that only old age could cure him of his discomfort with women. As a housemaster, a matriarch approached him on a cold St Andrew's Day, demanding to know how her son Nigel was doing.

'All right', came the nervous reply.

'All right, Giles? For the money I am paying you, I could keep two racehorses in training at Newmarket – and what is more, they would be winning prizes!'

Giles promptly agreed to make Nigel his next head of house.[8]

Uncle Jack's obituary in 1940 had noted how he had 'displayed great generosity towards' those wishing to visit St Michael's Mount. 'With a kindness that was typical of his character he threw it open to the public – with certain natural limitations – and arranged that one of his employees should explain its history and particular features to those who visited it.' The contribution this made to the growing tourist industry could 'be gathered from the fact that over 10,000 persons a year signed the visitors' book, and there were thousands who did not'.[9]

As Sam and Gwen had braced themselves for their Royal Court hearing in May 1949, they would have been keenly aware of the success of Longleat House, which a month before had become the first stately home to open its doors as a commercial concern, at a charge of half a crown for adults and a shilling for children. Lord and Lady Bath appeared on the front cover of *Tatler*, which hailed 'an event of great cultural importance'. In the same month, Chatsworth followed suit and soon country house visitors were spoilt for choice, if they were prepared to pay. The pre-war custom, adhered to by Uncle Jack, had been to frown on charging visitors for admission, unless the proceeds went to charity. Post-war, the owners of these enormous properties could not afford to keep them, unless charity began at home.

For others, the National Trust whose original object had been to protect outdoor spaces of great beauty, had become a safe haven through its 'Country House Scheme', which had been authorised by an Act of Parliament in 1937. This allowed families to escape inheritance taxes, if they gave their properties to the Trust, which was quite explicit in expecting visitors to contribute to the cost of running them. It so happened that Gwen's brother, Harold, had joined its Historic Buildings Committee in 1944, and he was now vice-chairman of the Trust's Executive Committee.

Longleat had 134,000 paying visitors in its first year of operation and in 1950 *The Times* published its first annual list of country houses open to the public. It counted thirty-nine private houses, plus another twenty-eight belonging to the Trust. Five years later, the total number had swelled to 250 of Britain's finest homes, none offering access for free.[10] So naturally the St Levans began to explore the potential to offer the Mount to a wider number of visitors. A year after Longleat had opened, the Cornish papers reported:

> A continuous stream of people passed over the Causeway to St Michael's Mount all day long on Tuesday, when ... proceeds were entirely devoted to the British Red Cross Society. Fine weather attracted well over 1,500 people, who paid a total of more than £100 to climb the Mount and look over the Chapel and some of the apartments.
>
> Outside on the Causeway the Marazion detachment of the British Red Cross Society were busy forming a mile of pennies, which amounted to over £16.[11]

Minds were concentrated when, as their Counsel had predicted, the chancery case in the Appeal Court was won decisively by the Crown. Sir Andrew Clarke KC prepared the family for the showdown before the Law Lords, whose final judgement would be read out in the Palace of Westminster, on 12 July 1951. This just happened to be Piers' thirty-first birthday, which he took as a good omen. But after listening to the judgement, which was intensely intricate in its reasoning, Piers and his brother John both came away convinced that the family had lost.

The judges certainly made it clear that the inheritance was liable for tax. Uncle Jack had provided for an income to sustain his lifestyle when he had settled his will in 1927. This meant that he retained an interest in property, on which duty was payable. But he had transferred the bulk of his estate into a separate fund, in which he held no interest. The mischief in the 1940 Finance Act was that it had 'hypothesised' that this should nevertheless be assessed as part of the property, from which Sam's uncle still drew his benefit.

Here, the senior Law Lord Gavin Simonds found in the Finance Act 'provisions which are, I think, of unrivalled complexity and difficulty and couched in language so tortuous and obscure that I am tempted to reject them as meaningless'. He answered the profound question at the heart of the matter by reasserting Lord Wensleydale's familiar dictum: 'It is a well-established rule that the subject is not to be taxed without clear words for that purpose'.

Lord Simonds' son had been killed in action at Arnhem, where he had been second-in-command of his battalion. Three months after giving judgement for the St Aubyns, Simonds was appointed Lord Chancellor by the new Conservative government. But the rule he affirmed was not partisan in any sense, which is why it still stands today; unless the taxpayer has indulged in elaborate tax avoidance and swum into deep waters.

The Devonport estate which Sam had inherited was much depleted. Of the houses originally granted on long leases, by 1945 about a quarter remained within the estate. But quite apart from war damage, many of their leases still had forty years or more to run. Meanwhile, the 1947 Planning Act removed the essential role of the lord of the manor, as a guardian of development and quality of life on his urban property. Lastly, Plymouth Council urgently needed to build social housing, to provide for families bombed out of their homes. Large tracts of land were therefore sold to the Council, for clearance and social housing projects, which would help the

St Aubyns to meet the far less onerous demands of the taxman, now their case had been settled.

The family determined on a disposal strategy in the town, which today has almost run its course, with leasehold reform since 1967 having speeded the process on its way. They also thought long and hard over how to protect the family's enjoyment of its prize possession and the farming estate in Cornwall. The price which Lord Beaverbrook had placed on the island, in making his tactless offer to purchase, emphasised that it dwarfed the value of anything else they owned. So the Mount would still have to be sold if the family was ever again caught by inheritance taxes.

Meanwhile, Harold Nicolson was finding his role at the National Trust deeply absorbing. James Lees-Milne, who was the Trust's Adviser on Historic Buildings, became Harold's biographer and later wrote: 'he was popular with his fellow members and the staff whom he never snubbed but always treated with respect, friendliness and dry humour'.[12] In 1947, Lees-Milne took Harold and Vita on tours of historic buildings in the West Country, including some visited quite by chance, where they were usually welcome. But at Ramsbury Manor, the owner, Sir Francis Burdett, had been having breakfast:

> He 'rushed down the steps, brandishing a newspaper in one hand and a piece of toast in the other. Puce in the face with indignation he shouted to us to stop and explain our extraordinary behaviour. Overcome with shame Harold tried to hide himself on the floorboards'.

Vita refused either to obey Harold's pleading or to drive away:

> With exquisite courtesy, she pretended she had mistaken the house for Littlecote Manor, which it in no way resembled. The incident greatly upset Harold … The rest of the morning we drove in painful silence.[13]

There can be little doubt that Harold discussed with Gwen and Sam the possibility of their giving the St Aubyn family home to the nation, even before their court case was decided. But in the case of Sissinghurst, Vita made her view well known to her husband, as she recorded in her diary: 'Never, never, never! Not that hard metal plate at my door! Nigel can do what he likes when I am dead, but so long as I shall live, no National Trust or any other foreign body shall have my darling'.[14]

If Gwen's island castle became national property, on the other hand, it might have occurred to Vita that this would redress some of the stark imbalance which had arisen in their circumstances, since Gwen's Cornish accession. Like everyone else, the Nicolsons were now encouraging visitors to their brilliant garden creation, but it was under sufferance. Piers had moved with Mary and their three children to Sussex and very occasionally they were all invited to visit his uncle and aunt for tea. Harold took his nephew, younger son in tow, to the top of the tower at Sissinghurst. Here they gazed down on the day trippers flocking past below. 'You know Piers', he remarked dryly, 'I do so intensely fear this age of the common man'.

This was not a feeling shared by his son Nigel. Nor by the St Levans, who by 1953 had managed to increase visitor numbers on the Mount to 40,000 a year, each paying 2 shillings (10p), plus the cost of a ferry to the island, if the tide was in.[15] As the family lawyer as well as his father's heir, John St Aubyn began to explore the possible role of the National Trust, to safeguard the future of the island and the position of the family. With Sam still in healthy middle age, the tourist revenue rising and Uncle Jack's taxes paid, there appeared the opportunity to achieve something far more ambitious than an orthodox 'Country House Scheme', or the mere transfer of property in lieu of inheritance tax.

The family was conscious that a momentous decision was being taken and proposals surrounding a gift to the Trust were discussed in meticulous detail.[16] Ever the ship's captain, John was determined to achieve the right balance, to maintain command on board the island, at the same time as co-operating with the Trust in London, whose advice and expertise were looked upon as significant benefits to come. These aims were aided by strong personal relationships, not least that with his Uncle Harold as Deputy Chairman of the Trust. They were also assisted by the offer of a generous slice of the Devonport portfolio. Finally, in August 1954, the National Trust announced 'the gift of St Michael's Mount from Lord St Levan ...[who] has provided a munificent endowment'. It is one of the very few Trust properties which has never yet had to call on central funds for assistance.

One could view the result as emblematic of the long running strand of Cornish particularism. Cornwall might no longer have its own parliament, but the Mount at least has retained its own management. The St Aubyns might also be said to have adopted a position akin to their forebear, Sir Mauger. He was tenant-in-chief to the king; the family now hold the same role in relation to the Trust, running the tourist trade and overseeing the key island staff themselves. In any event, it is a formula which has proved the most productive – as well as one of the most congenial – to compare with any gift in the record of the Country House scheme. It remains the only property in the Trust handbook which is described as a partnership[17] – yet one which has lasted seventy years and now includes the fourth generation of the St Aubyns.

This was greatly to the credit of the National Trust – large rule-bound organisations often find it hard to be so far sighted and flexible. In return, the Trust found that this partnership was only the start of John's contribution to their work. He was involved from the outset in the National Trust's Operation Neptune, pledging miles of unspoilt Cornish coastline to prevent future development. He persuaded many personal friends to donate their houses to the Country House scheme. When the Labour government of the 1970s launched Manpower Services, he was the first to realise its potential in assisting the National Trust to undertake restoration work, such as rebuilding the causeway which linked the island of St Michael's Mount with the mainland. The National Trust awarded John the Octavia Hill medal in recognition of his outstanding contribution to the charity over his lifetime. While today, nearly half a million visitors come to the island every year and over half of those make the pilgrimage to the summit.

By the time of his negotiations with them in 1953–54, John was well ensconced in a duplex apartment in Ennismore Gardens, one of the most delightful squares in Knightsbridge. Every Monday evening, he would hold court there, a weekly fixture on the London social scene for the next two decades. This was because no one else held parties on a Monday and so it increased one's chances when inviting along any attractive girl one might meet during the week. By 1970, his London parties still flourished but marriage to Sue Kennedy portended a new, more serious side to John, as his lifetime's mission on the Mount now loomed.

Sam and Gwen eventually retired to the mainland in 1974. Four years later, dozing in their garden on a summer's afternoon, Sam suddenly opened his eyes and said quietly: 'I do love you, Gwen'. Then he closed them again for the last time. She lived until she was 99, always keen for family news, not least of her twenty-six great-grandchildren, and alert to the very end.

Without delay, John and Sue set about modernising the family seat. Mr Ager retired to an estate cottage on the mainland, after fifty-three years in service. He and the nine live-in staff were replaced by a couple from New Zealand. An ancient army landing craft gave way to innovative amphibious vessels, to reach the island at awkward times. The historic barge was restored as one of the world's oldest working sail boats, later to feature in the 2012 Jubilee Thames procession. Weekends were enlivened with charity days for local causes.

In the House of Lords, like family members before him, John spoke only on county issues. But to secure a debate on planning blight in Mount's Bay, he agreed in return to take the Tory whip. His nephew Nicholas' family were living near Gulval at the time, and Jane, his wife, had come to meet him off the Penzance night train. Instead, she was hailed on the platform by John, who announced to startled onlookers, 'I'm quite exhausted. Just come down from London, where I've been whipped all night for a week!'

John's legal practice proved its worth again, during the Penlee lifeboat disaster of 1981, when there was an outpouring of grief and a flood of donations to a hastily announced relief fund. John corralled his old friend, Lord Goodman, into sorting out the ensuing mess, when lawyers started circling this pot of gold. Instead of acrimonious lawsuits, the money actually reached the bereaved families and so the tiny port recovered its strength. John later attributed their success to Goodman's production of a delicious cake for tea, which at a critical moment aroused the lawyers' hunger at the expense of their wallets.

On 1 April 2013, John received the medal of the Arctic Star, sixty years after his heroic actions and only days before he died, aged 94. Following Sue's death in 2003, he had retired to the mainland but remained a prominent benefactor of local causes. Piers had moved to Lugdvan after Mary died and the two brothers remained close. John bequeathed the family seat to Piers' son, James St Aubyn, who with his wife Mary and four children had already settled in Cornwall and become fully involved in the estate's affairs.

James and Mary St Levan, as they became on John's death, have now managed its business, while living on the Mount for two decades. They were honoured by a visit from the future Charles III and Queen Camilla in 2010, when matching teacups were in plentiful supply; and from HM Queen Elizabeth and Prince Philip in 2013. They oversaw the most comprehensive castle renovation project since the east wing was built. They also led the island community through the isolation of the COVID-19 pandemic.

All this and more has been done, while upholding the family's values at their best. During James and Mary's time alone, there have also been four family weddings and five christenings in the Mount Church. In this epoch, family members have again been found in the Guards, the Inns of Court and the House of Commons, while others have sought new horizons. So the family identity both continues and evolves, alongside that of the island whose history it has shared, ever since William de Sancto Albino witnessed a gift to the Priory, and Sir Henry de Kemyell granted the monks a cartload of wood, each week, from his grove of Clowance, eight centuries ago.

SOURCE MATERIALS

AUTHOR'S NOTE

Profound thanks for this history are due to the faithful transcribers of our nation's records since the Conquest. A. L. Rowse, Muriel St Clare Byrne, P. A. S. Pool, Eveline Cruickshanks, as well as Mark Stoyle and John Chynoweth more recently, have provided scholarly detail about the Tudor, Stuart and Hanoverian periods. The Royal Institute of Cornwall, Kresen Kernow, the Institute of Cornish Studies, the Morab Library and Hatfield House have shared key contributions. The recent Gascon Rolls and Agincourt 600 projects directed by Ann Curry have revealed the family members who fought in the Hundred Years' War. Above all, I thank the Parliament History project for letting me draw on the biographies of the eleven family MPs elected between 1414 and 1812, and those of many of their contemporaries.

Diana Hartley's history and my father's library have been essential resources. I am indebted to my brother, James, for access to the family archives on St Michael's Mount and to my sister, Fiona, for excerpts from her book with Stanley Ager. I am deeply grateful to Kate Gibson for her research notes on James St Aubyn's diaries and letters, and her permission and that of the Huntington Library to use their contents. Juliet and Adam Nicolson have kindly let me draw on the Nicolson literary estates, Michael Bloch likewise on behalf of the estate of James Lees-Milne. Nicholas Coleridge has shared his memories of Giles St Aubyn and Jamie Wemyss his notes on the battle of Loos.

I thank the Chicago University Press for letting me extract jewels from the Lisle Letters and Oxford University Press for excerpts from Frank Taylor's *Gesta Henrici Quinti*. The British Library, the Newberry Library and the Folger Shakespeare Library have also been most generous.

There are so many others on whom I have relied, but with special thanks to my wife Jane, to Charles Fox, to Mark Stoyle and to John O'Reilly; also to my editors, Laura Hirst and Sarah Hodder. All scholarly contributions are listed among the source materials, in the bibliography and the end notes that follow. My narrative, with its inductive reasoning, is entirely to blame for any errors of fact or judgement.

November 2024

SOURCE REFERENCES

Since the formation of the Public Record Office in 1838, a great many calendars of the historic records in its possession have been published. Owing to their size and complexity, the eight abbreviated categories marked below with an asterisk are not listed individually in this bibliography, but the endnotes should still enable the reader to find the reference page of the appropriate volume in question.

As examples, the entry **CPR, 5.H.IV Pt. 2, Vol. 2, p.397 (13/5/1404)** refers to the Calendar of the Patent Rolls for the fifth year in the reign of Henry IV. The year 1404 is to be found in Volume 2 of the calendar edited by H. C. Maxwell Lyte (1905), where the specific entry for 13 May 1404 is to be found on page 397 under the heading '5 Henry IV'. The entry **CIPM, 1.H.IV, Vol. 18, no. 312, p.100 (23/5/1400)** refers to the Calendar of Inquisitions Post Mortem, for the first year in the reign of Henry IV, to be found in Volume 18, edited by J. L. Kirby (1987), where the specific entry number 312 is to be found on page 100.

Other than these eight categories, full references are to be found in the bibliography, under the names of the editors with which each endnote begins.

Abbreviations

A&O	Acts and Ordinances of the Interregnum, 1642–1660*
AEM & D Angl.	Archives étrangères, mémoires et documents, Angleterre, Ministry of Foreign Affairs, Paris
APC	Acts of the Privy Council of England*
BL	British Library
CIPM	Calendar of Inquisitions Post Mortem*
CCR	Calendar of Close Rolls*
CFR	Calendar of Fine Rolls*
CRO	Cornwall Record Office at Kresen Kernow
CPR	Calendar of Patent Rolls*
CSP	Calendar of Spanish Papers*
CSPD	Calendar of State Papers Domestic*
E.	Thomason Tracts, kept at the BL
EHR	English Historical Review
FRDK	Fourth Report of the Deputy Keeper of the Public Records (1843)
FSL	Folger Shakespeare Library
HHA	Hatfield House Archives
HHL	Henry E. Huntington Library, San Marino, California

HND	Harold Nicolson Diaries, 3 Volumes, Nigel Nicolson (ed.) (1966–8)
HoC	History of Parliament: The House of Commons
HoC.org	History of Parliament online: ww.historyofparliamentonline.org/
HRO	Hampshire Record Office
JHoC	Journal of the House of Commons (1802)
JICS	Journal of the Institute of Cornish Studies
JRIC	Journal of the Royal Institution of Cornwall
LP	J.S. Brewer, R.H. Brodie & J. Gairdner, (eds.), Letters and Papers, Foreign & Domestic, of the Reign of Henry VIII (21 vols., 1862–1932)
ODNB	Oxford Dictionary of National Biography (2004)
OUP	Oxford University Press
PC	Privy Council records held at TNA
RIA	Royal Irish Academy
RIC	Royal Institution of Cornwall
Rot. Parl.	Rotuli Parliamentorum
STAC	Star Chamber records held at TNA
TNA	The National Archives
TRHS	Transactions of the Royal Historical Society
WSRO	West Sussex Record Office

List of Illustrations

1. Detail from: HHL reference RB 125774, The Register of the Most Noble Order of the Garter, Vol. 2 (1724) by J. Anstis (image opp. p.268).
2. Detail from Crabbe, W.R., *Monumental Brasses of Devonshire, Transactions of the Exeter Diocesan Architectural Society* (Vol. VI, 1856), Plate 2. Newberry Library Identifier LC: 09013876.
3. *Recueil des chroniques d'Engleterre*. Origin: France, N. E. (Lille?) and Netherlands, S. (Bruges). c. XV.

PART ONE

Chapter 1: Liegeman

1. *HoC 1604–1629*, Vol. 6, p.135. The Roll of Battle Abbey, the Conqueror's 'faithful record of all who shared in the glory of the victory' (Burke, *The Roll of Battle Abbey*), lists the name of 'Sent Albin'. The account of the Roll published by John Murray in 1889 suggests that his town was near Evreaux. Leland in his *Itinerary* (p.186) agrees that he came out of Brittany, as does Camden in *Remains concerning Britain* (p.93). Saint-Aubin-du-Cormier is one

of the many local places named after Bishop Aubin of Angiers, who was the sixth-century patron saint of hostages and refugees. It is the closest to Evreaux, and to the bastille of Mauger's patron, the Baron Judhael of Mayenne.

2. 'Chronicum Johannis Brompton' is the MS in Cotton, Tiber C. XIII.
3. Tregellas, Walter H., *Cornish Worthies*, pp.281–82.
4. Monmouth, Geoffrey of, *The History of the Kings of Britain*, pp.256–8. For a modern account of the migration to Brittany, see Todd, Malcolm, *The South West to AD1000*, pp.238–40, 273–5.
5. Maxwell Lyte, *Descriptive Catalogue Vol. 3*, C.6412, *'in the armed hand'*.
6. Camden, *Remains concerning Britain*, p.93.
7. Stenton, Doris (ed.), *Pleas before the King or his Justices, 1198–1202*, Vol. 2, pp.60–61.
8. Polwhele, The Rev. R., *The History of Cornwall*, Vol. 2, p.65ff.
9. A territorial concept refined in Ardrey, Robert, *The Territorial Imperative*.
10. Maxwell Lyte, *Miscellaneous Inquisitions*, Vol. 126, p.43.
11. Maxwell Lyte, *Descriptive Catalogue*, Vol. 3, C. 6412.
12. Ibid., Vol. 3, C. 3642.
13. Camden, *Remains*, p.90. 'About the year of our Lord 1000 ... surnames began to be taken up in France, and in England about the time of the Conquest, or else a very little before, under King Edward the Confessor, who was all Frenchified.'

Chapter 2: Devonshire Knights

1. Pole, William, *Collections towards a description of the County of Devon*, p.410.
2. *Doomsday*, Devon, f.6, counted 8 ploughlands and 50 acres of woodland in Martinhoe. (https://opendomesday.org)
3. Reichel, O. W., *Devon Feet of Fines*, Vol. 1, no. 149, p.77.
4. Hull, P. L., *The Cartulary of St Michael's Mount*, p.47 (no. 70); Cal. of Liberate Rolls (1228–33), pp.73, 117 & 238; Chaplais, Pierre, *English Diplomatic Practice in the Middle Ages*, pp.135–37; Orme, Nicholas, *Cornwall II: Religious History to 1560*, p.163.
5. Maxwell Lyte, *Miscellaneous Inquisitions*, Vol. 1 no. 19, p.5.
6. Maxwell Lyte, *Descriptive Catalogue*, Vol. 3, 432 D.228.
7. Holden, A., Crouch, D. and Gregory, S. (ed. and trans.), *History of William Marshal*, ll. 2069–92.
8. Vivian, J. L., *The Visitations of Cornwall*, p.437.
9. Pole, *Collections*, p.410.
10. Hartley, Diana, *The St Aubyns of Cornwall*, p.27.
11. Maxwell Lyte, *Miscellaneous Inquisitions*, Vol. 1, no. 647, p.198.
12. Moor, Charles, *Knights of Edward I*, p.166.
13. Camden, *Remains*, pp.232–233.
14. 'The Crusaders returned from the East as brothers-in arms...', Morris, Mark, *A Great and Terrible King*, p.116.

15. Calendar Roll, 22 Edward 1, 383 (12/08/1294).
16. Moor, *Knights*, p.166.
17. Ibid.
18. Ibid.
19. Ibid.; Morris, *Great and Terrible King,* p.190.
20. Moor, *Knights*, p.166.

Chapter 3: Sir Mauger's Heirs

1. Pollard, Alfred W. (ed.), *Chaucer's Canterbury Tales* (Vol. 1, p.17, prologue, lines 321–24 translated).
2. Reichel, *Devon Feet,* Vol. 2, no. 1067.
3. Burke, J., *A Genealogical and Heraldic History of the Commoners of Great Britain and Ireland,* Vol. 4, (1838) p.165. In July 1797, the St Aubyns rented Alfoxton to William and Dorothy Wordsworth, at the dawn of the Romantics.
4. Formerly 'Argalles'. Won at an inquisition in 1276: Concanen, G., *A Report of the Trial at Bar, Rowe v. Brenton,* Appendix, 13. Nearly 400 acres (*Doomsday,* Cornwall, f.7).
5. Rowe, J. H., *Cornwall Feet of Fines,* no. 373, p.211 (3/11/1302).
6. Maxwell Lyte, *Descriptive Catalogue,* Vol. 3, A.8806.
7. Wotton, Thomas, *The English Baronetage*, pp.543–4.
8. Mortimer, Ian, *The Time Traveller's Guide to Medieval England*, p.67.
9. Where, in 1321, he and his wife complained to the king that the Bishop of Bath had 'disseised them of their rights of common pasture'. TNA SC8/142/7098.
10. See Pole, *Collections* and 'Copies & Extracts of Old Evidences'; also see Reichel, *Devon Feet,* Vol. 2. *passim.*
11. Reichel, *Devon Feet,* Vol. 2, nos. 1019–20, pp.146–7.
12. Walter was patron of the living at Combe Coffyn and his kinsman, Sir Martin de Sutton, was appointed rector. (Grandisson, John de, *The Register of John de Grandisson, 1327–1369,* p.1508). Kinsman William de Sutton was patron of St Probus in mid-Cornwall and owned its manor (Grandisson, *Register*, p.709).
13. Sir John de Langford (Wotton, *Baronetage*, p.544).
14. Rowe, *Cornwall Feet,* no. 522, pp.305–6.
15. CFR, 11.E.III, Vol. 5, p.44 (25/9/1337).
16. Reichel, *Devon Feet,* Vol. 2, no. 1394, p.367.
17. Grandisson, *Register,* 1509.
18. Grandisson, *Register,* 1473 & 1509.
19. Maxwell Lyte, *Descriptive Catalogue, Vol. 3,* A.8537.
20. TNA C61/81 m.1 61.3, 68.1, 77.1 (16/1/1369).
21. Ibid.
22. Ibid.
23. Sumption, J., *The Hundred Years War*, Vol. 3, *Divided Houses,* p.60.
24. CIPM 43.E.III Vol. 12 no. 436 (27/12/1370).
25. TNA C61/83 m.9 22.1 (18/2/1370).

26. Froissart, *Chronicles*, Folio 332 r, v (Book 1, SHF 1–666). Macaulay, G. C. (ed.), *The Chronicles of Froissart*, p.201.

27. Jones, Michael, *The Black Prince,* pp.405–8.

28. Sumption, *Divided Houses*, p.743.

29. Ibid., p.777.

30. TNA C61/94 m.8 (18/2/1381).

31. TNA C76/65 m.10 (8/4/1381).

32. CCR, 5.R.II, Vol. 2, p.18 (28/10/1381).

Chapter 4: The Widows of War

1. *HoC 1386–1421*, Vol. 2, pp.573–74.

2. Vivian, *Visitations*, p.437.

3. Maxwell Lyte, *Miscellaneous Inquisitions*, no. 894, p.340.

4. CCR, 6.R.II Pt.1, Vol. 2, p.241 (22/1/1383).

5. CCR, 5.R.II, Vol. 2, p.18 (28/10/1381).

6. CIPM, 9.R.II Vol. 16, file 36, no. 145, p.55 (8/6/1387).

7. John had entrusted his estates to the others in September 1382 (see n.4 above) and these arrangements made at Combe Raleigh were acknowledged in Westminster on 22 January 1383, 'upon his going over sea in company of Edward de Cortenay earl of Devensir' (see n.5 above). The next month, the Courtenay faction in parliament were the key advocates of Dispencer's crusade (see *HoC 1386–1421* Vol. 2, p.691).

8. Sumption, *Divided Houses*, p.509.

9. During the forced retreat from Ypres, 8–31 August, it seems John died of his wounds on 29 August 1383 (CIPM, 8.R.II, Vol. 16, file 36, no. 143, p.54). The 'John Seynt Aubyn knight' listed in the hasty summons to guard the coast of Cornwall in May 1383 probably refers to a Parracombe or Clowance family member (CCR, 6.R.II, Pt.2, Vol. 2, p. 270); while the transcript of his Cornwall inquest two years later erroneously places his death in 1384. On 14 April 1385, the escheator 'took in hand' his tenures of the king in chief, in a long roll call of the deceased (CFR, 8.R.II, Vol. 10, pp.98–99), his son being a minor.

10. *HoC 1386–1421*, Vol. 4, p.573; Wykeham, *Register Wykeham,* ii. pp.378–9.

11. *HoC 1386–1421*, Vol. 4, pp.110–11.

12. Ibid.

13. CIPM, 14.R.II, Vol. 16, no. 146, p.55 (13/2/1391).

14. CIPM, 1.H.IV, Vol. 18, no. 312, p.100 (23/5/1400).

15. Sir Richard's father had been a contemporary of Guy's great-grandfather, Guy St Aubyn, with whom he had served as a Cornwall commissioner in the 1350s. CFR, 31.E.III, Vol. 7, pp.44–5 (1/8/1357).

16. *HoC 1386–1421*, Vol. 4, pp.506–7. In 1379, Sergeaux was accused of wanton criminal offences in Cornwall over the previous twelve years. He was acquitted under the aegis of Sir Robert Tresillian, whose executor he later became.

17. CCR, 2.H.IV Pt.1, Vol. 1, pp.228–9, (6/11/1400); see also CFR, 1.H.IV, Vol. 1 Pt.1, p.73 (4/8/1400).
18. CFR, 22.R.II, Vol. 11, p.291 (20/9/1398). Sir John Cornewall had charge of Alice & Joan Sergeaux's minority and demanded £100, or 20 marks a year until paid. Their inheritance was worth £20 a year each.
19. CPR, 5.H.IV Pt. 2, Vol. 2, p.397 (13 May 1404).
20. Longmate, Norman, *Defending the Island: from Caesar to the Armada*, pp.358–362.
21. Bell, Adrian. R., *The Soldier in Later Medieval England*, p.99. TNA E 101/43/32.
22. See n. 19 above. Sir William Marney, who married Alice's sister Elizabeth in 1388, was Guy's captain: TNA, E101/43/32, m3. Apart from Richard Fitzalan, earl of Arundel (one of Richard II's fiercest opponents), the sisters were also great-nieces of his brother Thomas, archbishop of Canterbury, and of Joan, countess of Hereford.
23. Longmate, *Defending the Island*, p.360.
24. Stafford, Edmund, *The Register of Edmund Stafford 1395–1419*, p.201.
25. GEC, *Complete Peerage*, Vol. 10, pp.234–6. Their son was born in April 1408, so they were married by July 1407.
26. TNA C138/22 no. 52, m.20; CIPM, 4.H.V, Vol. 20, no. 646, p.203 (16/2/1417).
27. *HoC 1386–1421*, Vol. 2, pp.508–10.
28. Ibid., Vol. 4, pp.276–7.
29. CPR, 12.H.IV, Vol. 4, p.252 (14/2/1411).
30. *HoC 1386–1421*, Vol. 4, pp.276–7.
31. TNA E101/44/30 no. 1, n.1_m.2; E101/47/39. Sir W. Marney's son probably drew John into Clarence's retinue: see Warner, Michael P., *The Agincourt Campaign of 1415*, pp.149–51, App. 2.
32. *HoC 1386–1421*, Vol. 2, pp.508–10.
33. TNA E101/45/4 m 3. Warner, *Agincourt*, App. 2.
34. Taylor, Frank, *Gesta Henrici Quinti: The Deeds of Henry the Fifth*, p.35. Reproduced with the Licensor's consent through PLSclear.
35. TNA E101/44/30 no. 1, n.1_m.2.
36. *HoC 1386–1421*, Vol. 2, pp.508–10.
37. Maxwell Lyte, *Descriptive Catalogue Vol. 3*, A.8535.
38. *HoC 1386–1421*, Vol. 4, pp.276–7.
39. Ibid.
40. Bell, *The Soldier*, p.113.
41. Sumption, J., *The Hundred Years War*, Vol. 4, *Cursed Kings*, p.530.
42. Chastellain, George, *Fragment relative a la Normandie*, p.276 (Appendix). Pole, *Collections*, pp.85 & 132. Curry, Anne and Ambühl, Remy, *A Soldiers' Chronicle of the Hundred Years War*, p.190 [which states John St Aubyn was appointed by Clarence].
43. Strecche, John, *The Deeds of King Henry V*, p.23. Easter Day was April 5, 1418.

44. Ibid., p.34.
45. CFR, 6.H.V, Vol. 14, p.239 (12/11/1418).
46. In the house of the Carmelite friars in London: *HoC 1386–1421,* Vol. 4, p.277.
47. CFR, 7.H.V, Vol. 14, p.303 (11/12/1419); CFR, 8.H.V, Vol. 14, p.351 (13/10/1420).
48. Vivian, *Visitations*, p.437.
49. For example, Geoffrey St Aubyn & Sir William Bodrugan both served in a Cornish Commission of Array: CPR, 6.H.V, Vol. 2, p.209 (5/03/1419).
50. Pole, *Collections*, pp.131–32.
51. CPR, 13.H.VII, Vol. 2, p.136 (14/7/1498). Chantries and guild chapels were abolished by Edward VI's sweeping reforms, through the Dissolution Act of 1547.
52. Polwhele, *History*, Vol. 2, p.57.

PART TWO

Chapter 1: The Kemyell Inheritance

1. CPR, 5.E.III Pt. 2, Vol. 2, p.180 (12/10/1331). On his return, Ralph was appointed receiver of St Michael's Mount. The last of his line, his descendants today are the Boscawens, Pole Carews and Prideaux Brunes. (Taylor, Rev. T., *St Michael's Mount*, pp.118, 145-6.)
2. Vivian, *Visitations*, p.437.
3. Hals, *The Compleat History of Cornwal[l]*, p.77; cited by Polwhele, *History*, Vol. 2, p.65. Tonkin, cited by Gilbert, Davies, *The Parochial History of Cornwall*, p.265. See also *Visitation of Cornwall* (1620), p.277. Kemyell also appears in the land tenure record of 1351 (*Magna Britannia*, Vol. 3).
4. Hull, *Cartulary*, pp.55–56 and then pp.50–51.
5. Vivian, *Visitations*, p.437.
6. Soulsby, Ian, *A History of Cornwall*, pp.48–50.
7. CFR, 26.E.III, Vol. 6, p.334 (also see pp.376 and 415).
8. CFR, 31.E.III, Vol. 7, pp.45 and 46.
9. Drake, S. J., *Cornwall, Connectivity and Identity in the 14th Century*, App. 1. But in October 1394, 'Geoffrey's complaint has shewn that contrary to the statute he is elected a coroner although he is no knight' (CCR, 18.R.II, Vol. 5, p.315). The Coroner examined any aspect of medieval life affecting revenue for the Crown. After 1066, killing a Norman incurred a village-wide fine called the 'Murdrum', unless 'Presentment of Englishry' was proved at inquest.
10. CFR, 22.R.II, Vol. 11, p.278 (17/11/1398); 1.H.IV, Vol. 12, p.1 (30/9/1399).
11. Botreaux, Geoffrey *et al.* were once accused with mining a tin works at Lamorna 'in contempt of the king', and threatened with a £200 fine if they did not desist: CCR 11.R.II, Vol. 3, p.430 (29/7/1387). The executorship: CFR, 1.H.IV, Vol. 12, p.46 (14/2/1400).

12. CCR, 3.H.IV Pt. 2, Vol. 1, p.569 (3/6/1402).
13. CPR, 6.H.V, Vol. 2, p.197 (11/4/1418).
14. TNA E101/49/34 m.10.
15. Pole, *Collections*, p.410.
16. Friel, Ian, *Henry V's Navy*, p.136.
17. Taylor, Frank, *Gesta Henrici Quinti: The Deeds of Henry the Fifth*, pp.163–7.

Chapter 2: Cornish Gentry

1. Nicolson, Adam, *The Gentry: Stories of the English*, p.12.
2. See Rowse, A. L., *Tudor Cornwall*, 106ff.
3. *HoC 1386–1421,* Vol. 2, pp.271–2.
4. Hals, *History*, p.77, cited by Polwhele, *History*, Vol. 2, p.65.
5. CPR, 9.H.V, Vol. 2, p.421 (12/2/1422); 10.H.VI Pt. 1, Vol. 2, p.197 (28/10/1431).
6. CPR, 6.H.VI, Vol. 1, p.428 (9/10/1427).
7. CPR, 9.H.VI Pt. 1, Vol. 2, p.87 (16/10/1430).
8. See. p.27 above. Arrallas was still in St Aubyn hands in the eighteenth century. (Tregellas, *Worthies*, p.285.)
9. GEC, *Complete Peerage*, Vol. 10, pp.234–6.
10. Ibid.
11. Vivian, *Visitations*, p.438.
12. Drake, *Cornwall*, p.14.
13. CPR, 13.E.IV Pt. 1, Vol. 1467-77, pp.399–400 (27/10/1473).
14. Taylor, *St Michael's*, pp.130–31; Carew, Richard, *The Survey of Cornwall*, pp.118–19.
15. Rowse, *Tudor*, pp.104–05.
16. Orme, Nicholas, *Cornish Wills, 1342-1540*, Devon and Cornwall Record Society (2007), p.93. She left him 6 marks, and 'wages and pension' of 4 marks, to run for two years after her death.
17. CPR, 1.R.III Pt. 1, Vol. 1476-85, p.371 (13/11/1483).
18. Borlase, Dr William, *The Natural History of Cornwall*, p.30.
19. CPR, 2.R.III Pt. 1, Vol. 1476-85, p.479 (4/8/1484).
20. Horrox, C. & Hammond, P. (ed.), *BL Harleian mss. 433,* Vol. 2, p.34 (9/11/1484).
21. Campbell, William, *Materials for a History of the Reign of Henry VII,* pp.208–9. [Mahenest: today Menheniot].
22. Chynoweth, John, 'The Wreck of the St Anthony', *JRIC (1968)*, pp.385–406.
23. Rot. Parl. Vol. 6, *Act of Attainder 1504.*
24. Taylor, *St Michael's*, pp.142–3.
25. Taylor, *St Michael's*, p.178; TNA E.101. 516 m.27. All the West Country had revolted; the twenty-two gentlemen heavily fined in Somerset included John St Aubyn of Alfoxton. (Arthurson, Ian, 'The Rising of 1497: A Revolt of the Peasantry?' in Rosenthal, Joel and Colin Richmond (eds.), *People, Politics and Community in the Later Middle Ages*, p.6.)
26. Borlase, William Copeland, *The Descent, Name and Arms of Borlase*, pp.31–2.

27. Chynoweth, John, *Tudor Cornwall*, p.47; BL, Harl. MS 6166, ff. 95–123.
28. Chynoweth, *Cornwall*, p.47.
29. CPR, 23.H.VII Pt. 2, Vol. 2, pp.578–9 (12/07/1508).
30. Taylor, *St Michael's*, p.144.
31. I am grateful to Sarah Whale and Robin Harcourt Williams, the archivists at Hatfield House, for identifying Peter St Aubyn's roll for 1508–9 (CRO, AU/66). The 1512 roll is held in their archive as HHA/General 104/7. They say it is a short, possibly incomplete, compotus roll of Peter as 'Firmarius' (or Lessee) for the year running from Michaelmas 1511 until Michaelmas 1512. It includes accounts for the period 1510–1511, written in English by Roger Morecroft, the Sexton for the Mount church, who makes no reference to Peter, (suggesting parallel authority from Sion Abbey). A summary account roll for 1527–1531 (HHA/General 104/3) refers to arrears due from Peter, as the former Lessee, carried forward from 1513 (when the French assault no doubt depleted his income from Marazion, along with the houses). Aged over 70, his death soon followed.
32. See *HoC 1386–1421*, Vol. 4, p.650.
33. CPR, 5.H.VII, Vol. 1, p.322 (19/6/1490).
34. CPR, H.VII, Vol. 1, Appendix, pp.483; Vol. 2, Appendix, p.633.
35. CPR, 9.H.VII, p.479. The inspector's report is from Peter, Richard (and Otto Peter), *The Histories of Launceston and Dunheved*, pp.294–95.
36. *JRIC*, 1915, pp.80–86. See also Rowse, *Tudor*, pp.120–21.
37. Local folklore. Marsh, F. G., *The Godolphins*, p.5, n.1. The National Trust has recently run commemorative snail's races at Godolphin.
38. Tregellas, *Worthies*, p.285.

Chapter 3: Star Chamber

1. Indlewick, F. A. (ed.), *A Calendar of the Inner Temple Records*, Vol. 1, pp.87 & 92.
2. Granville, Roger, *The History of the Granville Family*, cover page.
3. CSP, Vol. 3, Pt. 2, p.22 (19/1/1527).
4. Cottonian Library Mss. Nero B1 fo. 64.
5. STAC 2/16/101.
6. This would be by writ of *dedimus potestatem*, which 'gave the commissioners "full powers" to hear and examine the matters in variance between the parties, and to set a final end to the dispute if they could'. Guy, John, *The Cardinal's Court*, p.102.
7. LP, Vol. 4, no. 2815. Milliton became Mount 'captain' in 1521 (Fletcher, Canon J. R., *A Short History of St Michael's Mount*, p.52).
8. Holinshed, *Chronicles of England, Scotland and Ireland*, Vol. 3, p.715.
9. Indlewick, *Inner Temple*, Vol. 1, p.88.
10. Cheyney, E. B., *The Court of the Star Chamber*, p.xxii.
11. Whitely, H. M., 'The Treasure Ship of Gunwallo', *JRIC (1890)*, pp.107–8.
12. STAC 2/16/101; Chynoweth, *The Wreck*, p.398.

13. Guy, *Cardinal's*, pp.86–87. One miscreant had his ear nailed to the wall (see p.117).
14. British Library, Cotton MS, Nero B1 fo. 66.
15. CSP, Vol. 3, Pt 2, p.282 (13/7/1527).
16. CRO ART/3/96. The post holder received the revenues in England due to the Holy See.
17. LP, Vol. 4.ii., no. 4909.
18. St Clare Byrne, Muriel, *The Lisle Letters*, Vol. 2, no. 114.
19. See Guy, *Cardinal's*, p.112.
20. Holles, G., *Memorials of the Hollis Family, 1493–1656*, p.54.
21. In 1525, Densell had delivered a seminal paper on the Statute of Westminster of 1275. Baker, J. H. (ed.), 'Densell, John (d. 1536)', *ODNB* (Vol. 15).
22. LP, Vol. 20.i, nos. 828, 408.
23. Twiss, Sir Travers (ed.), *The Black Book of the Admiralty*, Vol. 1.
24. '*Le secret des grandes fortunes sans cause apparente est un crime oubli parce qu'il a été proprement fait.*' 'Le Père Goriot' (1835).

Chapter 4: The King's Mercy

1. St. Clare Byrne, *Letters*, Vol. 5, no. 1127a, p.76.
2. Pool, P. A. S (ed.), 'The Penheleg Manuscript (1580)', *JRIC (1959)*, p.192.
3. Indlewick, *Inner Temple*, Vol. 1, p.87.
4. Ibid., p.92.
5. St. Clare Byrne, *Letters*, Vol. 1, p.86.
6. Ibid., Vol. 4, no. 971, p.326.
7. Ibid., Vol. 1, no. xxxvi, p.343.
8. Carew, *Survey*, p.109.
9. e.g. Zenobia Mallet, Honor's matrilineal descendant, married Thomas and Mary's grandson in 1573 (see Chapter 6 below).
10. St Clare Byrne, *Letters*, Vol. 1, no. 80, pp.622–3.
11. Lewis, George Randall, *The Stannaries: A Study of the English Tin Miner*, pp.216–9.
12. St Clare Byrne, *Letters*, Vol. 5, no. 1095, pp.24–6.
13. Ibid., Vol. 4, no. 895, p.163.
14. Ibid., *Letters*, Vol. 4, no. 896, pp.167–8.
15. LP, XI, no. 8. Chapuys to Granville, 18 May 1536.
16. St Clare Byrne, *Letters*, Vol. 4, no. 899, pp.171–2.
17. Ibid., Vol. 4, no. 898, p.169.
18. Ibid., Vol. 5, no.1095, p.25.
19. Ibid., Vol. 2, no. 382, pp.477–8.
20. Ibid., Vol. 4, no. 971b, pp.328–9.
21. Ibid., Vol. 4, no. 971a, p.327.
22. Ibid., Vol. 4, no. 897, pp.168–9.
23. Ibid., Vol. 5, no. 1201, pp.196–7.

24. Ibid., Vol. 6, no. 1653, pp.33–4.
25. Ibid., Vol. 5, no. 1558, p.665.
26. Ibid., Vol. 6, no. 1673, pp.106–7.
27. Ibid., Vol. 6, no. 1661, p.48.
28. Cartwright (pub.), *The Records of the Honourable Society of Lincoln's Inn*, (Vol. 1, 1896), p.52.
29. St Clare Byrne, *Letters*, Vol. 6, p.116.
30. Ibid., Vol. 6, p.118–21. Gruffudd, *Chronicle* 'A soldier in the Calais retinue', f.552a.
31. Ibid., Vol. 6, p.118.
32. Ibid., Vol. 6, p.119.
33. Burnet, *History of the Reformation of the Church of England*, I iii, p.189.
34. LP, Vol. 16, 1331; St Clare Byrne, *Letters*, Vol. 6, p.277.
35. See St Clare Byrne, *Letters*, Vol. 5, no. 1125, p.70.
36. LP, 1542, no. 6, p.717; CSP, Vol. 6 Pt. 1, 1538–42, no.230, p.468 (9/2/1542).
37. Holinshed, *Chronicles*, Vol. 3, p. 824; St Clare Byrne, *Letters*, Vol. 6, p.183–4.
38. Chapuys, 10/6/1541; St Clare Byrne, *Letters*, Vol. 6, p.171.
39. Sandford, F., *Genealogical History of the Kings of England*, p.448.

Chapter 5: A Perilous Country

1. LP, Vol. 12.ii, no. 557, p.211. Haynes was the radical Dean of Exeter Cathedral, appointed in June 1537.
2. St Clare Byrne, *Letters*, Vol. 6, p.188.
3. Carew, *Survey,* p.62. His nose had been severed.
4. St Clare Byrne, *Letters*, Vol. 6, p.279–80; LP. XV 489 (59) and 926, Marillac to Montmorency, 29/07/1540.
5. LP, Vol. 20.ii, 451.
6. CPR, 1.E.VI, Vol. 1, p.82 (26/5/1547).
7. St Clare Byrne, *Letters*, Vol. 1, no. 58, p.580.
8. CPR, 1.E.VI, Vol. 1, p.142 (18/6/1547).
9. Stoyle, Mark, A *Murderous Midsummer*, p.16–17.
10. Rose-Troup, F., *The Western Rebellion of 1549*, p.119.
11. Bucholz, R. O. *et al.*, *Early Modern England, 1485–1714*, p.176.
12. Thomas Winter, the son of Cardinal Wolsey, was made Archdeacon in Cornwall in 1537, but leased the office to Body for £30 a year; in 1543 reduced to £10 a year. See Orme, *Cornwall II,* p.91.
13. Stoyle, *Murderous*, p.56.
14. Taylor, *St Michael's*, pp.79–86.
15. Stoyle, *Murderous*, p.57.
16. Stoyle, *Murderous*, p.62 and p.304 (n.73).
17. Worth, R. N. (ed.), *Calendar of the Plymouth Municipal Records*, p.16.
18. Arthurson, Ian, 'Fear and Loathing in West Cornwall', *JRIC (2000)*, p.88.
19. FRDK, p.217.

20. CPR, 5.E.VI., Vol. 5, Appendix p.404 (17/5/1548).
21. Stoyle, Mark, *West Britons – Cornish Identities*, p.28.
22. Stoate, T. L., *Cornwall Subsidies in the reign of Henry VIII:1524 and 1543 and the benevolence of 1545*, p.40.
23. Arthurson, 'Fear and Loathing in West Cornwall', p.91.
24. Pool, P. A. S. (ed.), 'The Ancient and Present State of St Michael's Mount, 1762, Dr William Borlase Mss', *JICS (1975(3))*, p.32.
25. Rose-Troup, *Rebellion*, pp.98–99.
26. His maternal grandfather was H. Calwodely. Rowse, A. L., *Tudor Cornwall*, p.263.
27. Sturt, John, *Revolt in the West – The Western Rebellion of 1549*, p.26.
28. FRDK, 222.
29. Ibid.
30. TNA, STAC 5/T34, f.32; Stoyle, *Murderous*, p.137.
31. Carew, *Survey*, pp.111–12.
32. Stoyle, *Murderous*, p.181.
33. Aubrey, John, *Brief Lives* (MS. Aubr. 6, fol. 80.).
34. See Chapter 6, n.35 above. *HoC 1509–1558*, Vol. 2, 248.
35. Sturt, *Revolt*, pp.100–101.
36. They had both been part of Henry VIII's fifty strong 'Spears of Honour' in the 1510s. St Clare Byrne, *Letters*, Vol. 1, pp.151–153.
37. St Clare Byrne, *Letters*, Vol. 6, pp.290–1.
38. S.P.10/9, 48; Rowse, *Tudor*, p.288.
39. The confused rebel aims are outlined in Rose-Troup, *Rebellion*, p.126; e,g. 'Cornishmen … utterly refuse thy new English' (Lambeth, *Articles*, f.15 sig.).
40. Stoyle, *Murderous*, pp.224–5 & 294-6 (which emphasises the Arundells' role).
41. Ibid., pp.225, 265–6; Skidmore, Chris, *Edward VI, The Lost King*, pp.130–134.
42. APC, Vol. 2, 1547-50, p.366. See also Rowse, *Tudor*, pp.288–9.

Chapter 6: Cousins

1. Siculus, Diodorus, *The Library of History*, Book 5, Para. 22. He records: 'The inhabitants of Britain who dwell about the promontory known as Belerium [*i.e. Cornwall*] are especially hospitable to strangers and have adopted a civilized manner of life because of their intercourse with merchants of other peoples. They it is who work the tin, treating the bed which bears it in an ingenious manner.'
2. Smith, Anthony D., *The Ethnic Origins of Nations*, pp.11–16.
3. Polwhele, *History*, Vol. 2, p.30.
4. Carew, *Survey*, pp.66–7.
5. Norden, John, *Speculi Britanniae: Description of Cornwall*, p.28.
6. Polwhele, *History*, Vol. 1, pp.188–89.
7. Rowse, *Tudor*, p.230.
8. Soulsby, *Cornwall*, p.65.

9. The merchant fleet had reached 68 ships by 1582. Soulsby, *Cornwall,* p.65.

10. Rowse, *Tudor,* pp.385–92; Chynoweth, *Cornwall*, pp.141–43.

11. Carew, *Survey*, 71ff, where 'Pastimes to delight the mind...' are fully described.

12. Lewis, *Stannaries*, p.217.

13. Chynoweth, *Cornwall*, pp.145–48. Thomas' assessment was £50 in 1522–6; his grandson Thomas' only £20 in 1593–1600.

14. Stoyle, *West Britons*, p.28.

15. Nicolson, *Gentry,* p.21.

16. Grose, Francis, *The Antiquities of Cornwall*, p.45.

17. John Milliton probably suffered during the rebels' attack. He was omitted from Russell's letter to JPs in September 1549 (Russell, Lord John, *Letter to Cornish JPs,* Ms.). The IPM for his son William (Exeter Castle, 4 Oct. 13 Eliz.) states that John's will was signed in November 1549, when Godolphin was at Pengersick (Arthurson, 'Fear and Loathing in West Cornwall', p.92). His death is confirmed by his IPM, 4.E.VI (1550): TNA, C 142/90/13.

18. Local folklore.

19. Baring-Gould, Sabine, *A Book of the West*, p.289.

20. Carew, *Survey*, p.153.

21. Lawrance, W. T., *Parliamentary Representation of Cornwall*, p.8.

22. HoC.org/periods/tudors.

23. Lawrance, *Representation*, p.11.

24. Elton, G. R., *The Tudor Constitution*, p.249.

25. *HoC 1509–1558*, Vol. 1, 252.

26. CPR, Philip & Mary Vol. 2, 1554-5, p.106.

27. St Clare Byrne, *Letters*, Vol. 6, pp.259–60.

28. Carew, *Survey*, p.64.

29. St Clare Byrne, *Letters*, Vol. 1, no. 307; Norden, *Harl. MS. 6252*.

30. Carew, *Survey*, p.153. See also Rowse, *Tudor*, p.55.

31. Carew, *Survey*, p.127. See also Rowse, *Tudor*, 55ff. 'Carn-sew' in Cornish means 'the black rock' (Polwhele, *History*, Vol. 2, p.37).

32. Rowse, *Tudor*, p.61; he remarks 'it really was not very intelligent of them'.

33. Rowse, *Tudor*, p.58.

34. SP 12 46/16. Pounds, N. J. G., 'William Carnsew of Bokelly and his Diary', *JRIC (1978 Part 1),* pp.32–33. (See also Rowse, *Tudor Cornwall*, p.55; *Court and Country,* p.145).

35. See Dodds, P. A., *Transcript of William Borlase's Draft Letters* (1718–1745), p.70 for Borlase's account of the smelting process at this time.

36. Carew, *Survey*, p.152. See also Wotton, Thomas, *The English Baronetage*, p.545. Robert Mallet was entrusted at Hastings with the dead body of King Harold; and was later High Chamberlain of England. Polwhele, *History*, Vol. 2, p.76.

37. St Clare Byrne, *Letters*, Vol. 6, p.260.

38. *HoC, 1604–29*, 136. For details of their holdings, see Tregellas, *Worthies*, p.285; Lysons, Daniel and Samuel, *Magna Britannica* (Vol. 3, Cornwall, 1814).39. Memorial in Crowan Church: Polwhele, *History*, Vol. 1 addendum.

PART THREE

Chapter 1: The Jewel in the Sea

1. See Taylor, *St Michael's,* pp.18–20. He argues monks from Normandy confused the facts with how Mont St Michel evolved, as described by early French sources. So Polwhele (*History*, Supplement, pp.14–25), Leland etc. are all erroneous.
2. *JRIC*, 1972, p.299.
3. Fletcher, *History*, pp.25–26.
4. Ibid., p.30; Rot. Parl. E.III, no. 19.
5. Taylor, *St Michael's*, pp.112–14.
6. Oman, Charles, *Castles*, p.105.
7. Ibid.
8. Taylor, *St Michael's*, pp.156–8.
9. Milton, Giles, *Big Chief Elizabeth*, p.271.
10. The others were Nicholas Parker, Hannibal Vivyan and Thomas Chyverton. Taylor, *St Michael's*, p.160; BL, Add. 34,224, f. 7, 8, 15, 25, 38, 39.
11. Carew, *Survey*, ff156–58. Rowse, *Tudor*, pp.404–07.
12. See Dickinson, Robert, 'The Spanish Raid on Mount's Bay in 1595', *JRIC (1988 (2))*, for the Spanish account, which estimated 50 English killed but no Spanish: *'The mosque, where they gather for their conventicles, was not burned... trust in God that mass would be celebrated in it again within two years.'*
13. SP 12/253, 30.
14. Roberts, R. A. (ed.), *Calendar of the Cecil Papers in Hatfield House,* Vol. 5, p. 466.
15. ODNB, Robert Cecil, Vol. 10, p.750.
16. Taylor, *St Michael's*, pp.160–61.
17. Ibid., p.163.
18. Hull, *Cartulary*, p.9.
19. Pool, *Mount*, p.46.

Chapter 2: Crown and Parliament

1. Prothero, G. W. (ed.), *Select Statutes and Other Constitutional Documents Illustrative of the Reigns of Elizabeth and James I*, p.293.
2. Stone, Lawrence, 'The Inflation of Honours 1558–1641', *Past & Present (no. 14, November 1958)*, p.67 (table).
3. *HoC 1558-1603*, Peter Wentworth, Vol. 3, pp.598–99.
4. *HoC 1558–1603*, Vol. 3, p.321; *HoC 1604–1629*, Vol. 6, p.136.
5. Croft, Pauline, *King James*, p.64.
6. HoC, *1604–29*, pp.136–7.
7. Ibid., Vol. 6, p.135.

8. Ibid., Vol. 6, p.136.
9. 'To be qualified for it, one must be a gentleman born, and have a clear estate of £1000 per annum', Beatson, Robert, *A Political Index to the Histories of Great Britain and Ireland*, p.250.
10. *HoC, 1604–29*, Vol. 6, p.136.
11. Ibid., Vol. 2, pp.67–68.
12. See Scantlebury, John, 'The Development of the Export Trade in Pilchards from Cornwall during the Sixteenth Century', *JRIC (1989)*, for expansion since 1500.
13. *HoC 1604–1629*, Vol. 2, pp.67–68.
14. Ibid.
15. Ibid.
16. Ibid., Vol. 6, pp.563–65.
17. Ibid., Vol. 6, p.137.
18. BL, *Diary of Bulstrode Whitelocke*, Year 23, ff. 91–94.
19. Author's translation of Whitelocke's quotation in Greek. Diodorus Siculus was a Greek historian in about 40 BCE. See also endnote 1. to Pt 2, Ch.6 above.
20. TNA, E178/7161.
21. *HoC 1604–1629*, Vol. 6, p.137; Vivian, *Visitations*, p.437.
22. The High Sheriff before Boscawen was Charles Trevanion, another who baulked at compounding for the knighthood and 'it is conceivable that the burden of the shrievalty was imposed on him later that year as a punishment' (*HoC 1604–1629*, Vol. 6, pp.563–5).
23. CSPD, Charles I, Vol. 325, pp.569–70 (19/6/1636).
24. Ibid., 25/11/1636, pp.208–9.
25. PC 2/48, p.136.
26. Parry, R. H. (ed.), *Essays on the Civil War*, p.27.

Chapter 3. The Spoils of War

1. Worth, R. N., *The Buller Papers*, pp.63, 71; Taylor, *St Michael's*, p.164.
2. *HoC 1604–1629*, Vol. 6, pp.563–65.
3. Ibid.
4. John Taylor's diary in 1649. See Gray, Todd, *Cornwall The Travellers' Tales*, p.36.
5. Barratt, John, *The Civil War in the South-West*, p.38.
6. Ibid., p.50.
7. CRO, B/35/26. Issued on 20 March 1643.
8. Barrat, *South-West*, p.62.
9. Taylor, *St Michael's*, pp.165–6.
10. Barrat, *South-West*, p.115 (Chpt.2, Lansdown).
11. Ibid., 164f.
12. Charles I, *His Majesties Declaration,* E.669, f.7, 37.
13. See 12n. above; also Stoyle, *West Britons*, pp.160–62.

14. Tregellas, *Worthies*, p.286.
15. Barrat, *South-West*, p.279; Stoyle, *West Britons*, p.76.
16. E. 35 (24); Stoyle, *West Britons*, p.81.
17. Stoyle, *West Britons*, pp.77–82.
18. Hyde, E., Earl of Clarendon, *The History of the Rebellion and the Civil Wars*, IV, pp.99–100.
19. Stoyle, *West Britons*, p.99; Green, E., 'The Siege and Defence of Taunton', *Somerset Archaeological Society Proceedings*, *XXV*, p.40.
20. Carte, T. E., *A Collection of Original Letters and Papers... Found among the Duke of Ormonde's Papers*, Vol. 1, p.105; Stoyle, *West Britons*, p.105.
21. Stoyle, *West Britons*, p.106.
22. Ibid., p.142; Coate, Mary, *Cornwall in the Great Civil War and Interregnum 1642–1660*, pp.206–09.
23. Rushworth, *Historical Collections*, pp.295–6.
24. *HoC 1640–1660*, Vol. 8, p.499.
25. Coate, *Civil War*, p.219; Tregellas, *Worthies*, p.94; BL, Egerton Mss., 1048, f 86.
26. CRO, AU/4.
27. Sandys, William, 'An Account of some of the Transactions in Cornwall during the Civil War', *JRIC (1866, Pt. V)*.
28. Stoyle, *West Britons*, p.114.
29. Cited by Stoyle, *West Britons*, p.120.
30. Ibid., p.125.
31. *HoC 1640–1660*, Vol. 8, p.499.
32. Stoyle, *West Britons*, p.132.
33. Coate, *Civil War*, p.368.
34. *JHoC* Vol. 7, pp.443–4 (22/10/1656): '... Lord Commissioner Whitelock, ... Mr. St. Aubin ... are to meet To-morrow in the Afternoon at Two of the Clock, in the Star-Chamber ... to consider of the Estates of Delinquents, which have continued under Sequestration, and who have refused or neglected to compound.'
35. CRO, AU/29; CRO AU/26/1, AU/26/2; Pool, *Mount*, p.46.
36. Thirsk, Joan, 'The Sales of Royalist Land during the Interregnum', *The Economic History Review*, pp.191–92.
37. *HoC 1640–1660*, Vol. 3, pp.450–459.
38. 31 Jan. 1663. FSL, X.d.483 (147b). Draft letter to lawyer Sir Henry Pollexfen. 17–24 December 1650. FSL, X.d.483 (75–6) & (77–8). Godolphin's cousin, Sir William, was detained in Bodmin at the same time. Basset had been involved in the 1648 uprising. In 1651, Sir Francis (only knighted later at the Restoration) was put in the Fleet prison for contact with the exiled Prince Charles. (*HoC 1604–1629*, Vol. 4, p.398.) So Bennett's suspicions were not unfounded.
39. CRO, AU/8.
40. CSPD, Interregnum, Vol. 180, p.320 (9/3/1658).

41. CRO, AU/6-8.
42. Ibid.
43. CSPD, Interregnum, Vol. 182, p.93 (13/7/1658).
44. Ibid., Vol. 182, 113 (12/8/1658).
45. Larminie, '*Interruption*', HoC 1640–1660 Blog.
46. *HoC 1640–1660*, Vol. 8, 499.
47. FSL, X.d.483(127); *HoC 1640–1660*, Vol. 8, 500.
48. *JHoC* Vol. 7, 750a; *HoC 1640–1660*, Vol. 3, 458.
49. Larminie, Dr Vivienne, 'The "Interruption" of Parliament and the quest for political settlement, October 1659'; *HoC 1640–1660* Blog. *HoC 1640–1660*, Vol. 9, p.720.
50. Coate, *Civil War*, p.308.
51. *HoC 1640–1660*, Vol. 3, p.458. JHoC Vol. 7, 820b (24/1/1660); FSL, X.d.438 (134–9).
52. CRO, AU/9.
53. A&O, Vol. 2, p.1425 (12/3/1660); CSPD, Interregnum, 1659–60, p.571 (13/3/1660).

Chapter 4: Restoration

1. Nichols, J. (ed.), *The History of the Worthies of England ... by Thomas Fuller*, Vol. 1, p.214.
2. Stoyle, *West Britons*, p.157.
3. Ibid., p.158.
4. CSPD, Charles II, Vol. 10, Addenda 1660-70, p.663 (25/9/1661).
5. *HoC 1640–1660*, Vol. 3, p.458.
6. Vivian, J.L. & Drake, H. (ed.), *Visitation of the County of Cornwall in the year 1620*, p.212; Hartley, *St Aubyns*, p.109.
7. Mount records, 29/9/1667.
8. Vivian, *Visitations*, p.439.
9. b.1616, d.1687 – Vivian, *Visitations*, p.438–9 (corrected).
10. Mount records, 13/7/1675.
11. Taylor, *St Michael's*, p.154.
12. Exwood, M. and Lehmann, H. L. (eds.), *The Journal of William Shellinks' Travels in England 1661–63*, pp.115–128.
13. CSPD, Charles II, Vol. 165, p.595 (31/7/1666).
14. Ibid., Vol. 182, p.370 (26/12/1666).
15. CSPD, Charles II, 1671, p.547 (30/10/1671).
16. CSPD, Charles II, 1671-2, pp.141–2 (17/2/1672).
17. *HoC 1660–1690*, Trelawny, Jonathan I (*c*.1623–81). In the 1630s, Noye's father had been Charles I's notorious tax adviser; in 1642, the son had cajoled a county meeting in Truro to outlaw parliamentarians like John St Aubyn.
18. CSPD, Charles II, 1680–1, p.228 (2/4/1681), pp.280–1 (14/5/1681).
19. *HoC 1640–1660*, Vol. 8, pp.499–500.

20. Habakkuk, *Landowners*, pp.132–3.
21. See Chapter 2, n.9, p.xiii above, for 'qualifications'.
22. CSPD, Charles II, 1671-2, p.124 (7/2/1672). The Badge of Ulster, the distinctive ensign of the order and rank of baronet, was added to the family escutcheon.
23. Cited by Polwhele, *History*, Vol. 2 Supplement, 10.
24. But his death was recorded in 'Archdeacon Transcripts' according to Vivian *et al.*, *Cornwall in 1620*, p.212.

PART FOUR

Chapter 1: The Jacobite Tendency

1. Cox (ed. *et al.*), *Survey of London, Volume 10, The Parish of St Margaret Westminster – Part 1*, p.44.
2. *HoC 1660–1690*, Vol. 3, p.380.
3. Ibid., pp.380–81.
4. GEC, *Complete Baronetage*, Vol. 4, p.52.
5. Pool, P. A. S. (ed.), 'The Ancient and Present State of St Michael's Mount, 1762, Dr William Borlase Mss', *JICS (1975(3))*, p.42.
6. RIC File no. RIC-HB/20/89.
7. Mary's will dated 13/6/1717, Mount records.
8. Pool, P. A. S., *William Borlase*, p.305; Taylor, *St Michael's*, p.154.
9. Pool, *Borlase*, p.2.
10. Ibid., pp.15–16.
11. Ibid., p.16.
12. Ibid., p.28.
13. Ibid., pp.19–20; Dodds, *Draft Letters*, p.11.
14. Dodds, *Draft Letters*, p.9 (by kind permission of the Morab Library).
15. Cruickshanks, Evelyn, *Political Untouchables: the Tories and the '45*, p.5.
16. Archibald Hutchison MP to Prime Minister Sunderland: Cruickshanks, *Untouchables*, p.6.
17. Fritz, Paul S., *The English Ministers and Jacobitism*, p.109.
18. Cruickshanks, *Untouchables*, p.16. Tory Jacobites in dark blue attire passed their drink over a jug or glass of water, a silent toast to 'the king over the water'.
19. The Molesworths traced their descent from Sir Walter de Molesworth, a knightly companion of Mauger de Sancto Albino on Prince Edward's 9th Crusade in 1270. (Gill, Crispin, *The Great Cornish Families*, p.58; Debretts, *Peerage & Baronetage*, B889.)
20. Cruickshanks, Eveline, 'The Convocation of the Stannaries of Cornwall: The Parliament of Tinners 1703–1752', *Parliament, Estates & Representation*.
21. Tregellas, *Worthies*, p.290.
22. *Gentlemen's Magazine*, 1734; Tregellas, W*orthies*, pp.291–2.

23. Plumb, J. H., *Sir Robert Walpole, The King's Minister*, p.333.
24. *HoC 1715–1754*, Vol. 2, p.401.
25. Tregellas, *Worthies*, p.294.
26. Pool, *Borlase*, p.56; Dodds, *Draft Letters,* p.21.
27. Pool, *Borlase*, pp.56–57.
28. Polwhele, *History*, Vol. 4 supplement, pp.43–45; Rowse, A. L., *A Cornish Anthology*, pp.74–5.
29. *HoC 1715–54*; Sedgwick, Romney, 'The Tories, Essay V', *HoC (1715–54)*.
30. From Glubb, 'State of the Borough of Callington, 3 March 1772', Mss. (*HoC 1715–1754*, Callington, n.2). James Tillie's appointment as 'Superintendent of the Royal Foundry' was announced in the *Gentlemen's Magazine* 1734, p.275. See also Baring-Gould, Sabine, *Cornish Characters and Strange Events,* pp.25–33.
31. Tregellas, *Worthies*, p.294.
32. ODNB, Sir John St Aubyn, 3rd Bt., Vol. 48, p.591.
33. Quarterly Review quoted in Tregellas, *Worthies*, p.294.
34. Trevelyan, G. M., *British History in Nineteenth Century and After, 1782–1919*, p.14.
35. Lawrance, *Representation*, p.192.
36. Ibid., p.320.
37. Ibid., p.323.
38. 5/5/1741. Tregellas, *Worthies*, pp.295–6.
39. Lawrance, *Representation*, p.325.
40. *HoC 1715–54*, Vol. 1, pp.475-7.
41. *Quarterly Rev.* cxxxix. p.378.
42. Hall, Hubert, 'The Sources for the History of Sir Robert Walpole's Financial Administration', *TRHS (Vol.4, 1910),* p.42.
43. *HoC 1715–1754,* Vol. 2, p.401.
44. ODNB, Sir John St Aubyn, 3rd Bt., Vol. 48, p.591; Sedgwick, Romney, 'The Tories, Essay V', *HoC (1715–54).*
45. AEM & D Angl., 82, ff. 4–23, 62–109 (translated from French original).
46. *Gentlemen's Magazine*, Vol. xiii; Tregellas, *Worthies*, p.299.
47. Pool, *Borlase*, p.67.
48. Ibid.

Chapter 2: The Morice Bequest

1. Tregellas, *Worthies*, pp.298–99.
2. Fritz, *Jacobitism*, 'Conclusion'; Cobbett, William, *The Parliamentary History of England from the Earliest Period to the Year 1803.*
3. Taylor, Stephen, 'Walpole, Robert', *ODNB* (Vol. 57), p.89.
4. Hartley, *St Aubyns*, p.31.
5. Ubiquitous, e.g. Hogg, Thomas, *St Michael's Mount in Cornwall, A Poem*, p.31 (line 168n); Rowse, *Anthology*, p.68.
6. Pool, *Borlase,* p.64.

7. Ibid., pp.61–63.
8. Ibid., p.67.
9. Borlase to Oliver, September 1744. Pool, *Borlase*, p.67.
10. *HoC 1715–1754*, Vol. 2, p.402.
11. Pool, *Borlase*, p.70.
12. *HoC 1754–1790*, Vol. 3, p.397.
13. Coode, Jonathan, *The Cornish Club 1768*, p.9.
14. Cornforth, John, 'St Michael's Mount Cornwall', *Country Life*, p.84.
15. Pool, *Mount*, p.37.
16. St Aubyn, John, *Memorandum on St Michael's Mount*, p.17.
17. Mount records, 29/8/1754.
18. Mount records, 1777.
19. St Levan, *Historical Guide*, p.29; Hartley, *St Aubyns*, p.35.
20. Cave, K. (ed.), *The Diary of Joseph Farington*, Vol. 11, January 1811–June 1812, p.3909.
21. St Aubyn, *Lady St Aubyn*, Mount records.
22. Vivian, *Visitations*, p.440; Burke, *Heraldic History* (1858), Vol. 1, p.42. She was buried at Orsett, the Baker family's Essex estate, which was inherited by her Wingfield nephew.
23. *HoC 1754–1790*, Vol. 3, pp.397–98.
24. Ballantyne (pub.), *Memorials of Brooks's*, p.xi.
25. St Aubyn, James, *Diary*, 1819–1859, p.196 (13/02/1843); Hartley, *St Aubyns*, p.43.
26. HRO, 21M65/E1/4/2531 see Affidavit by Martha Nicholls in 1814.
27. Jaggard, Edwin, 'The Political World of Sir Christohper Hawkins (1758–1829)', *JRIC (2000; New Series, Vol. 3, Pts. 3 & 4)*, p.100.
28. 'Cornishman, A.', '*A Letter to the Free and Independent Electors of the County*' (1790 election leaflet). p.10.
29. *HoC 1790–1820*, Vol. 5, p.83.
30. Cave, *Farington*, Vol. 11, p.3909.
31. HRO 21M69/37/8 Joan Wake to Mrs Carroll in 1970.
32. Hartley, *St Aubyns*, p.33.
33. Boase, G. C., *Collectanea Cornubiensia*, p.1153; clergydatabase.org.uk.
34. Steer, B. D. G., *Pedigree of Vinicombe of Madron* (May 1990). Mount records.

Chapter 3: Regency Style

1. Jane Austen, *Mansfield Park*, Chapter 22.
2. Winston Graham in conversation with Jane St Aubyn, 1981; Dr Bernard Deacon, Director of the Institute of Cornish Studies at Exeter University, also described Sir John as Ross Poldark's 'real-life equivalent'.
3. Cave, *Farington*, Vol. 11, p.3903.
4. Gibson, Kate, *Illegitimacy, Family & Stigma in England, 1660–1834*, p.181ff.

5. Ibid., pp.155–56.
6. Ibid., pp.189–90.
7. Ibid., pp.9–10, 101.
8. Mount records 19/9/1829.
9. Lord Byron, *Poems*; Rowse, *Anthology,* pp.156–60.
10. St Aubyn, Sir John, *Short Abstract of Letters received in 1795*, Mount records, 1795.
11. Tregellas, *Worthies*, p.302. The house originally belonged to Samuel Whitbread and in the twentieth century to the Bowes-Lyons, HM Queen Elizabeth's grandparents, whom she visited there as a child.
12. St Levan, *Historical Guide*, p.41.
13. Hartley, *St Aubyns*, p.75; Sir Edward St Aubyn Obit (Mount records, 1/12/1872).
14. Rogers, John J., *Opie and his Works*, p.153.
15. Ibid.
16. Ibid., p.28; Rowse, A. L., *West Country Stories*, p.142.
17. Boase, *Collectanea*, 1153.
18. See Molesworth, ODNB Vol. 38, p.526.
19. Opie's wife praised 'the support and sanction of Sir John St Aubyn's presence and advice' when he died. Reynold's similar funeral had cost £500. Earland, Ada, *John Opie & his Circle*, pp.226–7 & 231.
20. Tregellas, *Worthies*, p.302.
21. Mount records 6/8/1856 (Auction particulars).
22. St Aubyn, *The Will*, 1st Codicil *(*CRO: RH/1/759); Walford, Edward, *Old and New London*: Vol. 6, Chapter 36, pp.489–503.
23. www.geolsoc.org.uk/Geoscientist/Archive/December-2009/The-Collector.
24. St Aubyn, *Diary, 1819-1859*, p.135.
25. Hartley, *St Aubyns*, p.32.
26. Cave, *Farington*, Vol. 11, p.3909. Martha had a house in Lugdvan parish.
27. Gibson, *Illegitimacy*, pp.65–66.
28. Ibid., pp.159–60; St Aubyn, *Diary,* 1819, pp.84–85.
29. St Aubyn, James, *Diary, 1810–1819*, pp.25–6, 36–7, 39–40, 44–45.
30. St Aubyn, *Diary, 1810*, pp.54–55. As Dr Gibson remarks in her notes, 'the weirdest but fullest example of the paternal decision behind naming and christening children I have seen'. Sara was a niece of Gilbert White, the famous naturalist, whose family lived near Jane Austen. Her character Willoughby (*Sense and Sensibility*, 1811) rather takes after James.
31. Gibson, *Illegitimacy*, pp.185–86.
32. St Aubyn, *Diary, 1819*, passim; Hartley, *St Aubyns*, p.43.
33. St Aubyn, *Diary,1810*, pp.126, 128; St Aubyn, *Diary, 1819,* p.78. Henrietta's son William (see *Diary, 1810*, p.103) died in 1819 (Caldwell, *Genealogy Mss*). In 1854 she wrote to her friend, Marie Blaze de Bury, the Scottish-born political writer and *salonnière* (Caldwell, Henrietta, *Letter c.1854 to Marie Blaze de Bury*).

34. St Aubyn, *Diary, 1810,* p.250 (23 January 1818). His part of Octavian, first played by John Kemble, required 'consummate skill' (Inchbald, Elizabeth, *The British theatre, or A collection of Plays,* Vol. 21).

35. St Aubyn, *Diary, 1810,* p.221; *Diary, 1819,* p.40; St Aubyn, James, *Journal of a tour in France, Switzerland and Italy,* 1819.

36. Poole, John, *Papers,* HM 44295.

37. Thurrock, Local History Society, 'Interview with Fr Sir Hugh Barrett Lennard, Bt.', *Panorama* (no. 44, 2006).

38. Gray, Patricia, *The Haunt of Grave-Robbers and Murderers: The History of Stoke Damerel Church, Devonport,* pp.39–112. Hawker's father was a famous vicar; his nephew authored 'Trelawny' and other Cornish myths (Stoyle, *West Britons,* pp.175–79).

39. Gibson, *Illegitimacy,* p.194 (and n.88 below). She contrasts this with the leniency of the pre-Reformation age. Today, even Archbishops are illegitimate.

40. Naylor, Sir George, *Garter King of Arms,* 1826, 1828. (Some words italicised for clarity.)

41. Gibson, *Illegitimacy,* p.244 n.156; WSRO: PHA 8641, *Royal Licence.*

42. See Hartley, *St Aubyns,* p.44. She mentions a prayerbook with 'James' bookplate … coat of arms surmounted by the Cornish chough'. The author has a similar bookplate, framed and dated 1809.

43. Helmholz, R.H., 'Bastardy Litigation in Medieval England', *The American Journal of Legal History,* p.360.

44. St Aubyn, Sir John, *The Will of Sir John St Aubyn Baronet of Clowance (Parish of Crowan) 1835,* CRO: RH/1/759.

45. Gray, *Stoke Damerel,* p.113.

46. Gibson, *Illegitimacy,* pp.147–8. Sir John acted similarly to the 3rd Earl of Egremont, who in 1837 left Petworth to George Wyndham, but the original Wyndham estate to his legitimate heir.

47. *Morning Herald,* 17/11/1836.

48. Mount records 15/10/1836.

49. *The West Briton,* Issue of 6/9/1839.

50. Mount records, 3/9/1839.

Chapter 4: Victorian Values

1. The queen's diary noted the Cornish 'are a very noisy talkative race [who] speak a kind of English hardly to be understood.' Hartley, *St Aubyns,* p.16.

2. Gibson, *Illegitimacy,* pp.95, 190; St Aubyn, *Diary, 1819,* pp.243–45, 278, 286.

3. White, *Gazetteer,* pp.644–48.

4. Sterry, Wasey, *Annals of the King's College of Our Lady of Eton beside Windsor,* p.275.

5. Ibid., p.298.

6. St Aubyn, John, *Transcript of letters from Europe* (1848), Mount records.

7. Walford, *London,* Chapter 36.

8. Pool, *Borlase,* pp.50–54.
9. Jaggard, Edwin, 'Liberals and Conservatives in West Cornwall 1832–1868', *JRIC (No. 1, Series 2, 1993)*, p.19.
10. Mount records 16/1/1860 et seq. Palmerston had accompanied Queen Victoria's visit to the Mount in 1846. Hartley, *St Aubyns*, p.17.
11. *The Times*, 25/01/1860.
12. Mount records 4/7/1866. As with the first baronetcy, (see Pt.3 Ch.4 n.22 above), a hand *appaumée sinister* – the Badge of Ulster, the distinctive ensign of the order and rank of baronet – was once again added to the ancient family escutcheon.
13. Hartley, *St Aubyns*, p.60.
14. Mount records *c.*1880.
15. *Kelly's Directory of Cornwall*, Lelant, 1873.
16. Hartley, *St Aubyns*, p.53.
17. Roberts, Andrew, *Salisbury – Victorian Titan*, p.461.
18. *Falmouth Times*, October 1891, Mount records.
19. Cannadine, David, *Aspects of Aristocracy*, p.256, citing Bateman, J., *The Great Landowners of Great Britain and Ireland.* But Bateman seems to have counted as income not only rack rents, but also the capital proceeds and/or reversion of leaseholds. (Cannadine, p.166.)
20. *Western Mercury* 15/06/1892.
21. Club Season Card 1892–3, Mount records. The painting hangs in the castle.
22. *Daily Express* dated 1901. Mount records.
23. News report, 1953, Mount records.
24. News reports, 1900 and 1904, Mount records.

PART FIVE

Chapter 1: Men at Arms

1. This campaign is described in Raugh, Harold E. Jr, *The Victorians at War, 1815–1915.* The details of family members involved come from the Mount records.
2. AngloBoerWar.com/ Thorneycroft's Mounted Infantry; Bachelors' Club 1902, Mount records.
3. Ager, Stanley & Fiona St Aubyn, *The Butler's Guide*, p.23.
4. Lemon, Mark, *Up and Down the London Streets,* p.305. Cited in Hatton, Joseph, *Clubland* (1890).
5. Jones, Dr Spencer, *Stemming the Tide. Officers and Leadership in the British Expeditionary Force 1914*, p.19.
6. Jones, Dr Spencer, 'The Recapture of Gheluvelt', *Voices of War & Peace.* See also Jones, *Stemming the Tide*, pp.254–61.
7. Jones, *Gheluvelt.*
8. Jones, *Stemming the Tide*, p.18.

9. Mount records, 1916.
10. Storey, Richard A., '2nd Lord Montagu of Beaulieu (1866–1929)', ODNB Vol. 38, p.752.
11. Hall, Catherine, *Civilising Subjects, Metropole and Colony in the English Imagination 1830–1867,* pp.84–139.
12. From Phillippo, J. M., *Jamaica, Its Past and Present State,* pp.174–78.
13. Hartley, *St Aubyns,* p.77.
14. *West Briton,* October 1897.
15. *London Evening News,* 4/3/1914.
16. Ponsonby, Sir Frederick, *The Grenadier Guards in the Great War of 1914–1918,* Vol. 3, 207, p.17.
17. Ibid., Vol. 1, pp.246–249.
18. Wemyss, James 12th Earl of, *Gosford,* pl.266n.
19. Howard, *First World War,* pp.64–66.
20. Wemyss, *Gosford,* pl.266n.
21. Ponsonby, *Grenadier,* Vol. 1, pp.324–36; Wemyss, *Gosford,* pl.266n.
22. Howard, Michael, *The First World War,* pp.64–66.
23. Mount records, February 1916.
24. 'One of the greatest diplomats of his day.' ODNB, Arthur Nicolson, Vol. 40, p.885.
25. Glendinning, Victoria, *Vita – The Life of Vita Sackville-West,* p.60.
26. Lees-Milne, James, *Harold Nicolson – A Biography,* Vol. 1, p.36.
27. *Tatler,* 9/8/1916 (British Newspaper Archive).
28. *The Queen* magazine, 14/10/1916 (British Newspaper Archive).
29. Mount records, letter 23/7/1915.
30. Ponsonby, *Grenadiers,* Vol. 2, pp.149, 162, 175.
31. Glendinning, *Vita,* pp.82 and 83.

Chapter 2: The Lotus Eaters

1. Nicolson, Harold, *Good Behaviour,* p.396.
2. Fraser, Rebecca, *A People's History of Britain,* p.669.
3. Lambert, Anthony J., *Country House Life,* p.vii.
4. St Aubyn, Fiona, *The Butler's Guide,* p.21.
5. Cannadine, *Aristocracy,* p.218.
6. Nicolson, Harold, *Comments 1944–1948,* pp.222–23.
7. Glendinning, *Vita,* pp.264–5.
8. Ibid., p.265.
9. Ibid., pp.264–5.
10. Ibid., p.269.
11. HND, Vol. 1, p.164.
12. Glendinning, *Vita,* p.269.
13. HND, Vol. 1, p.167.
14. Ibid., p.171.
15. Glendinning, *Vita,* p.274.

16. Olson, S., *Harold Nicolson Diaries and Letters*, *1930–1964*, p.205; Cannadine, *Aristocracy*, p.222.
17. HND, Vol. 1, p.91.
18. Ibid., p.224.
19. Ibid., p.221.
20. Tinniswood, *The Long Weekend*, pp.60–62.
21. Her father, Sir George Wombwell 4th Baronet, as ADC to Lord Cardigan in 1854, had survived the Charge of the Light Brigade. Reaching the Russian guns, his horse was killed under him and he was briefly captured. But catching a loose horse, he escaped back to the British lines, hotly pursued by Russians.
22. Spicer, Charles, *Coffee with Hitler*, p.143.
23. Spitzy, Reinhard, *How We Squandered the Reich*, pp.95–107.
24. Hancock, Peter, *Cornwall at War*, pp.11–12.
25. Spicer, *Hitler*, p.144; *Western Morning News & Daily Gazette*, 5/4/1937.
26. Lanyon, Andrew, *Von Ribbentrop in St Ives,* p.85.

Chapter 3: Total War

1. *The Telegraph*, obit, 7/4/2013.
2. *Western Morning News*, May 2010 (Mount records).
3. *London Gazette*, 20/8/1940, 5090.
4. Kindell, Don, *Admiralty War Diaries of World War 2*, Home Fleet – April to September 1942.
5. O'Reilly, John, *From Delhi to Arnhem*, p.23.
6. *The Telegraph*, obit, 16/6/2006.
7. O'Reilly, *From Delhi*, p.82.
8. Verkaik, Robert, *The Traitor of Arnhem*, pp.329–39 (App. 1). The circumstantial evidence is overwhelming.
9. Verkaik, *Traitor,* p.5.
10. Gill, Crispin, *Plymouth. A New History,* pp.259–262.
11. Glendinning, *Vita,* pp.319–20.
12. HND, Vol. 2, 240.
13. Lees-Milne, *Nicolson*, Vol. 2, p.153.

Chapter 4: Gift to the Nation

1. St Aubyn, *The Butler's Guide*, p.28.
2. Ibid., p.25.
3. Ibid., p.7.
4. *The Spectator*, Long Life, 17/9/1994.
5. His skill in matching buyers and sellers enabled Piers to offer the finest margins. After hiring Gordon Pepper, 'the premier analyst in the gilt-edged market', W. Greenwell and Co. became 'the UK's leading gilt advisory company' (see Edinburgh Business School, *Financial Markets*).

6. As he related to the author in March 1974.
7. Nicholas Coleridge, Eton College Chapel, 13/11/2015.
8. As recounted to the author (with the name of the boy changed).
9. *Cornish Evening Tidings*, 11/11/1940.
10. Tinniswood, *Noble Ambitions: the Fall and Rise of the Post-War Country House*, p.224.
11. Mount records, 1950.
12. Lees-Milne, *Nicolson*, Vol. 2, p.177.
13. Ibid., p.209.
14. HND, Vol. 3, p.268.
15. Newspaper reports, August 1954 (Mount records).
16. Mount records.
17. National Trust, Handbook 2024, p.41.

BIBLIOGRAPHY

Books

Ager, Stanley & Fiona St Aubyn, *The Butler's Guide* (1980).

Ardrey, Robert, *The Territorial Imperative* (1966).

Aubrey, John, *Brief Lives* (Andrew Clark (ed.), Clarendon Press, 1898).

Ballantyne (pub.), *Memorials of Brooks's* (1908).

Baring-Gould, Sabine, *A Book of the West* (1899).

Baring-Gould, Sabine, *Cornish Characters and Strange Events* (1925).

Barratt, John, *The Civil War in the South-West* (2005, Ebook set to 407 pp.).

Bateman, J., *The Great Landowners of Great Britain and Ireland* (4th edn., 1883).

Beatson, Robert, *A Political Index to the Histories of Great Britain and Ireland* (Vol. 1, 1806).

Bell, Adrian. R., *The Soldier in Later Medieval England* (2013).

Boase, G. C., *Collectanea Cornubiensia* (1890).

Borlase, Dr William, *The Natural History of Cornwall* (1758).

Borlase, William Copeland, *The Descent, Name and Arms of Borlase* (1888).

Brown, H. Miles, *Battles Royal: Charles I and the Civil War in Cornwall and the West* (1982).

Bucholz, R. O. *et al.*, *Early Modern England, 1485–1714* (1958).

Burke, J., *A Genealogical and Heraldic History of the Commoners of Great Britain and Ireland* (4 Vols; 1835–38 edn. and 1858 edn.).

Burke, J., *The Roll of Battle Abbey* (1848).

Burnet, *History of the Reformation of the Church of England* (1679).

Camden, William, *Remains concerning Britain* (1629 edn.).

Campbell, William, *Materials for a History of the Reign of Henry VII* (1877).

Cannadine, David, *Aspects of Aristocracy* (1994).

Carew, Richard, *The Survey of Cornwall* (1602; Chynoweth *et al.* (eds.), 2004).

Carte, T. E., *A Collection of Original Letters and Papers ... Found among the Duke of Ormonde's Papers* (2 Vols., 1733–39) pp.124–5.

Cartwright (pub.), *The Records of the Honourable Society of Lincoln's Inn* (Vol. 1, 1896).

Cave, K. (ed.), *The Diary of Joseph Farington* (1983).

Chaplais, Pierre, *English Diplomatic Practice in the Middle Ages* (1981).

Chastellain, George, *Fragment relative a la Normandie* (Williams (ed.), 1850).

Cheyney, E.B., *The Court of the Star Chamber* (1913).

Chynoweth, John, *Tudor Cornwall* (2002).

Coate, Mary, *Cornwall in the Great Civil War and Interregnum 1642–1660* (2nd edn., 1963).

Cobbett, William, *The Parliamentary History of England from the Earliest Period to the Year 1803.*

Colman, George the Younger, *The Mountineers Play in 3 Acts* (1794).

Concanen, G., *A Report of the Trial at Bar, Rowe v. Brenton* (1830).

Coode, Jonathan, *The Cornish Club 1768* (Private edition, 2022).

Cox (ed. *et al.*), *Survey of London, Volume 10, The Parish of St Margaret Westminster – Part 1* (1926).

Crabbe, W. R., *Monumental Brasses of Devonshire, Transactions of the Exeter Diocesan Architectural Society* (Vol. VI, 1856).

Croft, J. Pauline, *King James* (2003).

Cruickshanks, Evelyn, *Political Untouchables: the Tories and the '45* (1979).

Cunliffe, Barry W., *Bretons & Britons* (2021).

Curry, Anne and Ambühl, Remy, *A Soldiers' Chronicle of the Hundred Years War* (2022).

Debretts, *Peerage & Baronetage* (2003).

Drake, S. J., *Cornwall, Connectivity and Identity in the 14th Century* (2019).

Duffin, Anne, *Faction and Faith: Politics and Religion of the Cornish Gentry Before the Civil War* (1996).

Earland, Ada, *John Opie & his Circle* (Hutchinson, 1911).

Ellis, H. (ed.), *Original Letters Illustrative of English History* (11 Vols. in 3 Series, 1825–46).

Elton, G. R., *The Tudor Constitution* (2nd edn., 1982).

Exwood, M. and Lehmann, H. L. (eds.), *The Journal of William Shellinks' Travels in England 1661–63*, (Camden 5th Series, Vol.1, Royal Historical Society, 1993).

Fletcher, Anthony, *Tudor Rebellions* (1987).

Fletcher, Canon J. R., *A Short History of St Michael's Mount* (1951).

Ford, J. D. M. (ed.), *The Letters of John III, King of Portugal* (1931).

Fraser, Rebecca, *A People's History of Britain* (2003).

Friel, Ian, *Henry V's Navy* (2015).

Fritz, Paul S., *The English Ministers and Jacobitism* (2019).

G.E.C, *The Complete Baronetage* (1904).

G.E.C, *The Complete Peerage* (1945).

Gairdner, James, *History of the Life and Reign of Richard III* (1898).

Gibson, Kate, *Illegitimacy, Family & Stigma in England, 1660–1834* (2022).

Gill, Crispin, *The Great Cornish Families* (1995).

Gill, Crispin, *Plymouth. A New History* (1993).

Gilbert, Davies, *The Parochial History of Cornwall*, 1838 (4 vols.).

Given-Wilson, C. (ed.) *et al.*, *Parliamentary Rolls of Medieval England* (16 vols., 2005).

Glendinning, Victoria, *Vita – The Life of Vita Sackville-West* (1983).

Gorris, J. J., *Etudes sur les colonies marchandes a Anvers* (1925).

Grandisson, John de, *The Register of John de Grandisson, 1327–1369* (1894).

Granville, Roger, *The History of the Granville Family* (1895).

Gray, Patricia, *The Haunt of Grave-Robbers and Murderers: The History of Stoke Damerel Church, Devonport* (1979).

Gray, Todd, *Cornwall The Travellers' Tales* (Vol. 1, 2000).

Grose, Francis, *The Antiquities of Cornwall* (London, 1786 edition).

Guy, John, *The Cardinal's Court* (1977).

Hall, Catherine, *Civilising Subjects, Metropole and Colony in the English Imagination 1830–1867* (Chicago, 2002).

Hals, *The Compleat History of Cornwal[l]* (1750).

Hancock, Peter, *Cornwall at War* (Halsgrove, 2002).

Hartley, Diana, *The St Aubyns of Cornwall* (1977).

Hatton, Joseph, *Clubland* (London and Provincial, 1890).

Heal, F., and Holmes, C., *The Gentry of England and Wales, 1500–1700* (1994).

HoC 1386–1421, ed. J. S. Roskell, L. Clark, C. Rawcliffe, 1993.

HoC 1509–1558, ed. S. T. Bindoff, 1982.

HoC 1558–1603, ed. P. W. Hasler, 1981.

HoC 1604–1629, ed. Andrew Thrush and John P. Ferris, 2010.

HoC 1640–1660, ed. Vivienne Larminie and Stephen Roberts, 2023.

HoC 1660–1690, ed. B. D. Henning, 1983.

HoC 1690–1715, ed. D. Hayton, E. Cruickshanks, S. Handley, 2002.

HoC 1715–1754, ed. R. Sedgwick, 1970.

HoC 1754–1790, ed. L. Namier, J. Brooke, 1964.

HoC 1790–1820, ed. R. Thorne, 1986.

Hogg, Thomas, *St Michael's Mount in Cornwall, A Poem* (1811).

Holden, A., Crouch, D. and Gregory, S. (ed. and trans.), *History of William Marshal* (3 Vols.), London: Anglo-Norman Text Society.

Holinshed, *Chronicles of England, Scotland and Ireland* (1808 edition).

Holles, G., *Memorials of the Hollis Family, 1493--1656* (A.C. Wood (ed.), 1937).

Horrox, C. & Hammond, P. (ed.), *BL Harleian mss. 433*, 4 Vols. (1979-83).

Howard, G., *Wolsey, the Cardinal and His Times* (1824).

Howard, Michael, *The First World War* (UOP, 2002).

Howarth, David A., *1066, The Year of Conquest* (1977).

Hull, P. L., *The Cartulary of St Michael's Mount* (Devon & Cornwall Record Society, 1962).

Hutton, Ronald, *The Restoration, A Political and Religious History of England and Wales, 1658–1667*.

Hyde, E., Earl of Clarendon, *The History of the Rebellion and the Civil Wars* (W. Dunn-Macray (ed.), 6 Vols., 1888).

Inchbald, Elizabeth, *The British theatre, or A collection of Plays* (1808).

Indlewick, F. A. (ed.), *A Calendar of the Inner Temple Records* (Vol. I, 1896).

Jones, Michael, *The Black Prince* (2017).

Jones, Dr Spencer, *Stemming the Tide. Officers and Leadership in the British Expeditionary Force 1914* (2013).

Kindell, Don, *Admiralty War Diaries of World War 2.*

Lambert, Anthony J., *Country House Life* (1981).

Lanyon, Andrew, *Von Ribbentrop in St Ives* (2011).

Lawrance, W. T., *Parliamentary Representation of Cornwall* (1926).

Le Patourel, John, *Norman Empire* (1976).

Lees-Milne, James, *Harold Nicolson – A Biography* (2 Vols., 1980, 1981).

Leland, John, *Leland's Itinerary*, Toulmin Smith (ed.), (1907).

Lemon, Mark, *Up and Down the London Streets* (1867).

Lewis, George Randall, *The Stannaries: A Study of the English Tin Miner* (1965 edn.).

Longmate, Norman, *Defending the Island: from Caesar to the Armada* (Grafton (ed.), 1990) pp.358–362.

Lysons, Daniel and Samuel, *Magna Britannica* (Vol. 3, Cornwall, 1814).

Macaulay, G. C. (ed.), *The Chronicles of Froissart* (J. Bourchier (trans.), 1904).

Maclean, Sir John, *Deanary of Trigg Minor* (1876).

Marsh, F. G., *The Godolphins* (Limited Edition, 1930).

Maxwell Lyte, H. C., *A Descriptive Catalogue of Ancient Deeds* (6 Vols., 1890–1915).

Maxwell Lyte, H. C., *Calendar of Miscellaneous Inquisitions* (Vol. 1 1219–1307 – Vol. 8 1422–85).

Milton, Giles, *Big Chief Elizabeth* (2000).

Monmouth, Geoffrey of, *The History of the Kings of Britain* (Folio Soc. (ed.), 1969).

Moor, Charles, *Knights of Edward I* (1929).

Morris, Mark, *A Great and Terrible King* (Windmill (ed.), 2009).

Mortimer, Ian, *The Time Traveller's Guide to Medieval England* (Vintage, 2009).

Nichols, J. (ed.), *The History of the Worthies of England ... by Thomas Fuller* (2 Vols., 1811).

Nicolson, Adam, *The Gentry: Stories of the English* (2011).

Nicolson, Harold, *Comments 1944–1948* (Constable, 1948).

Nicolson, Harold, *Good Behaviour* (Axios, 2009 edition).

Norden, John, *Speculi Britanniae: Description of Cornwall* (1728).

Olson, S., *Harold Nicolson Diaries and Letters, 1930–1964* (1980).

Oman, Charles, *Castles* (1926).

O'Reilly, John, *From Delhi to Arnhem* (2009).

Orme, Nicholas, *Cornwall II: Religious History to 1560* (VCH, 2010).

Orme, Nicholas, *Cornish Wills, 1342-1540*, Devon and Cornwall Record Society (2007).

Parry, R. H. (ed.), *Essays on the Civil War* (1970).

Peter, Richard (and Otto Peter), *The Histories of Launceston and Dunheved* (1895).

Phillippo, J. M., *Jamaica, Its Past and Present State* (1843).

Plumb, J. H., *Sir Robert Walpole, The King's Minister* (USA Edition, 1961).

Pole, William, *Collections Towards a Description of the County of Devon* (1791).

Polwhele, The Rev. R., *The History of Cornwall* (Vols. 1&2, 1803); (Supplement, 1804); (Volume 4 & Supplement, Kohler & Coombes, 1978).

Pollard, Alfred W. (ed.), *Chaucer's Canterbury Tales* (2 Vols., Macmillan 1894).

Ponsonby, Sir Frederick, *The Grenadier Guards in the Great War of 1914–1918* (3 Vols., 1920).

Pool, P. A. S., *William Borlase* (1986).

Prothero, G. W. (ed.), *Select Statutes and Other Constitutional Documents Illustrative of the Reigns of Elizabeth and James I* (3rd edn., Clarendon Press, 1906).

Raugh, Harold E. Jr, *The Victorians at War, 1815–1915*.

Reichel, O. W., *Devon Feet of Fines*, Vol. 1, 1196–1272, (1912); Vol. 2, 1272–1369 (1939).

Roberts, Andrew, *Salisbury – Victorian Titan* (1999).

Rogers, John J., *Opie and his Works* (1878).

Rose-Troup, F., *The Western Rebellion of 1549* (1913).

Rowe, J. H., *Cornwall Feet of Fines* (Vol. 1, Richard I–Edward III, 1914).

Rowse, A. L., *A Cornish Anthology* (1968).

Rowse, A. L., *Court and Country* (1987).

Rowse, A. L., *Tudor Cornwall* (1941).

Rowse, A. L., *West Country Stories* (1944).

Rushworth, *Historical Collections* (Vol. 6).

St Aubyn, Fiona, *The Butler's Guide* (2012 edn.).

St Aubyn, The Hon. Giles R., *The Year of Three Kings: 1483* (1983).

St Clare Byrne, Muriel, *The Lisle Letters* (6 Vols., 1981).

St Levan, Sir John 4th Baron, *The Illustrated Historical Guide: St Michael's Mount* (2004).

Sandford, F., *Genealogical History of the Kings of England* (1707).

Siculus, Diodorus, *The Library of History* (Books III-VIII), (C.H. Oldfather (trans.), Harvard University Press, 1935).

Skidmore, Chris, *Edward VI, The Lost King* (edn. 2008).

Smith, Anthony D., *The Ethnic Origins of Nations* (1986).

Smith, Sir Thomas, *De Republica Anglorum: A Discourse on the Commonwealth of England*, (L. Aston (ed.), 1906).

Soulsby, Ian, *A History of Cornwall* (1986).

Spalding, Ruth (ed.), *The Diary of Bulstrode Whitelocke, 1605–1675* (OUP/British Academy).

Spicer, Charles, *Coffee with Hitler* (2022).

Spitzy, Reinhard, *How We Squandered the Reich* (Eng. Trans. G.T. Waddington, 1997).

Stafford, Edmund, *The Register of Edmund Stafford 1395–1419* (1886).

Stenton, Doris (ed.), *Pleas before the King or his Justices, 1198–1202* (4 Vols., Selden Society, 1948–9 and 1966–67).

Sterry, Wasey, *Annals of the King's College of Our Lady of Eton beside Windsor* (1898).

Stoate, T. L., *Cornwall Subsidies in the reign of Henry VIII: 1524 and 1543 and the benevolence of 1545* (1985).

Stoyle, Mark, *A Murderous Midsummer* (2022).

Stoyle, Mark, *West Britons – Cornish Identities* (2002).

Strecche, John, *The Deeds of King Henry V* (Kenilworth edition, 2014).

Sturt, John, *Revolt in the West – The Western Rebellion of 1549* (1987).

Sumption, J., *The Hundred Years War*, Vol. 3, *Divided Houses* (2011).

Sumption, J., *The Hundred Years War*, Vol. 4, *Cursed Kings* (2015).

Taylor, Frank, *Gesta Henrici Quinti: The Deeds of Henry the Fifth* (1975).

Taylor, Rev. T., *St Michael's Mount* (1932) pp.142–3, 178.

Tinniswood, Adrian, *Noble Ambitions: the Fall and Rise of the Post-War Country House* (2021).

Tinniswood, Adrian, *The Long Weekend* (Vintage, 2018).

Todd, Malcolm, *The South West to AD1000* (1987).

Tregellas, Walter H., *Cornish Worthies* (1884).

Trevelyan, G. M., *British History in Nineteenth Century and After, 1782–1919* (1922).

Twiss, Sir Travers (ed.), *The Black Book of the Admiralty*, 2011 ed., Vols. 1–4.

Verkaik, Robert, *The Traitor of Arnhem* (2024).

Vivian, J. L. & Drake, H. (ed.), *Visitation of the County of Cornwall in the year 1620* (1874).

Vivian, J. L., *The Visitations of Cornwall* (1887).

Walford, Edward, *Old and New London: Vol. 6* (London, 1878).

Warner, Michael P., *The Agincourt Campaign of 1415* (2021).

Wemyss, James 12th Earl of, *Gosford* (Private Edition, 2022).

White, William, *Whites Gazetteer and Directory of Devon* (1850).

Wykeham, *Register Wykeham* (Hants Rec. Soc. 1896–9).

Wood, A. C. (ed.), *G. Holles, Memorials of the Hollis Family, 1493–1656* (1937).

Worth, R. N. (ed.), *Calendar of the Plymouth Municipal Records* (1893).

Worth, R. N. *The Buller Papers* (1895, Privately printed; at the RIC).

Wotton, Thomas, *The English Baronetage* (1741).

Manuscripts

BL, Add. 34,224 see Pt. 2 Ch. 1.

BL, Cotton MS, Nero B1 fo. 66.

BL, Cotton MS, Tiber C. XIII.

BL, *Diary of Bulstrode Whitelocke*, Additional Manuscript no. 53726.

BL, Harl. MS 6166, ff. 95–123, *The King's Book of all the Lords, Knights and Gentlemen of this Realm of England.*

BL, *Visitation of Devon & Cornwall 1531*, Additional Manuscript no. 14315.

Caldwell, *Genealogy Mss*, Caldwell Collection, RIA 12 R 39 – RIA 12 R 48.

Caldwell, Henrietta, *Letter c.1854 to Marie Blaze de Bury*, Morgan Library, New York (ID 432682 MA 14300.90).

Charles I, *His Majesties Declaration to all his Loving Subjects in Cornwall*, 10 September 1643.

'Cornishman, A.', '*A Letter to the Free and Independent Electors of the County*' (1790 election leaflet). Mount records.

Dodds, P. A., *Transcript of William Borlase's Draft Letters (1718–1745)*, Volume 13, from the Morab Library.

Froissart, Jean, *Chronicles*. www.dhi.ac.uk/onlinefroissart/index.jsp.

Glubb, 'State of the Borough of Callington, 3 March 1772'; at the RIC.

Gruffudd, *Chronicle* 'A soldier in the Calais retinue', see St Clare Byrne, '*Lisle Letters*, Vol. 1 p.361; Mostyn Ms. 158, University of Wales.

King John III of Portugal to Cardinal Wolsey, 10 September 1527. (Cottonian Library Mss. Nero B1 fo. 64).

Lambeth Palace Library, London, 'A copy of a letter containing ... the Articles... of the Cornish rebels' (1549).

Naylor, Sir George, *Garter King of Arms*, 1826, 1828. Mount records.

Norden, *The Survey of Cornwall*, Harl. MS. 6252 (pa. 27), f.28.

Poole, John, *Papers,* HHL: Mss HM 44280–44354.

Roberts, R. A. (ed.), *Calendar of the Cecil Papers in Hatfield House* (1894).

Russell, Lord John, *Letter to Cornish JPs*, 30 September 1549 (Bedford Mss).

St Aubyn, James, *Diary*, 1810–1819, HHL: Mss HM 80304.

St Aubyn, James, *Journal of a tour in France, Switzerland and Italy*, 1819, HHL: Mss HM 81168.

St Aubyn, James, *Diary*, 1819–1859, HHL: Mss HM 63181.

St Aubyn, Sir John, *Copy Letter from Sir John St Aubyn to Lady St Aubyn and of another Letter from Sir John to John Baker Esq*. Mount records.

St Aubyn, Sir John, *Short Abstract of Letters received in 1795*. Mount records.

St Aubyn, Sir John, *The Will of Sir John St Aubyn Baronet of Clowance (Parish of Crowan) 1835*. Copy held at CRO: RH/1/759.

St Aubyn, John, *Transcript of letters from Europe* (1848), Mount records.

St Aubyn, The Hon. John T., *Memorandum on St Michael's Mount*, Mount records (c.1890).

Steer, B. D. G., *Pedigree of Vinicombe of Madron* (May 1990). Mount records.

WSRO: PHA 8641, 'Instance of the confirmation by Royal Licence, of surnames of noble families, borne by acknowledged natural children.'

Articles

Arthurson, Ian, 'Fear and Loathing in West Cornwall', *JRIC (2000); New Series, Vol. 3, Pts. 3 & 4), pp.68–96.

Arthurson, Ian, 'The Rising of 1497: A Revolt of the Peasantry?' in Rosenthal, Joel and Colin Richmond (eds.), *People, Politics and Community in the Later Middle Ages* (Glosc., 1987), pp.1–18.

Baker, J. H. (ed.), 'Densell, John (d. 1536)', *ODNB*(Vol.15).

Blake, William J., 'The Rebellion of Cornwall and Devon in 1549', *JRIC (Vol. 18, Pt.1, 1910)*, pp.147–96.

Bond, David, 'Sir William Killigrew and the Royalist War Effort in Cornwall 1643-6', *JICS (1986)*, pp.53–62.

Brogan, Stephen, 'James I: The Royal Touch', *History Today (Vol. 61, Issue 2, February 2011)*.

Chynoweth, John, 'The Wreck of the St Anthony', *JRIC (1968)*, pp.385–406.

Cornforth, John, 'St Michael's Mount Cornwall', *Country Life* (3/6/1993).

Cruickshanks, Eveline, 'The Convocation of the Stannaries of Cornwall: The Parliament of Tinners 1703–1752', *Parliament, Estates & Representation* (Vol. 6, no. 1, 6/1986).

Dickinson, Robert, 'The Spanish Raid on Mount's Bay in 1595', *JRIC (1988 (2))*, pp.178–186.

Edinburgh Business School, *Practical History of Financial Markets* (February, 2011).

Geological Society: www.geolsoc.org.uk/Geoscientist/Archive/December-2009/ The-Collector.

Green, E., 'The Siege and Defence of Taunton', *Somerset Archaeological Society Proceedings, XXV* (1879).

Hall, Hubert, 'The Sources for the History of Sir Robert Walpole's Financial Administration', *TRHS (Vol.4, 1910)*, pp.33–45.

Helmholz, R. H., 'Bastardy Litigation in Medieval England', *The American Journal of Legal History* (Vol. XIII, 1969).

Jaggard, Edwin, 'Liberals and Conservatives in West Cornwall 1832–1868', *JICS (No. 1, Series 2, 1993)*.

Jaggard, Edwin, 'The Political World of Sir Christohper Hawkins (1758–1829)', *JRIC (2000; New Series, Vol. 3, Pts. 3 & 4)* pp.97–111.

Jones, Dr Spencer, 'The Recapture of Gheluvelt', *Voices of War & Peace*.

Larminie, Dr Vivienne, 'The "Interruption" of Parliament and the quest for political settlement, October 1659'(HoC Blog, 17 October 2019).

Morning Herald (London), 17 November 1836, Account of fire at Clowance, Mount records.

Pool, P. A. S (ed.), 'The Penheleg Manuscript (1580)', *JRIC(1959)*.

Pool, P. A. S. (ed.), 'The Ancient and Present State of St Michael's Mount, 1762, Dr William Borlase Mss', *JICS (1975(3))*, pp.29–47.

Pounds, N. J. G., 'William Carnsew of Bokelly and his Diary', *JRIC (1978, Pt.1)*, pp.14–60.

Sandys, William, 'An Account of some of the Transactions in Cornwall during the Civil War', *JRIC (1866, Pt. V)*.

Scantlebury, John, 'The Development of the Export Trade in Pilchards from Cornwall during the Sixteenth Century', *JRIC (1989)*, pp.330–359.

Sedgwick, Romney, 'The Tories, Essay V', *HoC (1715–54)*.

Stone, Lawrence, 'The Inflation of Honours 1558–1641', *Past & Present (no. 14, November 1958)* pp.45–70 (OUP).

Storey, Richard A., '2nd Lord Montagu of Beaulieu (1866–1929)', *ODNB* (Vol. 38).

Taylor, Stephen, 'Walpole, Robert', *ODNB* (Vol. 57), pp.67–90.

Thirsk, Joan, 'The Sales of Royalist Land during the Interregnum', *The Economic History Review* (New Series, Vol. 5, no. 2, 1952).

Thurrock, Local History Society, 'Interview with Fr Sir Hugh Barrett Lennard, Bt', *Panorama* (no. 44, 2006).

The West Briton, (West Cornwall newspaper, Friday 6/9/1839 – Account of Sir John 5th Bt.'s funeral).

Western Morning News, (19/11/1910 – Obit of Lady St Levan; Mount records).

Whitely, H. M., 'The Treasure Ship of Gunwallo', *JRIC (1890),* pp.107–8.

GLOSSARY

Advowson: right of nomination to an ecclesiastical position.

Amercement: discretionary fine for an offence.

***Appaumée sinister*:** the palm of a hand shown on the left-hand side, viz. the heraldic shield of a baronet.

Balinger: small boat under sail and oars.

***Baton sinister*:** a left slanting truncated strip on an armorial shield, denoting illegitimate descent.

Carrack: large square-rigged sailing ship.

Chevaler: armed horseman bound by fealty.

Coiner: maker of counterfeit coins.

Compotus roll: manorial or estate archive.

Compound: to pay a fine, to recover a confiscated estate.

Court-leet: manorial court ruled by its lord.

Demesne-lands: lands which belong to the Crown absolutely.

Dentices: marine ray-finned fish similar to sea bream.

Devasting: from *devast*, to lay waste, devastate (modern).

Escheator: holder of lands which revert to the Crown on the death, minority or forfeiture of a tenant-in-chief.

***Ex parte militum*:** in the armed hand.

Fealty: formal recognition of a feudal duty.

Frankpledge: surety which binds a tithing to observe the law, answer charges in court, etc.

Gravamen: core element of a complaint or accusation.

Hanaper: small wicker basket for holding official papers.

***In se teres*:** self-sufficient (c.f. Horace: *in se ipso totus teres*).

Indult: a papal licence to override a canon law.

LVO: Lieutenant of the Victorian Order.

Portreeve: bailiff or mayor of a port or market borough.

Reeve: official who oversees a town, district or estate.

***Supersedeas omnino*:** staying all legal proceedings.

Tandem: a carriage made for two, drawn by a fast horse.

Tenant-in-chief: one who holds land directly from the Crown.

Tithing: ten men and their families administered as a group.

INDEX

Reigning Monarchs

Dates	Monarch	Pages
1760–1820	George III	
1820–1830	George IV	156–57
1830–1837	William IV	
1837–1901	Victoria	173, 174, 184
1901–1910	Edward VII	185–86, 191, 194
1910–1936	George V	191
1936	Edward VIII	
1936–1952	George VI	
1952–2022	Elizabeth II	227
2022–	Charles III	149, 218, 227

St Aubyn Patrilineal Descent

Date	Name	Spouse	Pages
1066/1107	Mauger Kt.		1–3, 5–6
1107	Walter		6, 7
1180s	Mauger	Maude	7
1210/1233	William		8
1185–1255	Stephen Kt.		7, 8
1284	Gilbert Kt.		8
1267/1288	William Kt.		8
1272	John		8
1225–1291	Mauger Kt. ‡	Isabella Pidekswell	8–11, 12; Plate 2
1279–1325	Mauger		23
1280–1357	Guy	Margaret de Raleigh	12–13, 35–37
d. 1349	John		13–14
1330–1381	Thomas Kt.	Alice de Raleigh	13–19
1355–1383	John Kt.	Joan Chudleigh	14, 18, 20–22, 193
1377–1404	Guy	Alice Sergeaux	22–27, 42–43; [Plate 3]
1380–1418	John ‡	Katherine Chalons	22, 27–33
1335–1405	Geoffrey ¶	Elizabeth Kemyell	35–37
1380–1455	Geoffrey	Alice Tremere	37–39, 41–43; Plate 4
1385–1460	Peter		37–39, 41–43
1435–1510	Thomas	Maude Trenowth	44, 47, 48–51
1440–1515	Peter		44–48, 49, 89
1487–1558	Thomas ¶	Mary Grenville	51–63, 65–69, 71–75, 76, 78, 86
1545	Peter		74, 87
1513–1590	John¶	Blanche Whittington	72, 79, 86–88
1520–1558	William ‡	Elizabeth Borlase	67–68, 69, 85, 86
1543–1626	Thomas ¶	Zenobia Mallet	89, 93–94; Plate 5

Date	Name	Spouse	Pages
1577–1639	John ‡ ¶	Katherine Arundell	97–99, 102–103, 105
1578–1637	Thomas ‡	Katherine Bonython	96–97, 99–102, 103
1613–1684	John ‡ ¶	Catherine Godolphin	103, 105–06, 108–10, 112–29; Plate 16
1640s	Thomas		103, 106–109, 111, 127; Plate 17
d. 1687	Katherine		123–24, 128
1645–1687	John 1st Bt. ‡	Ann Jenkyn	127–28, 130
1670–1714	John 2nd Bt. ‡ ¶	Mary Delahay	130–31
1702–1744	John 3rd Bt. ‡	Catherine Morice	131–148; Plate 18
d. 1768	Margaret	Sir Francis Basset	152
1726–1772	John 4th Bt. ‡	Elizabeth Wingfield	139, 147, 148–151, [152, 156, 158, 250, n.22]
1758–1839	John 5th Bt. ‡ ¶	Juliana Vinicombe	151–162, 164, 165, 166–172, [173, 177]; Plates 19, 20
1757–1804	Elizabeth	Humphrey Prideaux	158
1760–1836	Catherine	John Molesworth	157, 158, 160, 169
b.1762	Anne	Robert White	
1769–1830	Dorothy	Sir T. Barrett Lennard Bt.	156, 158, 162, 165
1780–1844	Hebe	Edmund Prideaux	153, 158
1783–1862	James	Sarah White	153, 157–58, 162–69, 173; Plate 21
1794–1877	William	Dorothy Barrett Lennard	165–68
1799–1872	Edward 1st Bt.	Emma Knollys	169, 173–74, 177–78, 180–81; Plate 23
1829–1908	John 1st Ld. ‡	Lady Elizbth Townshend	174–186, 190, 195; Plates 24, 28
1857–1940	John 2nd Ld.	(1) Lady Edith Edgcumbe	184–94, 201, 206–7, 215, 221–22,
		(2) Julia Wombwell	255, n.21; Plate 29
1858–1915	Edward		189–90, 193, 194, 198
1867–1897	Arthur	Katharine Phillippo	194, 195
1871–1914	Piers		189–90, 193–94, 198
1878–1965	Lionel	Lady Mary Parker	193–94, 201
1895–1978	Francis 3rd Ld.	The Hon. Gwendolin Nicolson	194–99, 201–06, 208, [209], 215–19, 222–26; Plates 35, 36, 39
1919–2013	John 4th Ld. ¶	Susan Kennedy	205–06, 208–11, 217, 219, 223, 225–27; Plates 37, 39, 41

Date	Name	Spouse	Pages
1920–2005	Piers	Mary Southwell	206, 208, 211–14, 217, 218, 220, 223, 225, 227; Plates 38, 29, 40
1925–2016	Giles		208, 214–15, 217, 220–21; Plate 39
1950–	James 5th Ld. ¶	Mary Bennett	227–28; Plate 15
1952–	Fiona	The Hon. Robert Boyle	217
1955–	Nicholas ‡	Jane Brooks	225, 227; Plate 39

Notes: The dates between 1180 and 1540 which end in '5' or '0' are close estimates derived from historical documents. Dates in italics denote when documents show that the person was living. Square brackets denote references to the spouse only. MPs are marked ‡. High Sheriffs of Cornwall are marked ¶.

Military Contests

Date	Conflict
1066	Hastings 2, 89
1271	9th Crusade (Lord Edward's) 8–9
1277	Wales Campaign 9
1282	Orewin Bridge 9–10
1369–70	Aquitaine Campaign15–18
1370	Limoges, siege of 17; Plate 6
1383	Ypres 22; *see also* Gheluvelt
1404	Blackpool Sands 26–27
1415	Harfleur, siege of 28–30
1415	Agincourt 30
1417–18	Normandy campaign 30–32, 38–39
1549	Fenny Bridges 77
1549	Woodbury 77
1549	Clyst St Mary 77
1642–46	Plymouth, siege of 106, 108–10, 112
1643	Braddock Down 106–07
1643	Modbury 107
1643	Stratton 107
1643	Chewton Mendip 107
1643	Lansdown Hill 107–08
1643	Roundway Down 108
1643	Bristol 108
1644	Lostwithiel 109–10
1644	Newbury 111

General Index to Names and Places